# SECURITY IN THE PERSIAN GULF

1     **Domestic political factors**
*Shahram Chubin* (editor)

2     **Sources of inter-state conflict**
*Robert Litwak*

3     **Modernisation, political development and stability**
*Avi Plascov*

4     **The role of outside powers**
*Shahram Chubin*

The International Institute for Strategic Studies was founded in 1958 as a centre for the provision of information on and research into the problems of international security, defence and arms control in the nuclear age. It is international in its Council and staff, and its membership is drawn from over fifty countries. It is independent of governments and is not the advocate of any particular interest.

The Institute is concerned with strategic questions — not just with the military aspects of security but with the social and economic sources and political and moral implications of the use and existence of armed force: in other words, with the basic problems of peace.

The Institute's publications are intended for a much wider audience than its own membership and are available to the general public on special subscription terms or singly.

# Security in the Persian Gulf 4:

# The Role of Outside Powers

SHAHRAM CHUBIN
*Project Director, Regional Security Studies Programme
International Institute for Strategic Studies*

Published for
THE INTERNATIONAL INSTITUTE
FOR STRATEGIC STUDIES
by
GOWER

*Published by*

Gower Publishing Company Limited,
Gower House, Croft Road,
Aldershot, Hants GU11 3HR, England


British Library Cataloguing in Publication Data

Chubin, Shahram
    The role of outside powers — (Security in
    the Persian Gulf; 4)
    1. Security, International 2. Persian Gulf —
    Foreign relations
    I. Title    II. Series
    327'.116'09536      DS49.7
    ISBN 0-566-00449-6


Printed and bound in Great Britain by
Biddles Ltd, Guildford and King's Lynn

# Contents

# Introduction

For the decade of the 1980s, even with the greatest success for oil conservation, diversification of supplies and the substitution of other products, Western dependency on Middle Eastern oil will continue. The Persian Gulf, and particularly Saudi Arabia, will be the critical states yet their future political orientations and oil policies are uncertain.

Inhabiting a region undergoing rapid and fundamental changes, their political future cannot be guaranteed even with (perhaps especially because of) their financial assets. The types of challenges to these states' security are neither clearly identifiable nor easily met by traditional diplomatic instruments. Yet outside powers will be importantly affected by the consequences of change and instability in these states.

Not only are the challenges and threats to Western interests more inchoate and less soluble by traditional means, but those erstwhile instruments themselves, (such as raw military power) are progressively less valuable or indeed relevant to a broad range of foreign policy problems. The narrow utility of force has raised questions as to the effectiveness of the residual instruments in the armoury of Western diplomacy in their relations with their local allies. What, in short, does the West have to offer these states in a partnership? What is the currency to be offered in exchange for those governments' willingness to accommodate Western interests — the pursuit of moderate price increases, raising oil production or recycling petro-dollars?

1

The West is not without instruments for influencing these states. These range from implicit security relationships to mutually beneficial trading ties constituting a web of incipient interdependence. The manipulation of these instruments, and the mutual perception of common interests, however, are subject to limitation and even complete reversal, dependent as they are on political conditions within the region.

Political forces within the Persian Gulf (inter-Arab, and Iran-Arab) condition the political environment of the states in the region and hence the choices of their elites on how best to respond to assure their security. Although inherently marginal, the role of outside powers in responding to these forces and in addressing these priorities of the regional states, need not be insignificant, and indeed, may be decisive.

In addition external powers may, through their policies, aggravate indigenous instabilities — by inconsistent policies, by precipitate withdrawals of political support, or military over-reactions to local incidents. Policies designed to enhance immediate interests, such as encouraging higher oil production, may undermine longer term interests of stability and assured supplies. The manipulation of instruments of influence such as arms sales designed to aid military modernization, must be used with discrimination if they are not to endanger the regime they are intended to protect. In the long term, military modernization may itself prove a threat.

Apart from short versus longer term trade-offs, choices between regional and wider interests must be made. Both these elements are present for example in US policy choices on the Palestine question. Failure to tackle this problem will affect Saudi security and Saudi relations with the West, while energetic pursuit of a particular settlement may increase short-term problems with the Saudis. Similarly, responses to events in the Persian Gulf that see it as an autonomous region would have quite different implications for superpower relations to responses that link it with their rivalry elsewhere.

Primarily but not exclusively due to the region's oil wealth, both the West and the East have become progressively more interested in the Persian Gulf in the 1980s. This interest will endure. Each superpower will seek access to the region's resources on privileged terms, denial of the area to the other's predominant influence, and the use of strategic facilities in one form or another. This interest coupled with political and even military involvement will raise the stakes of the competition in the region and affect the capacity of the superpowers to manage indigenous conflict in the region. This intensified competition will in turn underscore the differing priorities and perspectives existing between local and outside powers. Seen from the standpoint of the superpowers, the Persian Gulf region will be a test-case for their relationship in which the extent of competition and its forms will unfold in the 1980s. Seen from the viewpoint of the international system, the volatility of politics in the Persian Gulf, together with the dependence of outside powers on the region (coupled with a narrow range of instruments of influence), will in combination be reflective of the international environment in the 1980s. Regional security will be an issue involving both local and outside powers, but the balance of responsibilities have yet to be worked out.

It is, however, with the responsibilities of the external power with which we are concerned. How can it meet these without exacerbating local tensions? What types of relationships are most conducive to regional order? Will its role be a primary or supplementary one? What formal structures, or informal patterns of co-operation hold the most promise for success in conflict management?

## The nature of 'influence'

Outside power 'influence' is limited both by the nature of the challenges confronting the regional states (such as modernization, which is open-ended and intangible), and by differing perspectives and priorities. Regional co-operation, or indigenous moderate forces, cannot be created by outside powers. They can only be stimulated and reinforced by them.

'Influence' as a concept is ambiguous. It may refer to a product (outcome) or a process (a relationship). It may be narrowly issue-specific or refer to a quality in an overall relationship. As a result it may be either declining or durable. It is usually difficult to identify with precision.

It is also difficult to operationalize. Often it reflects joint or parallel interests, sometimes it involves a tacit reciprocal bargain. The desired outcome may be achieved prior to the use of 'influence' due to an anticipated reaction. What are the indicators of influence? An extensive presence? A large aid commitment? A major aid commitment? Military dependency? An institutionalized channel for influence?

Our aim is not a discussion of the general theory of influence but rather a focus on the instruments of influence available to the super-powers in their relations with specific regional states. While not oblivious to the phenomenon of reverse influence which constrains the mighty, the focus is on the use of influence as a means of managing or ameliorating or promoting instability. In the Persian Gulf this leads inevitably though not exclusively to an examination of arms sales — as

3

a means of influence and as a source of security. Arms sales constitute a visible, tangible and central tool in the relations between regional and external power. The salience of arms transfers as an instrument of influence requires examination. Here the relevant distinctions are among supplies as an inducement, or as a coercive instrument; as a specific need, or as a *symbol* of a wider relationship. Under what conditions are they an effective means of influence? What is the salience of other, general, factors in a relationship, such as economic strength (technology transfers), or a reputation as an ally? Our emphasis is on influence as an 'ordering' mechanism, as a means for affecting the policies of states and their interactions, in the service of a larger goal.

## Arms transfers and policy

With the UK's withdrawal from the Persian Gulf, Western policymakers looked to local states with compatible interests to assume responsibility for security. This was generalized in the Nixon doctrine enunciated in June 1969 in Guam. In the Persian Gulf it meant reliance on Iran and Saudi Arabia as 'twin-pillars' of local strength. It implied a US willingness to build up these states for the execution of these responsibilities, by arms sales and military training.

With the dawning of the energy crisis and growing dependency on Gulf oil which was fully visible by mid-1973, the issue of Gulf security gained further prominence. Additional reasons for arms sales to the region sprang up, first the 'demand-pull' of the Shah, eager for new arms and wider responsibilities, and second, the 'supply-push' of the West, eager to 'recycle' the large revenue surpluses accruing to the oil producing states.

There remained nevertheless within the US foreign policy elite (if not in actual policy) a deep ambivalence about policy toward the region. Henry Kissinger emphasized the geo-political importance of the region, the necessity of buttressing friendly states and the imperative of maintaining a reputation for dependability and firmness; others were not so sure. Growing dependence on Gulf oil was a fact. That the answer to this fact was the buttressing of local states through arms sales which, it was argued, implied or necessitated an indirect US security commitment, was however seriously questioned by some. This school of thought did not see the choices as between a direct and indirect US security role in the region. It argued, rather, that Western interests (access to oil, moderate oil prices, and regional stability) could be achieved by different policies and policy instruments. It saw a natural conjunction of interests between the Gulf states and the West requiring little cultivation, and saw threats to security as primarily local, requiring little in the way of modern arms to meet them, and as essentially 'political', necessitating reforms rather than repression.

This broad (and over-simplified) dichotomy in approach which persists is noted for it serves as a useful benchmark in assessing the record of US policy in the region in the 1970s.

In the Persian Gulf, arms sales became a central part of the US relationship with the major littoral states. Iran and Saudi Arabia ordered arms worth $30 billion between 1973 and 1980 and were the largest importers of arms. Arms became the central component of this relationship due to the interaction of each state's requirements and needs rather than to any clear or autonomous decision by any one state.

The incentives for arms sales to the Gulf states were clear: for strategic (or defence) purposes to bolster their capacity to resist aggression; for 'influence' as a channel for creating a dependency; and for economic reasons — such as the improvement of balance of payments, to reduce the unit costs of one's own weapons, to provide employment, etc. A variety of benefits were assumed from arms sales. Joseph Sisco referred to their 'moderating influence' (1973), and Eugene Rostow to the maintenance of 'regional balances'. David Packard argued that the US would gain more influence as a supplier than as a bystander,[1] while James Schlesinger noted, astutely, that while the US sold arms for its own reasons, the views of the recipients were not necessarily identical to those of the US. If the incentives for selling arms were theoretically clear, which arms or weapons systems should be sold was not. This was the product of the buying state's own appreciation of its needs and its persuasiveness within and importance to the US.

The use of arms sales as the central instrument of foreign policy was neither totally purposive nor unilateral at this time. The general interests of the US argued for it and regional friends demanded it. Arms became the central component in the relationships because they were at once tangible, symbolic and available. Their importance transcended their practical utility or the ambiguity behind the suppliers' motives and particularly the recipients' assumptions about Western commitment, implicit in arms sales. They became the currency in relations between the US and Saudi Arabia and Iran.

From this certain consequences followed. Starting as an instrument intended to facilitate the achievement of certain goals (regional stability and advancing bilateral relations), they tended to take on a life of their

1 Also that the US by pre-emptive selling could actually reduce purchases by them from other sources.

own. As the symbol of the relationship, arms transfers became hard to deny or even to regulate.[1] It is even more difficult to manipulate arms transfers for other ends or interests. The arms relationship in short has its own dynamic: it is difficult to deny *Phoenix* air-to-air missiles if F-14s aircraft are sold, or *Sidewinder* missiles, if F-15 fighters are approved. Furthermore the large-scale provision of arms to a regime (whether the Shah or the Saudi Royal Family) restricts the ability of the supplier either to 'influence' that regime or to cultivate options with respect to it. Politically identified with the recipient regime, the supplier is locked further into it and finds it difficult to avoid acquiescence in that state's definition of its needs. Accentuating this is the arms sales constituency (the US armed services, MAAG, and the manufacturers among others), which comes to see military assistance as an end in itself rather than a means. Advocacy thus often replaces responsible criticism. Furthermore, as arms become a substitute for alliance, they take on almost mystical qualities. Impervious to arguments about their intrinsic worth, they acquire great political and symbolic value. If restricted or denied they can weaken or destabilize the recipient politically, domestically and regionally. For the supplier state too they acquire greater importance as they come to be seen as a product or service that it is relatively much easier to supply to fortify the bilateral relationship than alternatives such as a formal defence treaty or a solution to the Palestine question.

The nature of a relationship in which arms sales occupy a key role is thus inherently complex and muddied. The important question is whether the record of its use as an instrument in diplomacy in the Persian Gulf is clear as to its effectiveness. Has it contributed to the achievement of US goals, and with what consequences?

In the section that follows I examine US relations with Iran and Saudi Arabia and Soviet relations with Iraq. In the case of Iran and Saudi Arabia, I make a distinction between the phases 1973-76 and 1977-80. In Iran's case a further division is made in the second phase to distinguish between the pre-revolutionary and post-revolutionary periods. This enables us to assess arms transfers as an instrument for durable influence in quite different political settings. In the case of Iraq—Soviet relations, the arms relationship is especially important in that arms sales are one of the few instruments of Soviet influence in the Third World, while Iraq is one of their older clients, dating back two decades.

---

1 Many observers have noted that when a particular arms request is under consideration the wisdom of the specific item is not at issue. Rather the entire relationship and the dependability of the supplier become the stake.

The three states contrast in their relations with the superpowers. Unlike Saudi Arabia, Iran has had a military assistance relationship with the US dating back over three decades. This was originally a government-to-government relationship with US advisers (MAAG) and it was strengthened by a bilateral Executive Agreement on Defence (1959) and participation in CENTO, in which the US was an associate member. In addition, Iran has diplomatic ties with the USSR. By contrast a Saudi defence relationship with the US is recent — starting in the 1970s — and only in the late 1970s did it become government-to-government, and more intensive. It is still informal with no express security commitment. Moreover Saudi Arabia does not have ties with the USSR.

Iraq, like Saudi Arabia, has ties with only one superpower, the USSR. The 1972 Treaty of Friendship contains a defence clause roughly comparable to Iran's rather weak assurance under the Executive Agreement. The Soviet Union is Iraq's major though not exclusive arms supplier. As with the US, arms transfers have been the major instrument in Soviet diplomacy with her ally in the Gulf, perhaps even more so. What is its record of achievement?

The second part of the book examines the potential contribution of the outside powers to conflict management in the region against the backdrop of trends in regional politics. The role of regional powers and regional structures is the related concern of this section which also evaluates the regional potential for conflict management.

# 1 The Record of Outside Power Influence

## US—Iran 1973-80

*The background: 1973-76*

The US involvement in Iran's military programmes dates to the late 1940s. From the immediate post-war period onward, strains developed between the Shah's view of Iran's defence needs and those of the US. American assistance in the restoration of the Shah in 1953 increased the psychological dependency of Iranian leaders on Washington. To this was added a real material dependency on US grant and budgetary assistance until 1967. By the mid-1960s, as Iran's oil income increased, Iran moved from grant-aid to credit-purchases from the US. This in turn gave way to outright purchases in the late 1960s and Iran's choices and bargaining power increased. US views of the optimum size for Iran's armed forces, or the appropriate weapons-systems for them were still heard, but increasingly ignored. By the early 1970s these American views, which had counselled restraint on an arms build-up for over two decades, were no longer offered. In part this was because Iran's oil wealth enabled it to reject views which it earlier had no choice but to accept. But equally important was the changed international context within which the Shah's perennial appetite for arms appeared intelligible and even welcome.

Foremost among these was the need for a strong and friendly state to protect US (and Western) interests in the Gulf.[1] The Shah was not only eager for Iran to do this and at her own expense but was prepared to do so on a wider canvas including the Middle East and the Indian sub-continent. US interests thus coincided with those of the Shah and a relationship was fashioned that not only avoided the need for a direct US military role but also promised support for its growing interests at a very low cost. The (only) identifiable costs were the sale of arms to the Shah's regime, a dependable but not formal ally. The strategic benefits from the point of view of a Republican administration contending with a public intent on retrenchment and selective commitment, were obvious. Equally clearly, a role as principal arms supplier implied con-comitant influence which could be manipulated as the recipient's dependence (on spare parts and training) grew. Hence Kissinger's cryptic reference in 1974 that he was fashioning with these states 'reasons for restraint'.

Apart from the longstanding arms relationship with Tehran and a willingness to strengthen a 'moderate' state able to assume wider responsibilities, the US had concrete political–military objectives in the Gulf. The establishment of a regional security system was one priority. Another was the strengthening of Iran itself *vis-à-vis* the Soviet Union, which was increasing its military potential. An Iran assured of its defence needs would be less prone to buckle under Soviet pressure. Often forgotten today, the May 1972 Nixon–Kissinger decision to allow the Shah to buy any conventional arms he wished came a month after the Soviet–Iraqi defence agreement and several months after the dismemberment of Pakistan. It also came before the quintupling of oil prices at the end of 1973. It was thus something less than the *carte blanche* it has been made out to be. Nevertheless the 1972 understanding was an order of magnitude change in US policy which formalized the US' transition from restraining patron to acquies-cent partner. It could be argued that this reflected a new inter-dependent partnership rather than created it. Internationally this may have been the case. Domestically, it sealed the future of the US interests with the Shah's fate. Yet in 1972 this appeared neither avoid-able nor unwelcome. The Shah's was apparently the most stable and certainly the longest lived regime in the Middle East.

How successful was US policy in obtaining its objectives within Iran in 1969-76? As far as security interests were concerned the record is clear. The Shah's role enhanced Gulf stability by containing Iraq, pacifying the Dhofari rebellion which had been abetted by South

1  This is not to suggest that many of these interests did not coincide with what the Shah considered in Iran's interests.

Yemen and the USSR and establishing working relations with Saudi Arabia. Further afield, Iran's diplomatic initiatives in Egypt and in the Indian subcontinent also worked in favour of diminishing conflict and strengthening peace.[1]

Militarily Iran's arms build-up and their assimilation was not tested. Yet it was already clear that rather than diminish US involvement, in at least its initial stages, the military component of the Nixon Doctrine (arms sales) actually increased the US physical presence. By 1976 there were some 25,000 military-related personnel (and their dependents) in Iran.

On the other hand the build-up of Iran militarily held the potential for a regional equilibrium less susceptible to disturbance by outside powers. The fact that Iran's arms were US supplied and largely compatible with those of US forces, together with the availability of Iran's military facilities, enhanced US and allied capabilities for rapid reaction in grave contingencies. Furthermore use of Iranian territory for intelligence and Soviet missile test monitoring were useful by-products of the arms relationship.

In the area of oil pricing, Iran and US interests diverged. While Tehran saw its interest in increasing its revenues (and even thereby discouraging consumption), Washington saw oil price rises as politically unpalatable and economically inflationary. The Shah's pursuit of Iran's interests to increase its revenues were historically justifiable and economically defensible. The difference between the two states' economic interests here was not allowed to wreck the compatability of interests on other security questions. Suggestions from various sources to invade the oilfields (Robert Tucker), encourage the break-up of OPEC (Professor Adelman), stimulate divisions between Iran and Saudi Arabia (Treasury Secretary Simon and Senator Frank Church) or favour Saudi Arabia over Iran (Ambassador J. Akins) were rejected by Nixon and Kissinger. Whether real or not,[2] linkage between the security dimension of US–Iranian relationship and oil-price questions (and Iran's role as advocate of price increases) was never formally invoked. However, careful consideration was given to a policy of such a linkage in the closing months of the Ford Administration.[3]

---

1   To these could be added the supply in 1974 of F-5s to South Vietnam at US request; the provision of oil to the US Navy in late 1973, and the supply of oil to Israel.

2   Adherents to the view that the oil-price increases were the result of expensive arms sales which necessitated greater revenues, (cf. Dale Tahtinen, 'Arms in the Persian Gulf') and Senator Frank Church (among others of the American Enterprise Institute for Public Policy Research, 1974) are unpersuasive.

3   Leslie Gelb, *New York Times*, 12 November 1976.

The Nixon-Ford presidencies were the highpoint of US—Iranian co-operation in which a tacit partnership evolved covering defence and security affairs in the Gulf and Middle East. Iran's policies were largely congruent with those of Washington and furthered their joint interests; differences on oil prices were submerged; and bureaucratic procedures were circumvented to facilitate this close relationship. Something approaching a 'special relationship' had indeed evolved largely due to the personal relationships between Nixon, Kissinger and the Shah.

The stability and durability of this personal (rather than institutionalized-bureaucratic) relationship was, however, suspect — largely for this very reason. There was no real consensus within the US, either in the bureaucracy or in the public at large, as to the wisdom of this close relationship. Some argued that oil prices were more important than military—security issues; others that the 'over-arming' of Iran threatened either regional or domestic stability, or that Iran's arms expenditures diverted resources from her economic development.[1] There was also a general hesitancy to embrace any further a regime with an 'unattractive' record on human rights. No matter that there were few suggestions as to how the US might extricate itself from dependency on the region without greater, and more direct, military involvement, there was a clear trend toward questioning the wisdom of the Republican administration's policies. By 1976 the consensus was unravelling and the tone of comments in that election year affected US—Iran relations.

The relationship underwent a marked shift in that year, losing its special status and reverting to straight bargaining. Sensing the new mood in Washington, the Shah resorted to earlier and successful tactics. In 1976-77 he hinted obliquely in interviews that if arms sales to Iran were curtailed he would:

1  Retaliate by limiting trade with the US.
2  Reconsider Iran's regional role promoting stability.
3  Buy arms from the USSR.
4  Be 'difficult' on issues relating to non-proliferation. (The latter was in fact used as an 'inducement' — that is, to show

---

1  Senator Church (1977); Lincoln Bloomfield (1976); Edward Kennedy (1974); Theodore Moran (1978); Leslie M. Pryor (1978). None of these authors suggested how the US could expect Iran to support Western interests if the US did not in turn meet some of the Shah's concerns.

his good faith, he supported US policies noting that he had the option not to do so.)[1]

A much clearer example of Iranian bargaining was in November 1977 on the Shah's visit to the US. In Washington he announced his support for an oil-price freeze in that December's OPEC meeting (in his hosts' idiom) by 'giving the US a break'.

The mood in Washington reflected a marked change in US priorities. Less geo-political than the Republicans, the Democrats were also less comfortable with the Iranian Shah who appeared arrogant, demanding and aloof. Defining security in other than purely military terms, the Carter administration sought to promote universal values such as human rights, particularly among its Third World allies. This implied greater popular political participation and more debate within those countries as to their policy choices and direction. In this view, stability in a region began with political stability at home. As regards Iran, the close — even cordial — relationship was gradually changed to a correct, working relationship. Standard comments of respect and public reassurance were still forthcoming from Washington but they carried less conviction. In fact, the Carter administration subtly shifted to a twin-pillar policy in which Saudi Arabia rather than Iran was given pre-eminent weight.[2]

In arms sales this shift was most apparent. Iran's requests were now routed through bureaucratic channels rather than allowed to short-cut them. US arms sales guidelines announced in May 1977 shifted the 'burden of proof' on to those requesting a particular purchase (rather than those rejecting it). This less permissive approach had an immediate impact. In July 1977 Iran's request for 250 F-18L aircraft was refused.[3] In July 1978 a request for advanced electronics on the F-4G was also refused. In addition the Carter administration sought where possible either to defer, or to scale down requests. Iran's request for a second tranche of 150 F-16s was accordingly postponed in 1977-78.

The Carter administration, though insensitive to the domestic political impact of such refusals within Iran, still sought to maintain its

---

1  *Business Week.* Note also that in 1976 when questions were raised about the activities of Iranian security personnel in the US, the Shah hinted that any restriction of their activities would be followed by Iran imposing restrictions on CIA activities within Iran. This implied a *quid pro quo* with the intelligence facilities used by the CIA—USA in Northern Iran for monitoring missile tests and signals and radio communications in the USSR. *Washington Post,* 1979.

2  Jim Hoagland and J.P. Smith, 'Saudi Arabia and the United States'. *Survival,* vol. XX, no. 2, March-April 1978, pp. 80-7.

3  The reason given was that the aircraft was not operationally deployed with US forces, a qualitative control outlined in the May 1977 guidelines.

ties with Iran despite Iran's human rights record. It thus supported the arms commitments it had inherited from the preceding administration. It expended considerable political (and presidential capital) in the latter part of 1977 in convincing a sceptical Congress of Iran's need for six AWACs early-warning aircraft. It also supported the request for the first tranche of 150 F-16s for delivery to Iran early in the 1980s. The AWACs affair, exacerbated by the administration's own 'open' approach to government which revealed differences within its own ranks (notably the CIA's opposition) and its own innocence of relations with Congress, also demonstrated the difficulties of shifting policies in such a sensitive area. Commitments were hard to stop, not merely because they were inherited, but because they were part of a process symbolizing the overall relationship.[1]

The more sceptical view of arms transfers as a tool of influence for promoting either bilateral relations or regional stability was paralleled in Carter's more low-key approach to political crises in the Third World. In neither Afghanistan (1978) nor Somalia–Ethiopia (1977-1978) did the United States respond militarily to these events, despite indications of Soviet complicity in the disturbances. The divergence between Iran's (and Saudi Arabia's) perceptions of the threat and that of the US were quite clear. Washington used its closer relationship with Iran to prevent the transfer of US-supplied arms to Somalia.[2] This affected both states' perceptions of their ally's dependability and willingness to meet their security needs.

*The revolutionary upheaval*

With the emergence of widespread unrest within Iran in 1978, US policy shifted and with it the utility of its policy instruments. From pursuing a close but measured relationship with an Iran considered a 'force for stability in the area' and a dependable ally, pursuing policies supportive of US interests, it became necessary to seek to contain that country's turbulence before it disrupted those wider interests. In the fluid politics that characterized the disintegration of the Shah's regime, the arms relationship was of limited value. The US sought

---

1  'Our willingness to sell arms is seen by many, indeed most, friendly governments, as a litmus test of our bilateral relationships. . . . a refusal to sell invariably touches an extremely sensitive nerve, and tends to raise doubts in the minds of the affected country about the assumed strength of the bilateral relationship in security affairs and about the future reliability of the United States as an arms supplier'. Lucy Wilson Benson, 'Turning the Supertanker: Arms Transfer Restraint', *International Security*, Spring 1979, p. 17.

2  Under the traditional 'end-use' agreement governing arms transfers giving the supplier the right to veto third party transfers by the original recipient. This veto was not exercised by the US in Iran's involvement in Oman because the arms remained in Iran's hands.

'damage limitation' and counselled political rather than military 'solutions'. There was no identifiable or discrete military threat that could be met by new, better or more arms. The close military relationship with the Shah's regime, a crucial asset in the event of aggression from external sources, was too blunt an instrument for this contingency.[1] Nor could less equivocal US expressions of support for the Shah or even the deployment of US troops to Iranian territory have materially affected the outcome of the revolution unless perhaps they had been forthcoming early in the upheavals. This was not possible because the initial unrest was not seen as the beginning of a momentous revolution but rather as sporadic and isolated disturbances. In the event, the US arms relationship with Iran, symbolizing its close ties with the Shah,[2] was transferred from an asset for influence in a peaceful era into a liability in a revolutionary situation. Even as a deterrent against external intervention in Iran's crisis, the demonstrative use of force by the US could have been counter-productive. Hence Washington's reluctance to allow the sailing to the Gulf of a carrier task force from the Philippines, which it had initially considered. The danger that such a move might be construed domestically in Iran as opposition to the revolution and set off still wider disturbances[3] overrode the initial impulse either to signal support for the Shah or deter Soviet involvement.

As the Shah's fate was sealed in the streets of Tehran, Washington re-examined its options. It found that the military relationship still conferred on it certain advantages. The fact that Iranian officers had been largely trained in the US (over 12,000 since 1947), could speak English and were well acquainted with their American counterparts, gave the US a natural channel for communication to the still intact armed forces. It was evident to all that this could still be a considerable advantage in the bargaining that would shape the future course of politics in Iran. The dispatch of General Huyser (Deputy to the US Commander in Europe) in December 1978 was intended by the US to establish an independent line of communication to these military

---

1 Ironically the Shah's regime had planned its security forces to meet isolated low-level guerrilla violence through SAVAK, and high-level military threats through its armed forces. The interface of these two categories of threat, widespread civil disorder which might have been met by mobile, tactical police forces armed with shields, rubber bullets and incapacitating gases, was not anticipated probably due to bureaucratic jealousies and a refusal to admit, even privately, its possibility. This question is important for its potential relevance to other states in the Gulf.

2 In addition to the co-operation between intelligence services spanning the decades, with which we are not here concerned.

3 The British Ambassador Antony Parsons who was in close touch with US Ambassador William Sullivan has argued that this move would have enraged the crowds still further rather than cowed them. (Personal interview, London, 1979).

commanders. Despite the controversy surrounding the mission,[1] this much is clear — the existence of an independent channel to the armed forces derived from the close military relationship with the US. Second, this channel was an important and potentially crucial one for influencing politics in Iran after the departure of the Shah[2]. The maintenance of an intact military as an institution could confer considerable bargaining advantages in managing both the post-revolutionary politics of Iran and the transition. How this channel of communication was used and what other forces bore on it is however more contentious. For our purposes it is sufficient to note the US dilemma in using this channel. The impulse to use the military to support the Bakhtiar government to extract assurances and concessions from the Bazargan— Khomeini forces competed with the conclusion of many US officials that the victory of the latter's forces was inevitable. The argument for recognizing the 'inevitable' and urging the military to withdraw support from Bakhtiar by announcing 'political neutrality' (with specific assurances from Khomeini about the military's welfare) was especially tempting for a United States that wanted above all to maintain its position within the country. Whether it was this that precipitated the Iranian generals' decision to opt for 'neutrality' in mid-February is still not clear. Evidently the generals were divided. Some saw the Shah's exile as temporary, others sensed the end of an era and a shift in American policy toward accommodating Khomeini. Whatever the relevance of the various factors, the channel available to the US was not used productively. The neutrality of the military was followed by its destruction and its senior officers were executed. The US' ambiguous role was condemned by royalist and republican alike.

### Post-revolution

The immediate consequence of the revolution was the virtual disintegration of the armed forces (desertion ran at 60 per cent), the purging of senior officers, and the withdrawal of US technicians and advisers. (The MAAG for example was reduced to six from approximately 400). In addition six intelligence gathering bases run by the CIA and NSA were lost. Advanced military equipment like the 77 F-14 aircraft and their *Phoenix* missiles were also at risk in the anarchy that followed

---

1 The Shah believed the Huyser mission was intended to undermine him and expedite his exile. General Haig and others are sceptical about the US role as well. See also Michael Ledeen & William Lewis, 'Carter and the Fall of the Shah', *The Washington Quarterly*, vol. 3, no. 2, Spring 1980.

2 Ambassador William Sullivan appears to have recognized the importance of the military as a channel to post-revolutionary Iran. See 'The Road Not Taken', *Foreign Policy*, no. 40, Fall 1980, pp. 175-86.

February 1979. In this new era it was the task of US diplomacy to prevent a total break in relations that would jeopardize its economic and political-military interests in the country. To do so it had to show a less conspicuous presence in the country but to conserve what contacts it had initiated with the new regime, and patiently to await the emergence of order in the country. In time, it was expected, a hierarchy would be established, priorities would be identified, and pragmatic considerations, both strategic and economic, would impel Iranian—US co-operations — albeit on a lower key.

American caution after February 1979 was understandable. Totally identified with the Shah over three decades, it had a burdensome past to live down with the new authorities and in the new anti-Western ethos in Iran. At the same time important interests were at stake: the prevention of a communist or leftist takeover in Iran which would further unsettle the Gulf region; the continuation of the export of oil to the US and, more important, to her European and Japanese allies.[1] The US therefore attempted to 'normalize' relations and to avoid giving offence or fostering the notion that she was intent on containing or isolating the new regime. Care was exercised to prevent provocation, criticism of massive human rights violation were perfunctory, and the best possible construction put on statements of intent emanating from Tehran. Where possible the 'moderate' forces' comments were singled out, and stressed, implicitly distinguishing between PM Bazargan and Ayatollah Khomeini. In short Washington sought to show that it was prepared 'to do business' with the new authorities in Tehran.

Events in Iran in mid-1979 seemed to support this approach. Despite statements to the contrary, the armed forces were not completely disbanded. In May, relations with Iraq and in August, relations with the Kurds deteriorated sharply and the Iranian authorities rediscovered the need for a military system that functioned. Despite the cancellation of $11 billion worth of US arms ordered by the Shah, the country had taken possession of $8 billion worth which were still largely unassimilated. If these were not to become scrap, spare parts and maintenance assistance would be required from the United States. Furthermore continued technical training of Iranian personnel was necessary for much of this material.[2] In addition, the Iranian logistical system had been computerized by the US. Without adequate skilled personnel the

1 The US normally imported 9 per cent of her energy imports (4 per cent total consumption) from Iran. In Europe the proportions were higher. In Japan Iran accounted for 20 per cent of her imports which were 90 per cent of her needs.

2 This in fact still continued. Despite revolutionary rhetoric some 250 Iranian military were being trained in the US in November 1979 (contrasted with 2,500 in 1976).

location of spare parts already in the country's inventory would be impossible. In short the umbilical cord leading from Iran to the US was still very real. The US, aware of this objective dependency, was anxious to use it discreetly as a basis for preliminary co-operation. To do so, it needed to avoid any public reference to it or to appear to be driving a hard bargain. Washington was extremely sensitive lest an attempt to exploit it should backfire and terminate the only existing channel for contact and co-operation. Thus it was hoped that the military relationship would prevent too complete or too rapid a breakdown in an overall relationship that was politically strained. Any unwillingness to respond sensitively to any Iranian requests was thus seen in Washington as potentially damaging to US interests, for this would drive the new regime elsewhere. Moreover the option of outright rejection was discarded because it might force the regime's hand and drive it into a corner, and possibly toward the USSR.

Washington thus found that Iran's military dependency, far from strengthening America's hand, inhibited it from the exercise of influence lest it jeopardize that channel. No matter that Iran's dependence was real, that Iran had tangible security problems that needed to be met, that Iran still required a counterpoise to the USSR, and that shifting arms supplies is a lengthy and costly business in which the transition period could be particularly dangerous – and that all of these considerations could be expected to militate in favour of US not Iranian leverage – supplier leverage simply did not materialize.

In practice the reverse happened. In mid-1979 the US, while continuing the technical training of Iranians, agreed to provide non-lethal spare parts, which (it was argued) had already been paid for. In addition there were reports of supplies of diesel fuel for military vehicles used in Kurdistan. US refined heating oil was also made available to the Iranian government. Negotiations for the resale of F-14s to the US were also announced but not initiated in 1979.

The semblance of 'normalization' was as illusory as was Washington's expectation that 'moderates' would emerge in Iran's revolutionary condition. The cultivation of the moderates in this situation was the kiss of death. The fear of Iran's disintegration, of a replacement by a leftist regime or even of further chaos, were powerful incentives arguing for 'doing business' with Khomeini's regime. Yet it was difficult to establish direct contact with the Ayatollah, who had in any case a totally different frame of reference. For Khomeini 'security' was to be achieved through revolutionary unity and purity not through arms. This meant that practical considerations held less importance than the manipulation of symbols. The occupation of the US Embassy in October 1979, supported by Khomeini, brought down the Bazargan government. In this episode the limits of American influence were further exposed. Khomeini's willingness to invite an American military response, to claim martyrdom or to expose US weakness while objectively foolhardy, was nonetheless tactically irreproachable for mobilizing revolutionary zeal and unity.

The US' responses were limited by a variety of factors. The well-being of the hostages ruled out any precipitate military rescue while regional and global considerations deterred a major punitive military operation. Furthermore the use of force might consolidate Iranians behind Khomeini and frighten US allies in the region. However, the failure to respond would also be costly. It could strengthen Khomeini's image among the Iranian masses, advertise US impotence and frighten US allies. The use of non-military instruments, such as trade embargoes, would hurt the Iranian people rather than the government and might, in any case, have proved ineffective, at least in the short run. Multilateral actions with Western allies confronted the problem of the greater dependence of these states on Iran's oil.[1] Furthermore the American freezing of Iranian funds inside the US (applying also to foreign banks) created strong resentments among US allies about a unilateral measure which affected multilateral interests.

*The military relationship and the hostage episode*

The seizure of some sixty US citizens, mostly diplomats, in the US Embassy in Tehran by militant students on 4th November, supported by the Iranian authorities, ushered in a new phase in Washington's relationship with the revolutionary regime. No longer so anxious to reassure Tehran about its 'acceptance' of the revolution and its willingness to work with it, Washington now sought to convey to the Iranian leaders the costs involved in supporting such hostile activities. In attempting to communicate this over the next fourteen months, Washington was constrained both by its continuing interest in Iran's political cohesion and by the refusal of the authorities in Tehran to acknowledge their continuing dependence on the US for arms. This failure to recognize or act upon an 'objective interest' made the Iranian leadership impervious to the types of sanctions and incentives that could be manipulated in the arms supply relationship. Normal assumptions about dependency fostering a business-like attitude or inhibiting extreme measures did not therefore hold in a situation where the dependent partner was prepared to sacrifice his material interests for a 'higher' goal.

---

1 Especially Japan's reluctance to forego Iran's oil or jeopardize her reasonably good economic relations with the new regime.

The Bazargan government had quickly recognized the reality of this military dependency and the necessity for the maintenance of a defence establishment. With considerable pragmatism they had embarked in the summer of 1979 upon re-establishing links with the United States — which had proved to be equally business-like. Foreign Minister Yazdi had put the matter very simply: 'We have bought billions of dollars worth of military equipment from the United States, and for the maintenance of this equipment we need parts. So obviously there will be, and there are, some contracts — you may say a purchasing contract — for the parts'.[1] Yazdi was aware that the issue of any type of military relationship with the US was a potentially contentious one. This was not merely a matter of emotions or revolutionary rhetoric. In the continuing power struggle in Iran it was clear that the future role of the armed forces could be decisive. Who supplied, advised and influenced these forces could play an important role in Iran's future. Nevertheless he and Bazargan still underestimated the power of the militants within Iran. By showing a willingness to acknowledge the necessity of a continuing Iran—US relationship, they inadvertently provided a pretext for those seeking a total rupture of relations.

The subsequent details of the saga of the US hostages concerns us only to the extent that the military component of the relationship was utilized. On 9 November the United States halted and impounded a $300 million shipment of aircraft spare parts; the announcement for the resumption of deliveries having been made on 5 October. On 23 November, the US announced that flight training for the 273 or so Iranian military personnel[2] still in the United States would be terminated, although other instruction courses would continue. The effect of these measures was to inhibit any commercial relationship in the military field by independent businesses and contractors. US companies complied with a government request to reduce their number of representatives in Iran.[3]

A second set of pressures were set in motion in the Spring. On 17 April President Carter declared that the $300 million in spare parts which had been paid for would now 'be made available for use by United States' military forces or for sale to other countries'. The bulk of this equipment comprised aircraft and helicopter parts. The practical effect of this move was that, if future US—Iranian relations should

1   *International Herald Tribune*, 5 July 1979.

2   The figures vary but appear to have consisted of 249 undergoing training with the USAF of which 200 were pilots, and 24 with the Navy of which 19 were pilots. See *Air Force Times*, 19 November 1979.

3   *Boston Globe*, 15 November 1979.

improve to the point of a renewal of the arms relationship, 'it will be longer and harder for them (Iran) to recover' because now there would be no parts in the pipeline.[1] Ten days earlier the severance of diplomatic relations had ended the remaining military training relationship and all Iranian military personnel had been returned to Iran.[2] A consequence of the measures undertaken by Washington after November was the severance for all practical purposes of any form of co-operation — official or commercial — in areas related to technology likely to have potential military application. This was due as much to the anger of US companies at the seizure of the hostages as to specific or express government prohibition. Nevertheless the implication of Washington's actions was clear: no company could expect government support in any claim against Iran if no diplomatic relations existed. Washington's measures therefore had the wider effect of inhibiting the continuation of normal commercial contacts such as the provision of 'customer service' by aircraft companies such as Boeing.[3]

Frustrated by the failure of these and other economic sanctions to make an impression on the Iranian government, the United States launched a rescue mission to free the hostages on 24 April 1980. Two aspects of this aborted mission concern us: the decision to launch the incursion by air from eastern Iran; and the expectation of some co-operation by Iranian military units within the country. Both of these components relate directly to the military and arms relationship. The choice of approach site was almost certainly due to the United States' knowledge about the likely blindspots in Iran's radar coverage — information that was due to its own contribution in their construction. Second, the military assistance expected from within the Iranian armed forces was due to the longstanding and extensive contacts between the two countries' military services.[4] In the context of the April mission, James Schlesinger's remarks six years earlier are apposite. Asked whether the United States had considered the effects of the sale of arms to countries that it might in future have to fight, the Defence Secretary said: 'In the extreme and highly unlikely circumstances (suggested) . . . it is not clear that American forces would prefer to come face-to-face

1   For the text of Carter's statement see *The New York Times*, 18 April 1980. See also *Wall Street Journal*, 18 April 1980.

2   See *Aviation Week and Space Technology*, 14 April 1980, p. 23.

3   See *ibid.*, p. 15.

4   This expectation of assistance appears to have been justified. The Iranian Air Force's destruction of the helicopters left behind at Tabas before they could be examined for information was much remarked upon in Iran and appears to have been due only partly to caution relating to their physical security. The former Chief of the Iranian Air Force, General Bagheri was subsequently arrested on charges of collusion with the US. See *International Herald Tribune*, 26 February 1981.

with equipment supplied by some other power as opposed to the US'.[1]

It was soon clear that the severance of spare parts from the United States and the prohibition of all arms transfers to Iran from any country possessing US-made equipment[2] was exacting a price on Iran, particularly in aviation. Iranian agents attempted unsuccessfully to circumvent the embargo by purchases in Europe.[3] In November 1979 Western observers reported that the radar systems were unserviceable and that the F-14s (of which Iran had 77) were barely operational. The 380 F-4s and F-5s were said to be 50 per cent operational. The helicopter force of nearly 1,000 was reported to be largely grounded.[4] The computerized logistics system was now in total disarray. As a result it was impossible to locate the existence of spare parts or supplies which might exist in inventory. Whether this was due simply to the lack of adequately trained manpower and inadequate assimilation of the technology, or due to actual sabotage — as implied by President Bani Sadr — is unknown. He observed that the operational readiness of the three armed services in January 1980 varied between 5 and 25 per cent.[5] A more obvious case of US sabotage related to the *Phoenix* air-to-air missile. Sensitive components of this missile were disassembled and removed by American technicians before their departure from Iran — a clear case of supplier leverage.[6]

Iran's efforts to procure military supplies through West Germany and Italy proved unsuccessful.[7] By January 1980, Iran's helicopter force of 1,000 was down to an operational readiness of some 15 per cent, due in large part to the lack of support personnel and spare parts from the US. The Italian government refused to supply the fifty CH-47C *Chinook* (Agusta-Bell) helicopters ordered by Iran pending the release of the hostages.[8] The effect of this was felt not only in the

---

1 Department of Defense News Release, 14 January 1974 (Pentagon Press Conference), as cited in James Noyes, *The Clouded Lens*, Hoover Institution, 1977, p. 197.

2 Or with a licence to manufacture it.

3 *Baltimore Sun*, 19 November 1979.

4 The articles by Robert Fisk in *The Times*, 27, 28 November 1979 and US Defense Department evaluations in *International Herald Tribune*, 19 November 1979.

5 Bani Sadr, interview *Le Monde*, 8 October 1980. The logistical system cost, according to the President, $250 million.

6 See *Aviation Week and Space Technology*, 20 October 1980.

7 *Newsweek*, 31 December 1979, p. 17.

8 See *Aviation Week and Space Technology*, 28 January 1980, p. 11; 18 February 1980, p. 15; 14 April 1980, p. 20. Agusta had 100 technicians in Iran and had provided 60 helicopters before the revolution.

military field where Iran's new defence officials with extraordinary naiveté had recently discovered the usefulness of the helicopter force inherited from the Shah's regime.[1] In fields of civil application (such as in flood relief operations) the spare parts for helicopters were missed and this was readily and publicly admitted.[2]

By mid-1980 it was clear that Western sanctions, especially in the military field, were exacting their toll. In addition to the political purges, desertions and the decline in discipline and morale in the armed forces and the low esteem in which they continued to be publicly held, the loss of technical assistance together with the severance of spare parts had reduced the Iranian military's capabilities even further. In the context of its international isolation, Iranian officials used their one remaining bargaining card *vis-à-vis* the West — the 'threat' to become dependent on the USSR. This had already been implied by economic agreements with the Eastern bloc announced the day after EEC sanctions were agreed on 22 April. In May this threat was revived in the context of potential arms supplies from the USSR to reduce Iran's dependence on the United States.[3]

The threat was significant for it reflected Iran's awareness of the limits to Western pressures. US measures after 4 November had been intended to impress upon Iran's leaders the costs of supporting such illegal actions as hostage-taking while continuing to offer the prospect of a normal relationship once the issue was resolved. Washington's responses had been gradual and calibrated, sensitive to both political pressures building up within the United States and the need to avoid precipitate action by offering Tehran the possibility of a peaceful solution. After the Soviet invasion of Afghanistan, President Carter and, after the rescue mission, Secretary Brown, each offered to normalize relations if the hostage issue were resolved. Indeed Carter in January had even offered to resume the sale of arms to Iran.[4] The United States' strategic interest in Iran had now been heightened by the presence of Soviet troops close to the Gulf. As a result, Defense Secretary Brown observed: 'We are quite eager to restore good relations . . . We do want to be friends with the revolutionary government . . . A strong, stable Iran, neutral and Islamic would be good for the area and

---

1 See Defence Minister Mustafa Chamran's comments, *International Herald Tribune*, 22-23 March 1980.

2 See *Daily Telegraph*, 23 February 1980.

3 It was raised but not acted upon by Foreign Minister Sadeq Ghotbzadeh. See *Daily Telegraph*, 9 May 1980.

4 *International Herald Tribune*, 24 January 1980.

for the United States. Moreover it would help to block Soviet expansionism'.[1]

As long as US strategic interests required a strong Iran that remained independent of the USSR and these interests dominated the US approach to the hostage issue, there were bound to be limits to the effectiveness of its measures aimed at Iran. Particularly in the psychological dimension affecting bargaining, the US need for Iran was clearly more evident and more publicized than the Iranians' need for a connection with the United States. It was only with the arrival — and perception — of a new and greater threat that the Iranians were persuaded to negotiate the issue realistically.

## The Iran—Iraq war

The escalation from border clashes to more significant conflict — without a formal declaration of war — was a direct result of Iran's military weakness. Differences between the two neighbours had periodically surfaced in the past two decades, ostensibly on the issue of their riverine frontier on the Shatt al' Arab.[2] But, despite occasional clashes, skirmishes, and exchanges of fire in the border region, there had never been a serious risk of war due to Iran's acknowledged military preponderance and its interest in the maintenance of the *status quo*. Iran's international isolation and particularly her military weakness — in part as the result of the US' embargo — changed the military balance of power in the Gulf. Iraq perceived an opportunity to score a rapid and decisive military victory and took it. The onset of the first Gulf war in modern times may largely be attributed to Iran's military weakness, in part caused by the severance of its military relationship with the US.

The war from Washington's view was a mixed blessing. While it might convince the Iranians of the futility of retaining the hostages, it might also weaken that country either leading to its disintegration or driving it into reliance on the USSR. Constrained by domestic political requirements and regional and international interests, Washington sought to dangle the possibility of a military relationship before the Iranians while seeking to limit the adverse consequences of the war.

The constraints operating on the US government domestically were clear: a passionate distaste for the Iranian regime combined with a fervent desire both to see it punished and have the hostages released. Electoral considerations impelled President Carter to seek the release

1 *International Herald Tribune*, 28 April 1980.

2 For background see the companion paper in this series by Robert Litwak. 'Sources of Inter-State Conflict', *Security in the Persian Gulf*, Gower, Aldershot, for IISS, no. 2, 1981.

of the hostages without sacrificing US honour through making concessions to blackmail. Yet the Iranians would need to be enticed by subtle incentives for the threat of increasing punishment had not worked and, if applied, could prove counterproductive from the standpoint of US strategic interests. US regional and global interests also required a delicate touch to ensure that neither Iran nor Iraq won a decisive victory; to ensure that the USSR did not benefit from the war; to limit the escalation of the conflict through prevention of competitive arms supply policies; and to retain its credibility as a partner of the Arab oil-producing states, particularly Saudi Arabia. The difficulties of balancing these considerations were made more difficult both by Washington's lack of diplomatic ties with either contestant and by the growing daily need of returning the hostages before election day.

To reduce the possibility of misunderstanding, the US and USSR met on 25 September and co-ordinated their positions by agreeing to neutrality. A week later the US dispatched early-warning aircraft to Saudi Arabia to allay its regional partner's anxieties. At the outset of the war President Carter announced that the US was 'not taking a position' on it, going on to explain that the conflict might convince the Iranians of their need for friends 'and therefore induce them to release the hostages'.[1] This was followed by hints of US concern. Warren Christopher, Deputy Secretary of State, noted that while the US remained neutral it would certainly oppose 'the dismemberment of Iran'.[2] By the first week in October, Washington had publicly warned Jordan against the transfer of US supplied arms to Iraq.[3] On 19 October President Carter alluded to the US interest in a strong Iran and Secretary of State Muskie made public reference to Iraq's 'invasion'.[4] By the end of the month, Washington had returned to its by now traditional ploy, that of holding out the possibility of restoring a military supply relationship once the hostage issue was resolved.[5] A mouth-watering list of equipment paid for and ready for delivery was made public. It included parts for F-4s, F-5s, F-14s, C-130s, *Dragon* anti-tank missiles, land-mines, 155 mm howitzer and tank ammunition and air-defence missiles.[6] Explanations for the American readiness to supply arms were various. Secretary Muskie, for example, argued that

1 See *International Herald Tribune*, 26 September 1980.

2 See *International Herald Tribune*, 29 September 1980.

3 See *International Herald Tribune*, 8 October 1980.

4 See *International Herald Tribune*, 20 October 1980.

5 See *International Herald Tribune*, 25-26 October 1980.

6 See *International Herald Tribune*, 31 October 1980. See also *Aviation Week*, 3 November 1980, p. 15.

retention of the embargo on parts favoured Iraq. The President made a distinction between supplying equipment already paid for and selling additional equipment.[1] Within a week these signals to Iran had been further refined. It was now observed that much of the material formerly ordered by Iran might not now be required while other orders, such as ammunition, might present the US with diplomatic problems if supplied during a conflict. It was suggested that, if Iran requested supplies, perhaps the provision of non-lethal equipment such as aircraft parts (rather than ammunition) might be appropriate.[2]

In the event the Iranians failed to rise to this bait and neglected to ask for spare parts. Indeed, despite setbacks on the battlefield, the Iranians apparently concluded the final agreement on the release of the hostages without any specific reference to the military supply relationship, or even the material already bought and embargoed. After this agreement there were no immediate signs of Iran's interest in the resumption of supplies. It became clear in January 1981 that Iran owned $1 billion-worth in arms, equipment and cash held by the US Department of Defense. Of this, approximately half derived from a cash trust fund customarily maintained by large-scale customers of US arms, the remainder was in equipment, some of which had been ordered before the advent of the revolutionary government in Tehran.[3] The new Republican administration expressly rejected its predecessor's policy of using the arms as an inducement for Iranian good behaviour. It immediately ruled out any military supply relationship with Tehran, cancelling the standing order (with reimbursement) and rejecting consideration of any future requests that Iran might be inclined to make.[4]

Why was the United States unable to use its past (and potential) role as an arms supplier to improve relations with Iran? After all, with Iran now at war and militarily disadvantaged, the opportunity for the re-establishment of US influence seemed obvious. The manipulation of arms supplies might be expected to provide the US with increased leverage on the contestants and in the Gulf as a whole. The reasons why this opportunity had not materialized by the spring of 1981 are attributable to two sets of discrete factors rather than to the inherent limitations of leverage in an arms-supply relationship. The first set of constraints revolves around the nature of the war itself, the impact of

1 President Carter's Campaign Debate in Cleveland, 28 October in *Selected Statements*, 1 November 1980, p. 26; *International Herald Tribune*, 31 October 1980.

2 See *Washington Post*, 4 November 1980; *Washington Star*, 4 November 1980.

3 *Baltimore Sun*, 22 January 1981; *Washington Star*, 22 January 1981.

4 *The Times*, 28 January 1981.

the embargo on Iran's preparedness and Iran's immediate military needs. The second lies outside strictly military considerations and originated in the nature of Iran's (domestic) politics, the power struggle within and the pressures that this created on the prosecution of the war.

*Preparedness.* The war demonstrated at its outset the failure of the early warning system to detect intruding Iraqi aircraft that were able to strike more than 300 miles deep into Iran. Although this was attributed to US—Iraqi collusion,[1] a more plausible explanation, given the same phenomenon on the Iraqi side, was the lack of expertise in maintenance.[2] In its initial phases the air war was quite intense. By the end of the second week of the war, Iranian aircraft losses were believed to be up to 100, twice those of Iraq.[3] It was evident that Iran was relying on the F-4s and F-5s (rather than the F-14s which were more difficult to service) and that these remained operational partly because the large inventory (totalling 343) enabled technicians to cannibalize many for needed parts. By the end of the third week of the war, Iran had begun a limited use of its *Cobra* helicopters, *Tow* and *Dragon* anti-tank missiles and the *Maverick* air-to-surface missile. Their limited use in the war, despite large Iranian stocks, suggested that lack of ammunition was less a problem than the inadequacy of maintenance and a dearth of spare parts.[4] The infrequent use of the large helicopter fleet certainly sustained this reasoning. Despite its clear superiority in airpower, in training and in aircraft performance and the flying of up to 100 sorties a day, Iran made no systematic use of airpower for close support, for interdiction, or to gain air superiority. This suggested weakness in logistics and in command and control. In addition a shortage of pilots and navigators as a result of frequent political purges seriously impaired the Iranian war effort. The brunt of the air war was sustained by the F-4s and F-5s while the F-14 was only used infrequently, primarily as a radar platform. Iran's primary reliance on these two aircraft and on C-130s and Boeing 707s for transport and supply (together with its need for helicopter parts) had indeed been apparent before the war. As a result of the systematic use of these aircraft against Iranian Kurds in 1979, they had needed repair and maintenance and it had been parts and ammunition for these aircraft that Iran had sought before the events of November 1979.

1  By Iranian officials, see *The Times*, 25 September 1980.

2  See *Aviation Week and Space Technology*, 29 September 1980, p. 27.

3  *Ibid.*, 6 October 1980, pp. 20-21.

4  See *ibid.*, 13 October 1980, pp. 24-25.

After the first weeks of the war, the level of air activity declined appreciably, leading in the winter months to a static land war punctuated by the sporadic exchange of shelling and occasional tank battles. In this kind of warfare, military equipment of US origin was less important. With the exception of its tank force (which included US-supplied M-60s and M-48s though it consisted predominantly of British-built *Chieftains*)[1] most of Iran's artillery needs were obtainable elsewhere. For example 105 mm, 130 mm and 155 mm artillery shells could be bought in the arms markets of Europe. Furthermore the sheer number of weapons systems and bulk of ammunition bought and stored in the Shah's day provided the Iranian armed forces with a considerable buffer against any immediate needs. Stocks could be extended by cannibalization particularly since the diminishing tempo of the land war necessitated the commitment of only limited numbers of vehicles, tanks and artillery to battle.

*Substitution.* The move from an air to a land war and the diminution of the intensity of the conflict thus reduced Iran's needs for spare parts from abroad, and specifically removed any immediate necessity of compromising its revolution (as Iran saw it) by re-establishing direct or indirect links with the United States to obtain spare parts for its aircraft. While reducing Iran's immediate needs it did not eliminate the necessity of acquiring replenishment for an arsenal which was bound to need ammunition and parts as the war continued. There was considerable evidence of Iran's search for new sources of equipment. For the exclusively US-supplied Air Force (which included Army and Navy aviation) there was the most difficulty. Even six months before the war Iranian agents had reportedly been trying, with little success, to obtain parts for F-4s and F-5s.[2] Iran continued without success to press Italy for the release of *Chinook* helicopters it had paid for earlier.[3] Iranian representatives – again without success – sought assistance from Greece for spare parts and the servicing of F-4 aircraft.[4] The Iraqi government claimed that Iran had received US-made supplies particularly for its Air Force with US approval from Japan and Taiwan.[5] Another source alleged that Israel was providing Iran with US equipment, particularly spares for the F-4, but neglected to state

1  875 *Chieftain* and 250 (light) *Scorpion* tanks of UK origin, and 400 M47/48, and 460 M-60A1 US tanks.

2  NATO intelligence sources are quoted in *International Herald Tribune*, 6 October 1980.

3  *Aviation Week*, 24 November 1980, p. 26.

4  *The Times*, 2 October 1980; *International Herald Tribune*, 10 October 1980.

5  *The Times*, 2 October 1980.

whether this was with or without US assent.[1] Still another source reported that Iran had obtained 'American-made spares' manufactured under licence in Italy.[2] Despite these allegations, which were cloudy and confused, two points were clear. First it was highly unlikely that the US would supply Iran either directly or indirectly with spare parts for aircraft without some sort of political understanding or *quid pro quo*. This meant that, with the possible exception of captured US-built equipment (as in Vietnam),[3] no major recipient of arms would risk its arms relationship with the US by contravening US law and policy. Second, it was always possible for Iran to obtain certain categories of material such as some artillery pieces and ammunition for them on the open market.[4] Clearly however Iran could not easily find radar equipment, avionics packages or the spare parts for aircraft that would be needed routinely for maintenance. The more extensive usage made of equipment during warfare (such as aircraft tyres) and battle damage would require considerable quantities of such items.

Iran achieved some success in obtaining arms and parts from countries outside of the West. Syria, Libya and North Korea are reported to have provided Soviet-bloc material. This consisted chiefly of ammunition, explosives and medical supplies. They were ferried by Iranian transport aircraft who were permitted access to Soviet airspace.[5] Direct Soviet assistance was more limited. The report of an offer to supply arms to Iran was denied by Moscow.[6] However, it appeared consistent with the Soviet interest in increasing the USSR's role in Iran for the Soviets to depict the US as poised to invade that country — the implication being that the USSR would then 'protect the revolution'.[7] Soviet supply of jet fuel directly to Iran was

1  *The Observer*, 2 November 1980. This charge was denied by Israel, see *ibid.*, 9 November 1980. It was confirmed subsequently by various sources, see *International Herald Tribune*, 24 August 1981.

2  *The Observer*, 25 January 1980.

3  These arms may have reached North Korea, a limited supplier of arms to Iran. See *Aviation Week*, 13 October 1980, p. 24 and *International Herald Tribune*, 10 October 1980.

4  This would account for claims by Iranian officials including Bani Sadr that obtaining US equipment in the arms market had posed no problem. See *Le Monde*, 8 October 1980. Another official specifically exempted certain categories of aircraft from this. See *The Times*, 31 October 1980.

5  See *International Herald Tribune*, 10 October, 5 November 1980; *Financial Times*, 1 November 1980.

6  See especially *International Herald Tribune*, 9 October 1980; *Le Monde*, 22 October 1980.

7  See *Pravda*, 17 January 1981.

reported.[1] Soviet bloc equipment could be of assistance to Iran in several areas. In air defence, ammunition for the ZSU-23-4 anti-aircraft guns would be useful. Ammunition and spares for armoured vehicles, SA-7 man-portable air defence missiles, all of which could supplement Soviet supplied equipment already existing in the Iranian inventory, would be helpful to Iran's war effort. Yet none of these would provide Iran with anything other than a limited capability to remain in the war — they could not furnish the basis for victory.

In sum the impact of the US-led sanctions on Iran's military preparedness was considerable. Iran's isolation and apparent military weakness had invited an Iraqi attack. *Inter alia* lack of spare parts and poor maintenance impeded Iran's capacity to use its air superiority to great effect and was reflected also in poor air defence due to the incapacitated *Hawk* defence system. Exclusive reliance on the US for supplies of aircraft and helicopter parts hampered Iran's search for alternative sources of supply. Such equipment as could be bought on the open market was at premium prices[2] and consisted of ammunition or small artillery pieces. Eastern bloc material, though available, was of marginal rather than decisive importance for Iran's military capability. As the war shifted to ground engagements, Iran's war effort was hampered not only by an embargo on US equipment but also by Britain's refusal to supply arms or spare parts during the conflict. As a result Iran's tank force, split almost equally between US and UK tanks, was in potential jeopardy. Extensive use of *Chieftain* tanks would require the replacement of their power packs (engines) and in due course[3] this might result in Iran's armour grinding to a halt without even encountering its adversary.

Although the costs of the embargo for Iran's preparedness and military capabilities, for her hard currency reserves in seeking substitute sources, and for her pride in failing to expel the Iraqi invader, were considerable, they were still in fact mitigated. The winding-down of the war after two months necessitated the commitment of fewer resources to it. Equipment could be husbanded and reconstituted through improvisation. The air-war particularly became less important. This enabled the Iranian regime to avoid (or put off) facing the reality of its military needs — which were now less pressing. It also allowed the politicians in Tehran to continue their power struggle without

1  *International Herald Tribune*, 5 November 1980 (The report cites *Aviation Week* as its source.)

2  This was an additional cost, and admitted by Iranian officials. See Bani Sadr's comments quoted in *International Herald Tribune*, 10 October 1980.

3  After 700 miles. See *Financial Times*, 21 January 1981.

identifying their priorities. It meant that there was no need to choose between confronting Iraq or the United States; both would continue to be the implacable enemies of the revolution. For the United States, this slow-motion war meant that the leverage that would logically accrue to it as the main supplier of arms to Iran in a situation of conflict remained potential rather than actual. Influence unacknowledged is not real.

Quite apart from the slow pace of the war which provided Iran with a breathing spell to ponder the hard choices of the future, there were domestic political constraints in Iran impeding any acceptance of a renewed military relationship with the United States. This was evident in the curious fact that, throughout the negotiations on the release of the hostages, the issue of the resumption of supply of spare parts came up only once, and that was in an exploratory meeting in September. It was never raised again. Nor, evidently, was there an implicit expectation that once the issue was resolved, the acquisition of arms would be easier,[1] for Iran's leadership interpreted the war with Iraq as a conflict launched by a US proxy.[2] At the outset of hostilities Iran's Foreign Ministry had put this clearly:

> . . . we consider all our domestic and external problems, including the aggressions launched by the Iraqi regime and the provocations they are mounting in the borders, to be a product of the provocations launched by the US superpower against us and our Muslim nation before the triumph of the revolution.[3]

With the perception that 'the hand of the US had appeared from the sleeve of Iraq'[4] in the war, it would be difficult to justify negotiations for arms with the United States. Indeed political in-fighting combined with revolutionary self-image made it hazardous to support the idea of any negotiations with the US. For by acceding to negotiations, it could be argued, Iran would be conceding defeat and indicating its willingness to sue for peace on terms dictated by the United States. Others within Iran argued in less doctrinaire terms and sought to define Iran's

---

1   For an authoritative discussion of the course of negotiations see *New York Times*, 28 January 1981. The issue was brought up by Sadeq Tabatabai, a relative of Khomeini, in discussions with Warren Christopher in Bonn.

2   See the comments of Iran's Minister of State for Executive Affairs, Behzad Nabavi in *Le Monde*, 29 January 1981.

3   Text of Foreign Ministry statement, Tehran, 18 September 1980 in Sound World Broadcasts (SWB) ME/6528/A/3 20 September 1980.

4   This was Khomeini's comment in mid-September; he had prefaced it with the statement 'We are at war with America'. See *International Herald Tribune*, 15 September 1980.

priorities accordingly.[1] One exchange in the Majlis (Parliament) captured this nicely: 'The Imam (reported one cleric) has said we are fighting against America. How can we have discussions and talks with our enemy?' To which a leading secular moderate replied: 'This is the first time I have heard that we are fighting against America . . . it is very dangerous for us not to contact America'.[2] Prime Minister Rajai in October asserted that: 'Negotiations will not be considered even though they (the US) might for example offer to provide us with spare parts'.[3]

The political competition within Iran resulted in a cacophony of voices arguing for quite different responses to the war. In this context it was clear that no person, Ayatollah Khomeini included, felt strong enough to pursue negotiations with the United States to their logical conclusion. Such consensus as was to emerge would have to be the product of time, of battlefield losses, and of economic privation rather than of artful persuasion or logic. Even then domestic politics precluded any serious quest for the resupply of arms from the United States. Revolutionary rhetoric and self-image had created hostages of the Iranian leadership which now found itself imprisoned by the web they themselves had spun. A decision to seek to reactivate the military supply relationship with the US would be an admission of defeat on several levels. It would imply that Iraq's attack was not inspired by the US and that such an interpretation had been erroneous. It would also be an admission that such a relationship would not tarnish the purity or integrity of the revolution and that such ties did not necessarily entail either dependency on or subservience to the supplier. The domestic political implications of such a relationship would also have to be considered. Would the build-up of the army and the resurrection of an *ésprit de corps* and military morale, together with contacts with a foreign government, be neutral in its consequences for Iranian politics? An admission that that foreign government, the United States, was neutral and not an active foe of the revolution would erode one of the pillars of the revolutionary edifice so ardently constructed among the masses. For these reasons the costs of even tacit co-operation — let alone a military supply relationship — would be too costly for the Iranian government. Domestic ferment and revolutionary propaganda constrained the range of responses available to Iran during its conflict with Iraq.

---

1 For example, the notorious Ayatollah Khalkali strove to make the war with Iraq the priority item even if it meant a settlement with the United States. He apparently did not accept Khomeini's view that these were an inseparable menace.

2 See *The Times*, 30 September 1980.

3 *International Herald Tribune*, 22 October 1980.

*The limits and conditions of influence in wartime.* If the United States failed in the first six months of the war to gain influence commensurate with what might have been expected, given Iran's continued dependence on her for replacements, the reasons for this are many and relate only partly to the actual supply relationship. On the purely practical level, it was not yet clear that Iran had exhausted its existing stocks. Nor was it certain that Iran's major problems of resupply had yet crystallized. In the early phases of the war morale and leadership may have been the major shortages. The declining use of air power after October reduced attrition (and so temporarily Iran's need for parts) in the one area of undoubted US monopoly. The embargo on parts had exacted some costs through increasing the price of purchases on the open market, and in virtually grounding the helicopter fleet but it had not yet convinced the Iranian leadership of the need to seek a reconciliation with the US.

The political inhibitions against such a *rapprochement* were various but may be reduced essentially to one factor in the continuing power struggle any person or faction advocating ties with the United States was open to criticism as a counter-revolutionary and subject to removal. The very idea of a renewed arms connection — with all its perceived implications for the importance of the armed forces in politics, the re-assertion of American 'control' (i.e. leverage), and the consequences of this 'dependence' for Iran's revolutionary gains — was clearly too high a price to pay to expel Iraq from Western Iran. According to this mind-set, the risks of prolonged war *vis-à-vis* Iraq paled into insignificance when compared with the risks of renewed dependence on the US.[1] The Iranian government was thus not tempted by the inducements and signals emanating from the increasingly desperate Democratic administration in Washington in the Autumn of 1980 and, as noted earlier, it made no effort to include the issue of military supplies in the final negotiations over the hostages.

That Iran has been impervious to past US blandishments does not necessarily mean that it will remain frozen in its decision not to reactivate the military relationship. Two factors could decisively reverse the current decision, one political, the second an outgrowth of developments on the battlefield. A change in the leadership in Iran, or the emergence of a strong pragmatic figure from within the current leadership could enable Iran to reverse its policies, including its phobia about relations with the United States — an issue which has acquired the status of legend in the revolutionary mythology. Such a prospect does not seem to be too distant for neither sloganeering nor the

---

1 Indeed many of Iran's more militant revolutionaries saw in a long war with Iraq an opportunity to consolidate the revolution and suppress differences emerging within Iran.

preservation of the revolution's rectitude is sufficient to meet the needs of the Iranian people over time.

The second factor which would increase the attractiveness — indeed the necessity — for US arms and enhance US supplier leverage would be a reintensification of the conflict. Whether the war heats up to include large-scale engagements or drags on into a long war of attrition across the front, Iran's lack of spare parts will prove a major and growing weakness. The continuing lack of support for its aircraft will cripple its chances of success in the event that Iran seeks to launch a decisive counter-offensive to expel the Iraqis completely from Khuzestan.

Unable to win the war without spare parts and unable during a conflict to shift weapons-systems and sources of supply, Iran will find itself ineluctably drawn toward the US. Unless the war winds down with the tacit consensus of the belligerents, or Iraq withdraws unilaterally, Iran will be forced to expel the Iraqis and to do this without adequate air cover will be hazardous indeed. As a result, it may well be that the point of leverage accruing to the supplier of arms has yet to be reached.[1]

*Conclusion*

What was the arms relationship with Iran designed to achieve?
With what degree of success and with what limitations?
How does the Iranian experience translate elsewhere?
What are the conditions for influence?

The intensification of the arms relationship with Iran coincided with the increased importance of the region and the growing willingness of Iran to assume responsibilities which the UK was shedding and the US was unwilling to assume. The emergence of parallel interests and the Shah's requests for arms made this intensification inevitable. It reinforced relations between Tehran and Washington. It brought nearly ten years of relative political stability to the Gulf region at a time when no other littoral state could assure the region's security. In the event, the arms and the relationship with Iran were tools ill-designed for the test that confronted them in late 1978 — a widespread Revolution. Whether Iran's arms purchases decisively contributed to the economic

---

1 This is not to deny that Iran still retains residual leverage. The threat in extremity to 'go to the USSR' or the possibility of disintegration may prove so damaging to US interests that Washington would allow a discreet, indirect resupply operation without requiring any political conditions from the regime.

problems and hence the Revolution is not at all clear.[1] What is clear is that the refusal of the Shah's request for arms would have weakened the US–Iran relationship.[2] In some respects this had already happened after 1976.

The military supply lever of the US was thus in practice of limited utility in the revolutionary period in Iran. In theory access to the senior military officers should have been a considerable asset; in practice it proved irrelevant at best. As a base on which to build with a new government in Iran, it proved, despite the tangible dependency it entailed, disappointing. It locked-in the supplier to an accommodating posture lest that channel be jeopardized. Despite palpable security problems, the new Tehran regime preferred political posturing to pragmatic policies. The upshot was a dependency that remained real but politically irrelevant in the short run. As long as no overwhelming security threat was perceived by Khomeini, the suppliers' leverage remained notional. The liability of intimacy with the Shah's regime still overshadowed everything else. In this setting the only consolation for the supplier was itself bitter-sweet; the deterioration of Iran's military machine, while constraining any effective aggression by Tehran in the region, also limited its capacity to deter aggression. A weakened, unstable Iran might threaten US interests as much as it did its own leadership. Iran, militarily weak, had proved a far more destabilizing regional force than ever was the case when the Shah's legions were intact. If this proved anything it was that a fixation on arms transfers as regionally disruptive had obscured the less tangible but more real threats to the region. The US' continued interest in a strong Iran also laid to rest the hoary notion that US entanglement derived from the arms transfers, rather than an antecedent interest which these arms transfers only reflected.

1 Despite T. Moran, *International Security*. But it is a relevant question for the rest of the Gulf. Contrast S. Neuman, 'Iranian Defense Expenditures and the Social Crisis', *International Security*, vol. 3, no. 3, Winter 1978-79, pp. 178-92. Stephanie Neuman, 'Arms Transfers, Defense Production and Dependency: The Case of Iran' in H. Amirsadeghi (ed.), *The Security of the Persian Gulf*, Croom Helm, 1981.

2 As Barry Blechman has argued: 'The sale of sophisticated weapons is a significant political act. It associates the seller with specific personalities and policies of the purchasing government, thus involving the seller in the foreign government's domestic politics. A decision to sell arms is viewed as a sign of approval and encouragement; a decision in favour of restraint is taken as a signal of disapproval'. *New York Times*, 2 April 1980.

*The nature of the relationship*

The US relationship with Saudi Arabia is at once more complex and simpler than that with Iran — more complex in that it embraces much more than arms in its mutual dependence, simpler because it is not one of near equals in a partnership.

From the US perspective, Saudi Arabia's importance is obvious. Saudi Arabia produces 30 per cent of OPEC's oil output and it supplies 10 per cent of total US consumption (20 per cent of imports). Only Saudi Arabia has the spare productive capacity to unilaterally determine the scale of price rises agreed in OPEC. As the most important single country in OPEC, Saudi Arabia is thus important as a dependable supplier of oil, able to moderate price increases to minimize their damage on the international economy, and in a position to increase its own production capacity to ameliorate world shortages, and largely to regulate prices.

In addition to this, Saudi Arabia as a monarchy is instinctively hostile to communism and radicalism. It is interested in stemming these forces in the Middle East and in supporting 'moderate' governments that seek evolutionary change. Oil revenues have enabled Saudi Arabia to exercise influence in its diplomacy in the Middle East in a direction generally favourable to Western interests.

Though delicate, the relationship with Saudi Arabia is less brittle than that with Iran. Saudi ambitions and capabilities are limited and there are fewer misgivings regarding her military build-up. With a population of at most six million and with a land-mass as large as the US east of the Mississippi, her vulnerability and insecurity in a region full of threats is easily acknowledged. In addition, Saudi policy, the outgrowth of consensus in the royal family, is more subtle, given less to posturing than to allusion and indirection and to postponing issues rather than risking confrontations. There is no question in American minds of Saudi Arabia playing a security role in the Persian Gulf comparable to that entertained in the past for Iran. Her military build-up is clearly 'defensive' and her foreign policy goals are circumscribed. She is often exasperatingly reticent rather than overly activist.

The Saudi military build-up has also given critics in the US less cause for concern. Although Saudi Arabia has been the largest importer of US arms in recent years and spends vast amounts *per capita* on military expenditures (and more than 10 per cent of GNP on the military), the results have not been spectacular or divisive of US public opinion until the AWACs deal. This is principally due to two reasons: Saudi

Arabia's evident importance and military weakness; and the large amount of money allotted to services, training and the improvement of physical infrastructure (calculated to be as much as 60 per cent of 'arms' imports). (These services were exempt from the Carter May 1977 guidelines limiting arms exports.) Also the scale of Saudi Arabia's military modernization and expansion has involved fewer US government personnel. It has created fewer problems for US governments because the Saudi style of diplomacy acknowledges its limitations. Fewer requests are made of the US for weapons that are 'inappropriate' and the Saudi style builds fewer resentments within the US bureaucracy than did the Shah's, with its pretension to equality and partnership. Again this may be tending to change if arms sales to Saudi Arabia are seen to be at the expense of Israel's security.

As with Iran, the security dimension is central to the relationship but it has given rise to fewer problems than with Iran. Unlike the relationship with Iran, which was orientated at times almost exclusively on the military dimension of the partnership, involving mutual expectations which could, and frequently were disappointed, with Saudi Arabia this is but one component of a more complex package. The military ties with Saudi Arabia are, in any case, relatively new (dating back a decade) and have been, until recently, less intensive and formal. In part this is due to the constraints on Saudi foreign policy arising from inter-Arab politics which militate against any formal or conspicuous alignments ('the Baghdad Pact syndrome').

The genuine interdependence existing between the US and Saudi Arabia is not more stable or impervious to disruption because it is very real. Indeed its very stability depends on political assumptions and expectations which may be reversed overnight by a change either in the orientation of the Saudi elite, or its physical replacement. It is nonetheless based on a partnership which has tangible benefits — for both parties.

What Saudi Arabia brings to this partnership is an ability to moderate oil prices, to increase its own production, to assure supplies, and to play a constructive role in preserving stability on the Arabian Peninsula. The willingness to pursue these policies depends very much on what is to be gained from doing so. For example, the willingness to expose itself to political attacks in OPEC or within the Gulf, by policies limiting its own potential oil revenues, or decisions to increase its maximum sustainable daily production capability (which involves technical and investment judgements), all involve important political calculations and decisions which converge on one question: is her security thereby enhanced? Another way of putting this is that Saudi oil and foreign policy decisions will depend on her leaders' assessments of the forces at work in the region and the instruments available to deal with them.

It is here that Saudi expectations of the US role enter the Saudis' part of the package deal. The principal point to be made is that Saudi expectations of the US have been excessive. This is due both to an exaggerated view of superpower omnipotence and to a 'psychological dependency' that reflects both a genuine acknowledgement of indigenous technical deficiencies and an acute sense of insecurity and military weakness. Excessive expectations derive from immense needs. A primary requirement is for 'reassurance'. This pertains most concretely to security-related matters such as guarantees for the Kingdom (and regime) and to a more general measure of assurance in a volatile *milieu* and against an uncertain future. By its very nature, this type of 'requirement' is difficult to meet — yet it underscores the importance of 'atmosphere' and 'symbolism' in an unequal relationship. The development of a modern armed force positioned in the border regions is one response to insecurity. The Air Force with F-5s, F-15s, and *Maverick* air-to-surface missiles is also being developed for defensive operations on the periphery of Saudi territory. Where specific weapon systems (such as the F-15 in 1978 and 1980-81, and AWACs) become an issue in Saudi-US relations, they become symbolic of the entire relationship and critical to its continued well-being.

Other regional threats, particularly if they involve any form of Soviet activity as an arms supplier, or arms transporter, or through surrogate forces (such as the Cubans), are expected to be met by Saudi Arabia with the assistance of the US in a similar capacity — as arms supplier, transporter, or even as ultimate guarantor. The US' willingness to use force demonstratively for political purposes to assure Saudi security is not new. In 1963 a US squadron of aircraft was despatched to Saudi Arabia both to reassure King Saud and to deter Abdul Nasir from any involvement in Saudi Arabia. In February 1979 and October 1980 both aircraft and ships were despatched to warn the PDRY (and Iran) and to give substance to the US (implicit) commitment to Saudi Arabia's security.

Against major threats to its security emanating from beyond the region, for example from the USSR, the Saudis rely on US assistance and involvement. This is primarily a deterrent function but also includes a requirement for rapid and major interventionary forces (by sea and air). This in turn requires both the strategic infrastructure for rapid deployment and political relations facilitating it. In addition what Saudi Arabia tangibly requires of the US can swiftly be enumerated but it is important to stress the significance of 'atmosphere' and perceptions to the lesser partner. For the US arms are far easier to provide for their very concreteness as a visible symbol of the bond can satisfy the recipient, reassure it and serve to advertise its importance to other states in the region. Arms act as symbolic substitutes for alliances.

Saudi 'concerns' or demands for 'reassurance' are nonetheless real for being intangible, inchoate and difficult to assuage. For example, Saudi fears of Soviet 'encirclement' through the PDRY, Iraq and Ethiopia, and the emphasis on the geo-political,[1] on the importance of American 'will' and the credibility of her commitments should not be understood in concrete or literal terms. Their importance derives rather from the shift they may give to the balance of indigenous political forces, and hence to Saudi political calculations made to meet them. A circle of adversaries would increase pressure on the Saudi government to accommodate them and inhibit the Saudis from adapting the best means of securing their defence. Increased indirect pressure, in short, will mean a loss of autonomy and choice for Saudi leaders directing foreign policy.

Saudi security concerns start with regime survival and stability. For internal and lesser contingencies, Saudi Arabia expects arms and training in modernizing its National Guard and improving its intelligence agencies. To deter regional threats emanating from other states, such as Iran or Iraq, a floating 'over the horizon' presence is likely to be useful in most military contingencies.

In this as in other aspects of relations with Saudi Arabia there are paradoxes:

1　Only the US can provide a balance (often psychological) to the Soviet threat but the physical presence of the US could exacerbate regional problems of instability and US over-reactions could stimulate Soviet responses.

2　Against regional threats, specific or ideological, the US potential role is also important especially its reputation for reliability and commitment. A strong arms relationship is central for advertising Saudi Arabia's importance but an overt alliance is still impossible politically.

3　Against factors strengthening radicalism, the US connection also has a role to play. For example, only the US is in a position to defuse the political pressures that bear on Saudi Arabia from a 'no-war, no-peace' situation, by pushing a Middle Eastern settlement. Yet the path chosen to achieve that goal (Camp David) may itself exacerbate those pressures on Saudi Arabia in the short run.

4　In a period of sustained instability, the US connection becomes a liability yet the option of cutting loose from the

1　Saudi geo-political concerns can sometimes be met more easily by marginal actions than their other worries. The US supply of arms to King Hussan of Morocco in late 1979 was undertaken partly to reassure Saudi Arabia, for example.

US is limited by the lack of a realistic alternative for security. Thus 'distancing' occurs to reduce the Kingdom's exposure.

The relationship between Saudi Arabia and the US is by no means exclusively related to security, even on the Saudi side. Interdependence constrains and channels choices. Saudi Arabia's leaders have looked to the West for technology and training to develop their country, diversify their economy, build their infrastructure and train their people. This requires the provision of services, large-scale imports and access to technology. The accumulation of revenues, which cannot be absorbed domestically, has been met by making large investments in the West, thereby increasing its interest in Western stability.

Saudi Arabia has the largest foreign exchange reserves of any country ($60 billion), and most of it is invested in the United States. This and her diversified investments provide her with several assets and (potential) economic levers in her relations with the US, including:

1  A reduction in US dollar holdings.
2  Withdrawal of deposits from US banks.
3  The sudden sale of large quantities of US government scrip.
4  Discontinuance of purchases of additional US government securities.
5  Closure of US portfolio accounts on fixed income and equity securities.

Saudi funds are a potential source of international financial instability and provide potential leverage *vis-à-vis* the US. Yet this can be over-stated. Saudi Arabia would itself be affected by these actions. Saudi development (as well as defence) is dependent primarily on access to Western technology as well as to investment markets. As a large foreign investor it has a vested interest in international stability.

Saudi oil and investment policies are particularly sensitive to Western economic policies and subject to change. For example weakness in the dollar could eventually encourage an oil pricing policy on a basket of currencies or Special Drawing Rights (SDRs)[1] (though the effects of this would be complex). More important, the Saudi oil production rate is strongly dependent on two factors. In the short run, willingness to increase production temporarily to assist the West in its difficulties (or in the long run to increase its production capacity)

---

1  The Saudis' strong economic involvement with the US in particular results in a shared commitment to a strong dollar and to Saudi concern in the absence of a strong US energy policy. Saudi officials are said to refer to 'our dollar' in private talks with their US counter-parts (Interview, Washington, October 1979.)

turns on the willingness of the US in particular to implement a strong energy policy. Second, a production rate which is geared less to investment needs than to alliance considerations requires at least assurances that its surplus investment will be safeguarded against inflation (or confiscation)and that such policies are 'appreciated' politically, by the consumers.

This requires amplification. In the oil market up until 1979, Saudi Arabia's oil production-rate has been in excess of its own economic needs. In an inflationary world economy, the return on investments overseas could scarcely be economically justified (given their vulnerability to confiscation) against the conservationists' argument in the oil producing countries that the best possible oil investment was to leave it in the ground where it would appreciate in value without being a hostage to the West. Saudi willingness to produce more oil than was justified by its revenue requirements has been in essence political, though admittedly the economic argument for preventing a world recession or contributing to inflation which would increase the price of its own imports is also important.

As in its foreign security policy, its oil policy is also subject to reversal depending on the balance of multiple considerations. Some of these it is in the power of the US to effect:

1  A strong US energy policy, conservation and realistic prices.
2  Protection of Saudi investments, and perhaps privileged status for them (guarantee of real value for surplus revenues) to encourage a stake in moderation.
3  Assurances of access to advanced technology.
4  Revision of tax laws making the employment of US personnel in the Kingdom less costly.

Perhaps most important in the short run is the first. The continuous pressure on Saudi Arabia to increase its maximum sustainable daily production-rate to meet other shortfalls (especially in 1979-81 when the Saudis' official ceiling of 8.5 million b/d was surpassed by 1 and on occasion by 2 million b/d for a year) may be short-sighted.[1] It increases Saudi Arabia's political isolation and her identification with the West at a time of strong conservationist and nationalist trends in the region. It therefore threatens the long-term security of supplies by

1  Saudi capacities are a source of dispute. In mid-1979 estimates were revised downward from 16 to 10.5 million b/d. At the end of 1979 Saudi officials declared that it had now risen to 11 million b/d and would increase to 12 million b/d within a few years. Clearly production capacity is not the same as actual production-rate, which will be dependent only partially on technical questions.

exposing the Saudi regime to the charge of collusion with the West and to parting with the national patrimony at a discount.

Related to Saudi production-rates is the general question of Saudi development. There exists a basic quandary for Saudi developmental planners in a tight oil market. Cuts in production do not automatically adversely affect revenues, indeed they rather stimulate increases in prices with the resultant effect of equal (or possibly) increased revenues for a diminished quantity of oil exported. This situation may vanish as worldwide production picks up or demand dries up and the scarcity vanishes. It is important nevertheless that Saudi planners are not encouraged by the West to pursue indiscriminate industrialization programmes in order to foster a false appetite for revenues designed to increase their incentives for maximum oil production to alleviate Western problems. This too will undermine the regime politically with long-term implications for the security of oil supplies.[1]

The interdependence between the US and Saudi Arabia is real. Each brings something to the relationship that the other requires. In economic terms the US is acutely dependent on Saudi Arabia but the dependency is by no means one-way. For its ultimate security Saudi Arabia is almost totally dependent on the US. Each has assets and instruments in the relationship but these cannot be converted into 'leverage' except with political will in a specific context. The components of the package comprising the relationship are linked implicitly. In a web of interactions both sides exert general influence. Saudi dependence on the US goes beyond the material. The US is the only congenial superpower and it is a preferred and trusted economic partner. The US is the only state that can reduce pressures on Saudi Arabia by a settlement of the Palestine issue and is the only market large enough for investment on the scale of the Saudis. Saudi sensitivity to US policies and its reputation are intelligible by reference to this broad enmeshment of ties. This interdependence militates against any sudden swings in the political relationship, barring any fundamental political reassessments by either party. The military component of the relationship is designed to deal with the exogenous threats to the Kingdom and it is with its dynamics that we are concerned.

*The record of the military relationship*

Saudi Arabia's importance in US security policies was marginal in the 1950s and 1960s. Government-to-government relations scarcely existed.

---

1 See the companion paper by Avi Plascov, *'Modernization, Political Development and Stability'*, Security in the Persian Gulf, no. 3, Gower, Aldershot, for IISS, 1981.

ARAMCO represented the major US institution doing business with Saudi Arabia. The UK remained paramount in the Gulf and the major arms supplier to Saudi Arabia in the 1960s. Saudi interest in developing relations with the US government was nonetheless clear. Partly this was due to its experience with ARAMCO and to the trust and respect that had been engendered in that relationship. It also arose partly from a degree of scepticism regarding the UK (for example over London's support for Abu Dhabi on the Buraimi dispute). The importance of the US connection had already been demonstrated in 1963 by the rapid deployment, as noted above, of US aircraft to Saudi Arabia for reassurance at the time of the Yemen civil war, when President Nasir's ambitions in the Arabian peninsula were suspect.

The importance of the US for assuring the security of the Gulf after the British withdrawal made relations even more important on the eve of the 1970s. Though militarily weak, the Kingdom was relied upon by US policy-makers and encouraged to become one of the 'twin-pillars' designed to assure the security of the region. Interest in Saudi Arabia picked up slowly as the recognition of an imminent and growing 'energy crisis' seeped through the Washington bureaucracy. By April 1973, when Saudi Arabia made its first allusion to the 'oil weapon', the central importance of that country's resources to the health of Western economies was, at last, painfully clear. The 1973 war also brought Saudi Arabia directly into the issue of Israel and the occupied territories.

The Saudi government began to look to the United States as a partner in security affairs at the turn of the 1970s. Initially this meant an interest in the United States for arms and advice, while Washington was keen to assist in strengthening Saudi Arabia and to promote close political and economic ties. A study of a possible Saudi naval expansion programme was initiated in 1968 and agreed in 1972. In the spring of 1971, a request for assistance in modernizing the Saudi National Guard led to an initial survey by mid-1972 which was completed by the autumn of 1973. An overall defence study requested in December 1973 was completed by September 1974. Despite the spectacular growth in Saudi military-related purchases in the 1970s there is thus considerable evidence of planning rather than *ad hoc* purposes unrelated to any programme. By the end of 1973 it had become a deliberate part of US policy to 'entangle' Saudi Arabia into a nexus of relations which would give it a tangible stake in moderation and would constrain any sudden, disruptive, policy reversals. Saudi Arabia, for its part, welcomed this new attention. Its experience with the US Army Corps of Engineers in various projects in the Kingdom had been an agreeable one. The expansion of contracts covering ports and general infrastructure grew apace.

As part of the new emphasis on Saudi Arabia, two government-to-government Joint Commissions were set up in 1974. One covered economic affairs, the other security affairs. Meeting twice a year, the Commissions increased the number and breadth of official consultations between the two states.

The sale of arms to Saudi Arabia came to symbolize the deepening relationship with that state. Unlike Iran, however, Saudi Arabia's value came primarily from her oil, not from her potential as an ally with regional influence.[1] Thus, although for Saudi Arabia the prime importance of the US was as a guarantor of her security, arms as such were less important as a currency of that relationship. This was evident in the nature of the Kingdom's arms build-up. Limited in particular by deficiencies in technically trained manpower and in physical plant facilities, the great bulk of her 'arms' purchases (60–65 per cent) were in fact spent on training, spare parts, and on the construction of infrastructure — roads, airports, barracks, and ports. The scope of the military build-up is exemplified by the comment of a US official in 1976 that, while other states in the Gulf dealt with divisions in their armed forces, Saudi Arabia counted only brigades. The military co-operation programme was also less 'intensive'[2] involving fewer US government personnel and more contract personnel.

Between 1973 and 1976 Saudi Arabia ranked second only to Iran in arms purchases and signed $8 billion-worth of foreign military sales agreements with the US. Military expenditure leapt from $1 billion to over $9 billion in the same period. Military expenditures per capita were the highest in the world after 1975 (averaging $1,250). The principal component of the military training mission was the US Army Corps of Engineers.

Necessarily the American presence in Saudi Arabia increased in proportion to the expansion of the military modernization programme. In 1976, US defence-related personnel in uniform numbered 300, with another 900 civilians working on defence-related contracts. Including dependents military-related US personnel totalled 3,450 comprising some 21 per cent of the 16,000 Americans in the Kingdom. By 1978 the number of Americans had doubled to 30,000 but military-related personnel still numbered only 3,200, accounting for less than 11 per cent of the American community.[3] These figures show that the size of

1 That is there was no question of Saudi Arabia playing a regional military role.

2 The number of Saudi military officers trained by the US, even allowing for differences in armed forces size, was considerably fewer than Iran. See *Security Assistance*, (1979). By 1981 the US had 400 military personnel in Saudi Arabia with an additional 750 Defense Department civilians (excluding AWACs personnel loaned to the Kingdom). See *International Herald Tribune*, 28-29 March 1981.

3 Uniformed military in 1978 had been reduced by one-third, to 200. These figures are taken from James Noyes, *The Clouded Lens*, Hoover Institution, 1977, p. 65.

the US military contingent remained small in relation to other activities by Americans.

The United States' involvement in Saudi development covers a wide range of fields:[1] planning (Stanford Research Institute); construction (Bechtel); oil (Aramco); and military modernization. The use of private enterprise in this last area is especially notable. The Saudi government contracted with the Vinnell Corporation of California to assist in the modernization of the National Guard. This force is comprised of the most loyal Bedouin elements, known as the White Army, and is structured primarily for an internal security mission. While Vinnell is responsible for training this force (with 1,500 US personnel on contract), the US government is involved in sales of armoured cars and tanks. In 1979 the US approved the sale of $1.23 billion-worth of equipment as part of this modernization programme. There is little doubt that the Saudi government values the involvement of the United States in its defence build-up. Although it is keen to keep the US military presence in the Kingdom limited, the presence of a sizeable US military training mission is a form of reassurance that a security commitment would be activated in a crisis. As such it is a substitute for a formal defence arrangement which the Saudis are unable to accept.

The Saudi military expansion programme encompasses five principal areas: the modernization of the air force; the creation of a coastal navy from scratch; the modernization of the National Guard; the construction of an air defence capability; and the establishment of the basic infrastructure required for defence and civilian projects. The modernization and construction of a very modest but technically advanced armed force has created problems for a state lacking trained manpower or a well-developed system of communications. The physical size and climatic inhospitability of the country makes the assurance of the territorial integrity of the country difficult. The defence of long borders against hostile incursions requires air mobility for troops and supplies necessitating multiple airfields, depots and long-range capabilities for aircraft.

It would be surprising if such an ambitious development programme progressed without complications and serious problems abound. While Western critics often emphasize the dollar value of 'military sales' they neglect to note the percentage of expenditure that relates to civilian-sector infrastructure. Reports of large contracts, such as the recent $2 billion in construction, services and spares for the Saudi navy

---

1 As a result in most years US—Saudi trade was in the US favour despite the heavy importation of oil.

and air force,[1] should not therefore routinely be equated with military capability. Similarly the shortage of skilled manpower has acted as a serious constraint on the programmes. Foreign personnel have to be contracted, often at high price and with potentially disruptive consequences for society. Over 950 specialists were sought in the US for two years' service in Saudi Arabia to train the Saudi Air Force on the F-15s purchased in 1978.[2] Manpower from Pakistan has also reportedly been sought.

A third issue is the general impact of the military build-up on Saudi stability. In its extreme form, Western critics argue that the arms build-up destabilized the Shah and contributed to the revolution in Iran. Sometimes this argument is made (as by US Representative Rosenthal) as a means of denying Saudi Arabia arms: 'We're seeing the exact same scenario that we saw in Iran — dumping a vast amount of highly sophisticated American equipment into an area where the stability of the government is highly unpredictable'.[3] Others, like George Ball, appear to have changed their minds. Ball had argued against the military build-up in Iran — a country with six times the population, a greater manpower base, and a more prominent security problem in the shape of the neighbouring USSR. However, Ball now writes:

> We sold military hardware to the Shah on the assumption that he would be the protector of the Gulf and we would stay out of it. If today the Gulf is to be protected we ourselves must pull the laboring oar, yet, to be fully effective, we shall need the co-operation of the Saudis.[4]

The distinction is unconvincing as it begs the question how much the Saudis need if the US back-up is there as the 'laboring oar'.

It is evident that the United States' prominent role as arms supplier to the Saudi government entails a measure of support for and identification with the current Saudi regime. Intrinsically involved in the supply of arms, in the advice offered on the structure of military forces, and in the choice of weapons systems are assumptions about domestic stability and the impact of military modernization on the society. Rapid expansion of the military may, as in Iran, dilute the base of

1 See *International Herald Tribune*, 21 January 1981.

2 See *Aviation Week and Space Technology*, 2 June 1980.

3 See *International Herald Tribune*, 28 February–1 March 1981.

4 George Ball, 'Reflections of a heavy year, America and the World 1980', *Foreign Affairs*, vol.59, no.3, 1981, p.484 *et seq*.

loyalty in the ranks. In Saudi Arabia tribal loyalty of the White Army may survive military modernization but the experience elsewhere in the Middle East is mixed on this issue. In the military relationship it will be important, as Bill Quandt has reminded us, that the United States does not promote its own ideas of military organization and seek to ensure their rationalization at the expense of traditional procedures which exist. The Saudi leadership may prefer reliability to efficiency in their military.[1]

We should not be surprised at the difficulties of building effective modern armed forces rapidly in a society lacking infrastructure and trained manpower, and constrained both by domestic political considerations and dependence on a supplier that is sometimes uncertain of its goals. It was bound to lead to high expectations that could not be met and to consequent frustration. Despite the commitment of over $35 billion in orders for military equipment largely over the past decade, by the 1980s the Saudis were still not in a position to meet their primary security threats by themselves.[2] As we shall see, both this inescapable dependence and the difficulties encountered in obtaining some of their arms requests from the United States have led to disenchantment in Saudi Arabia about the arms relationship with the United States.

*The F-15 aircraft: a case study in supplier-recipient relationship*

*The first round: 1978.* In its programme of air force modernization, the Saudi government in the 1970s sought to replace its aging *Lightning* aircraft (sold by the UK in the mid-1960s) with an aircraft that was capable, long-range and most important, advanced. The Ford administration promised a sympathetic hearing but it fell to the Carter presidency to reply to the Saudi request for 60 F-15s. A military case for the F-15s could be made: their range was a necessity given the Kingdom's area, and their greater capabilities did not entail correspondingly greater difficulties in maintenance or a significantly larger manpower requirement. But from the Saudi perspective the importance attached to the request was political. The supply of arms is above

1 William Quandt, 'Saudi Arabia's Foreign and Defense Policies in the 1980s', unpublished paper prepared for the *European–American Institute Workshop*, June 1980, p. 18.

2 For a parallel view see the Report of the Delegation to the Indian Ocean Area Committee on Armed Services, House of Representatives, 96th Cong., 2nd Session, Washington DC: USGPO 1980, pp. 26-27. For an excellent if overstated analysis see Abdul Kasim Mansur (pseud.), 'The Military Balance in the Persian Gulf: Who will Guard the Guardians?', *Armed Forces Journal International*, November 1980, excerpted as, 'The American Threat to Saudi Arabia' in *Survival*, January-February 1981.

all a political act representing for both parties a concrete indicator of the relationship. For the Saudis it was supremely important that its intimate and evolving ties with the United States be given tangible and public expression and that the worth and importance of the Kingdom's importance be publicly acknowledged in this way.

The Saudis saw in the request a test case for the overall relationship and a symbol of Saudi—US ties. An American decision to sell the planes would be an affirmation of Saudi Arabia's importance. A denial, deferral or reduction of the request would be a concrete indicator that the Kingdom was taken less seriously than either Israel or Iran, both states which were receiving state-of-the-art military equipment. Such a rebuff would have adverse consequences domestically and regionally. Within the Kingdom it would undermine those factions arguing for close ties with the United States and provide them with little to show for an accommodating oil policy. Regionally it would have been damaging to Saudi prestige, raising questions about US perceptions of Saudi reliability and stability and of its importance in relation to Israel or Iran. By undermining the Saudis, a refusal would have weakened the prospects for political co-operation on the southern littoral of the Gulf.[1]

The Saudi request for the F-15s thus represented far more than a preference for a particular weapons system. It was a demand for a political response, for reassurance, and for 'hand-holding' that could not be understood in technical terms or in relation to strictly or solely military criterion. The United States' response was indicative of the difficulties in the relationship.

The actual passage of the request with the administration's support through Congress in the spring of 1978, need not detain us here. The sale was agreed in the Senate by a vote of 54—44. It comprised part of a 'package' deal in which sales to Saudi Arabia and Egypt (50 F-5Es of the 120 requested) were 'balanced' by selling to Israel an *additional* 20 F-15s over the original Israeli submission of 15 F-15s and 75 F-16s. The end result was however less important than the process through which the Saudi request passed. To gain assent, the Saudi government was subjected to questioning of its motives and final agreement was made conditional on restrictive conditions that constituted a political embarrassment to the Kingdom.

1 These arguments apply equally to a US refusal of the subsequent Saudi request in 1980 for additional equipment. For the 'political' importance of arms sales and the relationship between the Saudi defence build-up and its credibility in the Arab world, see Andrew Pierre, 'Beyond the Plane Package: Arms and Politics in the Middle East', *International Security*, vol. 3, no. 1, Summer 1978, pp. 150-51, and Abdul Kasim Mansur, 'The American Threat to Saudi Arabia', *passim*.

It was no surprise that pro-Israeli forces within the US Congress exaggerated the potential of the F-15s for strikes against Israeli positions or for possible transfer to some other Arab state for it was clear that the most galling aspect of the Saudi request, and the subsequent package for the Israelis was the political symbolism of 'relative evenhandedness for US arms transfers'[1] to the region. But the requirement of an assurance from the Kingdom on the stationing of the aircraft away from its western frontier and their configuration to preclude their use against Israel was needlessly humiliating to the Saudis. Prince Fahd publicly declared: 'We only purchase the weapons necessary for defending our borders and our vast territory'. King Khaled in a letter to President Carter acknowledged a 'linkage': 'I would like to emphasize that the planes are being acquired for defence and Saudi Arabia is continuing to make every effort in pursuit of a just, comprehensive and lasting settlement in the Middle East'. The specific restrictions governing the sale included:

1   No transfer of F-15s or the training on them of third country nationals.
2   No equipment or special auxiliary tanks would be permitted to increase range.
3   Saudi Arabia would not request multiple ejection bomb racks or seek them elsewhere.
4   Saudi Arabia would not acquire other combat aircraft pending delivery of the F-15s.

Secretary of Defense Brown assured Congress that the planes would not be based at Tabuk, 125 miles from Eilat.

It was clear that these conditions and US hypersensitivity to Israel's security needs embarrassed the Saudis who publicly chafed at the restrictions. Prince Saud, the Foreign Minister, observed: 'As far as I am concerned, why should Saudi Arabia be the sole country to have a condition imposed on it? We are as much threatened as anyone'.[2] Politically these restrictions shed doubt on Saudi Arabia's Arab commitment, implying the acceptance of conditions separating the Palestinian issue from its own defence.

Saudi Arabia made the sale of the F-15s a test case of the overall relationship. It used the willingness of France to sell the F-I *Mirage* aircraft, with a quicker delivery schedule and no restrictions governing their deployment or re-transfer to third countries, as a lever to pressure

1   See Andrew Pierre, 'Beyond the Plane Package', *ibid.*, p. 155.

2   US TV interview. In fact similar, and equally embarrassing conditions had been demanded of Iran the previous year during the hearings on the sale of AWACs. Saudi Arabia has so far consistently rejected conditions on the AWACs sought by them.

Washington. Both Cyrus Vance and Harold Brown warned Congress that if the F-15 sale was not approved, Saudi Arabia would obtain its needs from France without controls guaranteeing Israel's safety.[1] In the event, the agreement to sell the aircraft was a pyrrhic victory for the Saudis who had been subjected to Congressional criticism and to what amounted to a pro-Zionist veto. Treated as a second class client rather than a regional partner it had been somewhat less than successful as an exercise in reassurance.

*The second round: 1980-81.* The bitter after-taste of the experience in 1978 however was not a deterrent to a new contentious Saudi request made in 1980. As in 1978, it is best understood for its political connotations — as a demand for reassurance and as a reaffirmation of a US commitment. But in the wake of Iran's revolution and the Soviet invasion of Afghanistan, it is equally intelligible in terms of a changed security environment in the region. Although annoyed by the 1978 experience, the Saudis had reason to suspect that a more acute security problem in the Gulf would now make the US more amenable to a request for arms, and that the conditions imposed in 1978 were in any case subject to bargaining.

The issue was first raised in February 1980 when Saudi officials discussed Gulf security with Zbigniew Brzezinski and Warren Christopher in Riyadh. Rather than offer the US military facilities in the region, Saudi officials sought to improve their own defence capabilities. The Saudis sought extra fuel tanks for the F-15, together with an aerial refueling capability in the shape of 4 KC-135 tankers, plus an unspecified number of AWACs early warning and command and control aircraft for directing the F-15s. In addition, Saudi Arabia asked to purchase the improved *Sidewinder* air-to-air missile (the AIM-9L). The additional refueling capability would have stretched the range of the F-15 from 450 to at least 1,000 miles.

The initial response by the US Executive Branch was encouraging. Brzezinski is reported to have told Crown Prince Fahd: 'For the defence of Saudi Arabia we will do anything'. General Jones and the Joint Chiefs of Staff were also keen to see the Saudis purchase the AWACs originally ordered by Iran.[2] The Saudis were then (a) asked to 'justify' the request; (b) told to be aware of possible political problems

---

1 Also it would deny the US influence over their use in conflict in the manipulation of spares, ammunition etc. An identical argument is being used over British Nimrod as an alternative to AWACs.

2 *Washington Star*, 18 July 1980.

in Congress in an election year and (c) appraised of the US doubts' about its absorptive capacity for new equipment.[1]

When the Saudi request for 'enhanced' F-15s became public, the responses were similar to 1978. Some, like Senator Jackson, saw 'blackmail' in the Saudi request. This phrase, most commonly used by pro-Israelis, was not confined to that group. Many in the United States saw its own influence as 'leverage' while other states' power was seen as 'blackmail'. *The New York Times* saw no difference between Saudi Arabia and the other states, and showed no recognition of a partnership and asked: 'If every Saudi desire is America's command', it asked 'then what of Iraq's desires and Libya's . . . ?[2] A more sophisticated response came from the *Washington Post* which saw the issue as balancing reassurance and credibility with Israel with consistency and reliability with the Saudis. It accurately diagnosed Saudi motives as being at least part psychological 'to remove the stigma of being a second class arms recipient' and it identified Israel's anxiety as political as well: ' . . . it is a reminder that Saudi Arabia is cutting into Israel's political edge in Washington'.[3] With the 'attentive public' as split as the US government (between NSC and Defense for, and Congress against) the possibility of a bruising public debate again looked imminent in mid-1980.

A major problem for those legalistically inclined was the express denial in May 1978 by the administration that the Saudi government would seek to add to the capabilities of the F-15. Secretary Brown had sent a letter to the Chairman of the Senate Foreign Relations Committee: 'Saudi Arabia has not requested nor do we intend to sell any other systems or armaments that would increase the range or enhance the ground attack capability of the F-15'.[4] Congress could now argue that this request was in violation of the administration's promises. Sixty-eight Senators (more than two-thirds of the Senate) duly did so in a letter to the President in the summer.[5] Senator Byrd, Majority leader, referred to the equipment requested as 'offensive' implying some imaginary criteria for distinguishing between arms

1  *Washington Star*, 20 April 1960.

2  *New York Times* (Editorial), 18 June 1980. The Editorial sought to balance between those who would confront the Saudis and those who would appease them.

3  See the Editorial, *Washington Post*, 20 June 1980.

4  John Sparkman, Alabama.

5  *The Times*, 9 July 1980; *International Herald Tribune*, 9 July 1980.

legitimately needed for 'defence' and other purposes.[1] By mid-1980 it was clear that the Saudis had decided not to press for a decision before the elections which were now looming large. In deferring the request, however, they made it clear that they would expect a rapid answer on the morrow of the election results.[2]

The administration was relieved at the Saudis' willingness to await the elections. It anticipated problems in Congress and did not expect President Carter to court electoral problems by raising the issue. It denied however that this 'breathing spell' constituted a 'back-door rejection'.[3] In October, as a prelude to a subsequent decision, the Defense Department undertook a study of the Saudi request to be completed by 30 November. By this time the eruption of the Iran-Iraq war and the request for the stationing of 4 US AWACs on Saudi soil had further changed the political environment in the Gulf. As a result many Defense Department officials were hopeful for more intensive military relations in the future between the two states.[4]

At this point one of those events which are explicable only in terms of US domestic politics intervened. President Carter, anxious about the softness of his support in New York State, appealed to the Jewish vote by observing on 24 October that the US would not reverse its May 1978 assurances; it would not provide 'offensive' equipment to Saudi Arabia. Subsequently it transpired that the President was attempting to distinguish between 'bomb racks' and refueling capability.[5] Besides undermining the Pentagon study, the President annoyed the Saudis. He lost the state anyway.

*The Saudi perspective.* From the outset the Saudis made it clear to their American counterparts that the request would be an 'important test case' which could damage relations.[6] In part the Saudis were motivated by competitiveness with Egypt and the need to be reassured that Cairo had not replaced Saudi Arabia as the centre of US attention. Egypt, which had felt able to ignore the Arab consensus and had allowed US F-4s and AWACs to be stationed on its soil, had also under-

1   *International Herald Tribune*, 23 June 1980.

2   The report in *Aviation Week and Space Technology*, 14 July 1980, p. 17, that the Saudis sought 'an immediate answer' which Defense Secretary Brown answered would not be forthcoming, is not corroborated elsewhere.

3   *International Herald Tribune*, 23 June 1980.

4   *International Herald Tribune*, 22 October 1980.

5   See *International Herald Tribune*, 27 October 1980.

6   See *International Herald Tribune*, 18, 23 June 1980.

taken joint military exercises with the US. The US had provided and subsidized Egypt's purchase of the AIM-9L *Sidewinder* missile which the Saudis now sought.[1] It was important in terms of regional politics and the Saudis' reputation that the Kingdom be allowed to buy for cash what another Arab state was obtaining at a discount.

More important, the Saudi government believed that a change in its security environment necessitated an acceleration of its military build-up which had been shown to be inadequate to meet even minor threats.[2] The Saudi government expressly rejected two types of linkage (or *quid pro quo*) in exchange for US arms: firstly, the provision of military facilities to the West on Saudi soil and secondly, support for the Camp David peace process.[3] Either of these concessions in the Saudi view would compromise rather than strengthen Saudi security. In combination they would entail a departure from the Arab consensus which has been the mainstay of Saudi foreign policy, resulting in an isolation which would increase the Kingdom's vulnerability to terrorism and subversion. Western expectations along these lines were, in the Saudi view, evidence of ignorance rather than malice, an ignorance that neglected to note that Saudi security was underwritten in large part by the sanction of the Arab–Islamic world which constituted a defence and psychological umbrella for Saudi Arabia that it could ill afford to destroy. Attempts by US Congressmen to link the sale of arms with explicit changes in Saudi policy toward Egypt and Israel were, in the Saudi view, unacceptable.[4]

The area of linkage or reciprocity in the Saudi view was in the Kingdom's oil policies. Saudi officials hinted that 'civilian authorities' were beginning to ask what the Kingdom was getting in return for stepped-up crude oil production and the establishment of oil prices several dollars per barrel lower than that being charged by other

---

1 See *Washington Star*, 15 June 1980.

2 The border war between the Yemens, the Mecca incident in November 1979 and now the Iran–Iraq war contributed to the feeling of weakness. In addition there was a regional perception of Saudi military weakness, that Saudi Arabia was a 'cheque book' state that had to be reversed. On the latter see Abdul Kasim Mansur, 'The American Threat to Saudi Arabia', *passim*.

3 The most authoritative report is in the *Washington Star*, 18 July 1980.

4 Eighteen of thirty-five members of the House, Foreign Affairs Committee (including three Republicans) opposed the sale arguing that if the sale was a 'test of friendship' that friendship was reciprocal and demanded in effect Saudi support of the Camp David Agreement before approving the sale, *International Herald Tribune*, 27 February 1981. This was supported by a *New York Times* editorial, see *International Herald Tribune*, 8 April 1981. The tendency of US legislators to link everything indiscriminately must baffle the Saudis. During the 1980-81 AWACs debate some argued that the Saudis' failure to restrain Syria in Lebanon constituted an argument against the sale.

producing states.[1] Oil Minister Zaki Yamani put this clearly: 'We've gotten no sign of appreciation for everything we've done'. Saudi development needs would require oil production of only half the current rate of 10.3 million barrels per day. 'Why should we accumulate a surplus of funds'?[2]

As in 1978, it was particularly galling to the Saudis to have their arms requests subject to what they saw as an Israeli veto. The Saudi Ambassador in Washington argued that the US was putting Israel's interests before its own and hinted (as in 1978) that there existed other sources for arms 'without restrictions and conditions'.[3] This was put more strongly after Carter's electoral gambit. A Saudi press statement noted that: 'Nobody has the monopoly on the Kingdom's friendship'. The Saudi press agency pointed out that 'if the Kingdom does not get a response it may knock on all doors to obtain necessary requirements to realize the defence of the homeland'.[4] In the Saudi view its ability to buy arms should be subject only to the limits imposed on it by the United States nuclear non-proliferation policy.[5]

The Saudi arguments[6] to the US government illustrate their perception of the nature of the relationship. In considering their request for the arms as a test of the relationship, they see the relationship as one 'carefully balanced' between the two parties and subject to adverse consequences if refused. While not threatening specific retaliatory action, they imply that a rejection would make future co-operation politically difficult. Furthermore although much of the equipment is available elsewhere, the Saudis insist that ' . . . as a matter of principle we want to purchase it from the US'. Conceding that the election posed problems for the administration, the Saudis did not push for an early decision but they did not conceal their belief that with more courage the United States government could always stand up to 'Zionist pressures'.

1  *Washington Star*, 18 July 1980.

2  *New York Times*, 19 October 1980. In 1978 Yamani had related Saudi oil production level and support for the dollar to US arms sales. *Washington Post*, 2 May 1978.

3  Sheikh Faysal al-Hejelan, *The Times*, 10 July 1980.

4  See SWB BBC/ME/6563/i 31 October 1980; *Financial Times*, 30 October 1980; *New York Times*, 31 October 1980; *The Times*, 31 October 1980.

5  See the comment by Mohammed Abdu Yamani, Information Minister, *New York Times*, 19 December 1980.

6  These are well compiled in a report in the *Washington Star*, 18 July 1980. Other useful sources on the Saudi perspective include George Ball, 'Reflections on a Heavy Year', *Foreign Affairs*, America and the World 1980, pp. 488-494 and Abdul Kasim Mansur, 'The American Threat'. I have drawn on all three in the next two paragraphs.

The Saudis' arguments in support of their specific request is enlightening. Reference has been made to a refusal to accept a *quid pro quo* between arms and either bases or support for Camp David. In the Saudi view the key linkage that exists is between its oil policies and western security. The arguments in favour of the Saudi request are subtle and relate to the impact of a rejection on Saudi security. Allusions are made to domestic pressures and public dissatisfaction over the Saudis' return on the relationship. This is not argued as a future possibility: 'That point has already come. The questions are being asked today'. The Royal Family implies that it is under considerable pressure from the military for equipment, and that the greatest threat to stability is internal and possibly from a discontented military. 'We are talking about helping the stability of our government'. A refusal may entail instability. Finally the argument is made that the USSR provides arms to its allies in the region, why then should the US remain unresponsive to its allies' needs?

*The denouement.* The election of a Republican President to the White House reduced the US domestic political calculations surrounding the Saudi request. Seeing the world largely in East—West terms, the new government could view both Saudi and Israeli needs as complementary. In February 1981 the pro-Israeli elements in Congress moved towards dropping their opposition to the Saudi request, provided the United States' offer to Israel was 'sweetened'. It became clear that, as in 1978, opposition to Saudi requests had become a means of increasing Israel's leverage for better terms from Washington. By the end of February the elements of a new package were discernible. In addition to the earlier 40 F-15s Washington would provide Israel with ten more on preferential financing terms. In addition Israel would have the restrictions on the sales of her *Kfir* aircraft (with a US engine) to the Third World removed, and would receive an enhanced early warning capability — probably a ground radar station and access to US intelligence. Thus in FY 1982, $2.18 billion in aid is to be allocated to Israel, of which $1.4 billion will be military aid and the remainder economic. In addition $600 million is to be provided for the building of new bases to substitute for those given up in the Sinai.[1] The Saudi request therefore seemed set for eventual approval by Congress in 1981 but it then ran into further difficulties. The agreement when it comes will not be a resounding affirmation either of Saudi importance or of the weight attached to the relationship with the Kingdom by Washington.

1   See *International Herald Tribune*, 21-22, and 27 February 1980.

After massive expenditure on the modernization and expansion of defence capabilities, Saudi Arabia still remains severely limited in its ability to meet threats to its territorial integrity, and is likely to remain so for the next decade. Despite exasperation in certain quarters with this state of affairs, the Saudi leadership is aware of the inevitably lengthy process that military modernization entails especially for a country starting from 'scratch' with little in the way of infrastructure and skilled manpower. This recognition does not however diminish the Saudis' quandary: how to maintain a defence link with the United States to meet the major threats to its security while diminishing its own political exposure to criticism within the Arab world of collusion and collaboration with Israel's foremost ally. The acute tension arising from the attempt to balance these two requirements has not been eased either by recent US foreign policy or by the intensification of threats to Saudi security within the region. Reliance on the United States remains a principal feature of Saudi defence planning but the political costs of identification with Washington have risen. Saudi attempts to reduce the conspicuousness of this link and to distance itself from the US have taken various forms including the diversification of arms suppliers (see below), and the refusal to support US policies in the region, but this has not severed that nation's continued *ultimate* dependence on the US for security. As its credibility as an ally declined and its liability as a partner increased, the US' ability to influence or persuade the Saudis on various issues has accordingly shrunk. The leverage of the arms supplier diminished as that supplier itself became at once less credible as a supplier of security and a magnet attracting regional hostility likely to undermine the recipient's security.

Doubts about the United States as a security partner can be traced to developments in 1978-79. It was not the fact that the United States could not prevent regional instabilities that impaired the US' reputation, but rather the nature of its lackadaisical and equivocal responses to them. It was not US military capabilities but rather its political judgement that was thrown into doubt, confusing and unnerving its regional partners.

The revolution in Iran was a traumatic event for the Saudi leadership. It took the (for it) unusual step of condemning the disturbances against the Shah in August 1978. The replacement of a pro-Western monarchy, which was moderate, with a militantly anti-Western republic was bad enough. But the uncertainty of the region in the face of the unpredictability of the new regime generated further insecurities. The very nature of the revolution, the alliance between secularists and fundamentalists, and between the middle and lower classes could not fail to find an echo elsewhere in the Gulf. Furthermore the prospect, in the Saudi view, was for the emergence of the Left as victors as the revolution became increasingly radicalized. The incapacity of the United States either to save the Shah[1] or to diminish the repercussions of his removal were closely studied in Riyadh. The parallels for themselves of US acquiescence in the change of leadership was obvious: 'better to lose a Shah than a nation' implied a priority commitment to the flow of oil, not to regime security. The inability of the US to influence the new Iranian authorities after the revolution was a continuing source of concern in Riyadh. For, whatever worries may have existed about Iran under the Shah, the Saudis had counted on the US' influence in Tehran as a potentially restraining factor. Now this had gone, to be replaced by tension between Washington and Tehran which caught Saudi Arabia in the centre of contradictory pressures. Above all though, the revolution in Iran raised questions about the relevance of the security relationship with the US. If threats materialized internally or in murky conditions, it was now clear that the US could not be counted upon for support.

The second regional event that unsettled the area was the unveiling of the Camp David agreements with simultaneous deterioration of stability in Iran later in 1978. The failure of the United States to consult with the Saudi leadership in advance and its assumption that Saudi Arabia's support (or at least its neutrality) would be automatic, demonstrated an egregious insensitivity to Saudi political concerns. From the Saudi perspective, any departure from the security reassurance provided by the umbrella of the 'Arab consensus' risked the intensification of pressures and threats to the Kingdom not only by radical Palestinian elements but by militant governments including Libya, South Yemen and possibly Iraq. The need to reinsure by maintaining its credentials as a good Arab nation was all the more pressing in the light of the wave of anti-Western sentiment emanating from Iran and finding responses in the region and beyond. To much of the Arab world, the Camp David agreements looked like an American sponsored plan to eliminate the Arab military option and hence to reduce any Israeli incentive to compromise. To expect Saudi Arabia's support for this in the light of its military weakness, the pressures of inter-Arab politics and the revolution in Iran, was to expect rather more influence than the arms relationship alone could muster.

In response to these developments (together with the brief Yemen war) the US in early 1979 sought to lay a new basis for its relationship

---

1 Or to grant him and his family a haven after thirty-seven years of 'friendship', something which is understood in personal terms in the Kingdom.

with Saudi Arabia. On a tour which also embraced Egypt, Israel and Jordan, Defense Secretary Brown in February 1979 offered the Saudi leadership a more explicit defence arrangement. This was apparently tied to Saudi support both for Camp David and a greater US military presence in the region. The Saudi response, while acknowledging the 'Communist threat', was to emphasize as a priority the necessity of revising the Camp David accords. The Defense Minister, Prince Sultan, argued that 'the situation in the region will become more critical unless Israel withdraws completely from the occupied territories, including Jerusalem, and grants the Palestinian people the right to self-determination in their homeland'.[1]

Nevertheless the US—Saudi military co-operation increased. Commercial sales, the hiring of civilian personnel, the building of infrastructure ('pouring concrete') continued. But to these activities was added in 1979 a new dimension: the US now assumed a direct training and advisory function with the Saudi armed forces including field and combat manoeuvres and the identification of contingencies and missions — in short a role more direct than that of mere salesman. This reflected a recognition in the aftermath of events in Iran that Saudi Arabia, with vast land space and limited military potential, could not soon expect to become self-reliant for defence against local threats.[2]

More generally it meant the effective end to the Nixon doctrine, for with local states unable to assume primary responsibility for the region's security, the US would have to play a more active forward role. In pursuit of this, talk of 'pacts' with states in the region and 'bases' for access to it increased. The prospect of an increased naval presence either within the region or 'over the horizon' was discussed publicly. In this connection, while consideration was given to the permanent deployment of a larger naval presence (perhaps by the creation of a Fifth Fleet), the MIDEASTFOR naval operations in Bahrain were reinforced in mid-1979 by the addition of two destroyers. Implicitly acknowledging the relationship between security in the Gulf, access to the region and the Palestinian issue, the US sought without success throughout the year to obtain the support of 'moderate' Arab regimes for the Camp David approach to a settlement.

1  *Okaz* (Riyadh) 12 February 1979; quoted in Adeed Dawisha, 'Internal Values and External Threats: The Making of Saudi Foreign Policy', *Orbis*, vol. 23, no. 1, Spring 1979, p. 143 f.n. Particularly annoying to the Saudis was the attempt by some quarters in Washington, e.g. Frank Church, Chairman of the Senate Foreign Relations Committee on February 1 1979 to link the sale of US aircraft with Saudi support for Camp David.

2  The acquisition of a purely defensive capability requiring air-mobile units and the construction of an air defence network would require time during which the US role as guarantor would be indispensable.

*The case of the Yemens.* Lacking military power, Saudi Arabia has sought to use its vast financial assets to strengthen its security. Dispensation of subsidies to friendly governments has been a feature of this 'chequebook diplomacy' while financial incentives have been held out tantalizingly to poor and hostile neighbours. The limits of this as a substitute for military power are nowhere better illustrated than in Saudi Arabia's relations with the People's Democratic Republic of Yemen (PDRY). Saudi offers of up to $125 million in aid in 1977 were unable to persuade the Aden government to stop backing radical movements in the Arabian Peninsula. The PDRY's disruptiveness in the region increased, culminating in June 1978 in the assassination of the relatively pro-Saudi President Ghashmi. The Saudis were successful in obtaining sanctions, including the severance of economic and technical assistance against the PDRY, the first such decision by the Arab League against a member state.

Despite this success, relations between North (the Yemen Arab Republic) and South Yemen (PDRY) deteriorated and led to border clashes in February 1979. The pro-Saudi regime of the North Yemen formally requested an Arab League meeting on the PDRY's 'military attack' on 25 February. Saudi Arabia responded by cancelling all military leave and placing its forces on alert. Three days later the United States agreed to speed up arms deliveries previously promised to the YAR. By the beginning of March, South Yemeni forces were reported to be deep inside North Yemen and close to cutting the Taez-Sana road. Despite a ceasefire arranged by Syria and Iraq in the Arab League, South Yemeni planes attacked North Yemen. While Arab League meetings continued to seek agreement on a ceasefire proposal and on a mediation committee to visit both countries, the United States assumed a more direct role. On 6 March a naval task force was despatched to the Arabian Sea to strengthen a warning given the previous day by Secretary Vance to the USSR against any USSR–Cuban involvement in the conflict. On 9 March, under emergency provisions of the 1976 Arms Export Control Act (circumventing the need for Congressional approval), President Carter approved the delivery to the YAR of $300 million-worth of arms including twelve F-5E aircraft within two weeks. A squadron of US F-15s together with ninety military advisers were also rushed to Saudi Arabia and, in addition, the US made an offer to provide early-warning (AWACs) aircraft if the Saudis required them. By the end of the month the crisis had subsided and the YAR and PDRY were engaged in discussions about eventual 'unification'. The incident underscored Saudi Arabia's military impotence in the face of even a limited regional threat.

Saudi Arabia's relationship with North Yemen — always ambivalent because of the persistent Saudi desire to control its more populous neighbour[1] — was at least partly responsible for that government's military weakness. The United States' reaction, in part a response to Saudi Arabia's panic, was designed primarily to reassure the Kingdom of its reliability as an ally. Whether the PDRY attack was a Soviet-sponsored probe was unclear, but it was manifestly Soviet-assisted as relatively large infusions of Soviet arms in the preceding months had made it possible. The Saudis' perception of the incident was that it represented a carefully calculated PDRY—Cuban—USSR probe designed to unseat the YAR government and to test Saudi and Western reactions. Though grateful for the prompt US response, the Saudi government was also embarrassed by the revelation of its military weakness and by the publicity surrounding the provision of assistance. It continued to remain opposed to any public support for either Camp David or an American military presence in the Gulf. This reluctance was if anything reinforced by the diplomatic assistance furnished by Iraq in the dispute — for Iraq remained adamantly opposed to both elements of American policy.

*The Iran—Iraq conflict.* Towards the end of 1979, two distinct but inter-related developments in the Gulf region punctuated the evolution of the US—Saudi security relationship: the crisis between Iran and the US over the seizure of American hostages; and the invasion by the Soviet Union of neighbouring Afghanistan. Both underlined the continuing instability and tension in the area and both focussed attention on the growing need for the West to develop military facilities in the region for rapid access and to the necessity for Western countervailing power to offset nearby Soviet forces. Yet neither was able to shake the Saudis from their resolve not to increase their identification with the West.

This determination if anything increased throughout 1980 as the Carter administration reversed its earlier policies and loudly proclaimed a rhetorical doctrine which it admitted it was incapable of supporting. Pleased by the willingness of Carter to at last question Soviet policies, and at being courted by National Security Adviser Brzezinski in early February 1980, the Saudis still remained adamant, seeing this as only the latest and not necessarily the last American 'flip-flop'. Accordingly they rejected a further US request for the use of military facilities on 8 April, 1980.

---

1 For a useful discussion see the Congressional testimony of US officials, in *Aviation Week*, 26 May 1980, pp. 79-83.

In the course of the year this judgement hardened. Washington's alternation between threat and whimper on the hostage issue was unimpressive. Threats to use force, to mine the Gulf's waters or to exact reprisals by military attacks did little to encourage Saudi Arabia (or the other Gulf states) to formalize any military relationship with Washington. The April rescue mission in Tabas was seen as a further indication of the erosion of American power.[1] Nor was Washington's response to the invasion of Afghanistan impressive enough to encourage the solidification of ties. Having failed to fully mobilize its allies on the issue, Washington failed also to convince Pakistan that it was seriously concerned and could be counted upon.[2] Subsequently it found, in the weakness of the Pakistan regime, in the sensitivity of India and in the disunity of the Afghan opposition, reasons for not supporting resistance to the Soviet occupiers. The US failure to 'draw the line' in Afghanistan[3] but to respond by flexing military muscles elsewhere did little to reassure the Saudis about the astuteness of American political judgements. The sheer volubility of US statements, punctuated by political rhetoric and contradictory leaks, gave the impression neither of consistency nor of purpose. Yet it was precisely at this time, with Washington in the throes of a premature election campaign, that the Carter administration sought from its regional partners open identification, oblivious to their political needs and domestic constraints.

The conflict between Iran and Iraq which had festered since the spring of 1979 escalated into large-scale hostilities in the second half of September 1980. Initially the Saudi response was low-key, advocating restraint and cautioning against an 'over-reaction' by the West. Saudi Foreign Minister Faisal specifically referred to the dangers of a superpower action-reaction syndrome and to the dynamic of a logic which, in seeking to meet 'every eventuality', actually 'tends to increase the threat'. In his view the dangers of Saudi involvement or the closure of the Straits was exaggerated. Outside forces, he believed, would 'only complicate the situation'.[4]

---

1 The fact that it was launched via Oman embarrassed that country and cast even more doubt on the predictability of US actions and on US judgement. For the general Arab perception of the pressures building up on them see *The Sunday Times* (Mohammed Heikal), 28 April 1980, and *International Herald Tribune*, 18 April 1980.

2 Reportedly the Saudis offered to participate in a 'joint consortium' with the US — 'Saudi Arabia would organize Arab funds, the United States would rally the West'. — Washington ignored this and failed to inspire Pakistan by itself. See *International Herald Tribune*, 19 February 1981.

3 On this issue see 'The Comments of a Saudi Leader', *The Times*, 10 February 1981.

4 See the reports based on interviews with him in *The Washington Post*, 28 September 1980; *Wall Street Journal*, 30 September 1980.

As a result of developments in the war (specifically the use of other Gulf states' territories by Iraq for the dispersal of its aircraft, and for access through them to the islands in the Lower Gulf), this initial Saudi evaluation was hastily discarded.[1] Fearing Iranian air attacks because of assistance to Iraq, the Saudis looked to the US for aid. On 29 September, US and Saudi officials conferred on the text of an announcement regarding US assistance. In Washington consideration was given to the provision of air defence aircraft (F-14s or F-15s). The subsequent decision to send four AWACs was considered a minimal response by Washington. In its deliberations Washington was guided by several considerations:

1 A need to reassure the Saudis about the US commitment.
2 A desire to meet the Saudi request to encourage Saudi Arabia later on to replace whatever oil short-falls occurred as a result of the war.
3 To stop the 'mindless gravitation' of Saudi Arabia toward Iraq.

Consideration was given in Washington to the opportunity presented by the Saudi request for military assistance to press for a longer-term arrangement but this was discarded. It remained nonetheless part of the US motive for its swift response that its actions might make the Saudis more prepared to envisage military co-operation to meet future contingencies.[2]

The upshot of these considerations was a formal Saudi request for defence assistance from the United States. Four AWACs early-warning aircraft, to be flown, maintained and protected by American personnel (numbering 300), were sent to the Gulf on 30 September. The cost of the operation was to be largely borne by the US with some contributions from Saudi Arabia. The aircraft were based in Dhahran. Two tanker aircraft (KC-135s) with support personnel (40) were also sent. The AWACs were considered an appropriate response, symbolizing US commitment (with its advanced early warning capability against air attack), yet remaining unprovocative. The US position was made clear; neutrality in the war did not mean that the US was '. . . neutral in meeting the legitimate defense needs of our friends'.[3] The US commit-

---

1 Indeed the differences between Prince Faisal's comments in the US and the activity of the Saudi government *at the same time* suggests differences in their evaluation of the problem that is greater than a simple matter of information. The subsequent Saudi request for assistance may well have been controversial within the Saudi leadership.

2 See the reconstruction of US decision-making by Richard Burt and Bernard Gwertzman, *International Herald Tribune*, 13 October 1980.

3 See the *Wall Street Journal*, 1 October 1980; *The Times*, 1 October 1980.

ment was augmented the same week by a mobile ground radar station and by additional communications equipment and 96 support personnel. The following week the US offered to share the information derived from the AWACs with the other non-belligerent Gulf states provided they eschewed any involvement in the conflict.

The US' aims during the conflict were straightforward: to keep open the Straits of Hormuz and to maintain access to the non-belligerents in the region. In showing its concern for its vital interests in the region it sought to protect the oilfields from any expansion of the war which might arise from Iranian reprisals for the involvement of the other Gulf states. At the same time as it asserted its own interest in the course of the war, and responded to its ally's needs, the US was constrained by two other necessities: the avoidance of any military action inconsistent with neutrality which might provoke a commensurate Soviet response; and the continuing need to demonstrate to its regional friends that its military activities were geared to the protection of the oilfields rather than from any design to seize them.

Within these constraints the US role in the war was successful.[1] The Iranian government on 1 October, 'fully aware of its international obligations', pledged not to attempt to block the Straits. The Saudi leadership's willingness publicly to request US military assistance demonstrated that *in extremis* their reticence could be overcome. It was a clear sign of the Kingdom's dependence on the US in an emergency. Even Iraq temporarily dropped its loud objections to a US presence after the Saudi request. The American action was a clear extension of US involvement in the region and an assumption of a direct military responsibility for the defence of Saudi Arabia's oilfields. It went beyond even the Carter doctrine which had claimed a right to involvement against an 'outside' threat to the region, for this was a local issue.

The war clearly showed that sources of threat to the region's security lay principally in the Gulf region itself and not, as had become a hardened cliché, from the Palestine question. It also demonstrated that the 'exclusion of the superpowers' from the Gulf could not be a realistic formula if one of the principal Gulf states had rapid recourse to one of those superpowers in the face of threats emanating from a regional conflict. Yet, despite the inadequacy of this formula for meeting even contingencies within the region, the political inhibitions on accepting alignment with the US persisted for the Saudis. To be sure Riyadh increased its oil production to full capacity (10.5 million

---

1   The best initial discussions of the war and its political repercussions are *Wall Street Journal*, 15 October 1980; *International Herald Tribune*, 15 October 1980.

b/d — 20 per cent more than its official ceiling) to compensate for any shortfall due to the war. But it still remained reluctant to cement its military relationship more formally. While it may have become more receptive to a discreet American presence in the region, it is doubtful, given the nature of US government, that this is feasible. To justify a US military presence on its territory, the Saudi government would need something tangible to show for it, not merely to its own populace but to the Arab world at large which would be in a position to undermine its security.[1]

So, despite the continuing need for a security guarantee from the US, Riyadh finds itself unable to provide the means to make this credible. It reverts to the traditional formula — 'We can't accommodate your security interests without substantial progress on our political problem, the Palestinians'[2] — and it indulges in flights of fancy with no relationship to reality but of great political appeal within the Arab world. Even as the conflict continued, Prince Fahd was quoted as saying that there were no threats to the region from within but rather from dangers 'converging in the region from remote areas'. He asserted that the Gulf nations do not need foreign help in maintaining their security because 'Gulf security is exclusively the affair of the Gulf nations'.[3]

How this Gordian knot will be cut continues to mystify observers. In his 'farewell comments', Secretary Brown noted the dilemma without suggesting any solution by observing on the one hand the Saudis' increased need for a US security commitment in the light of the War and of events in Afghanistan and, on the other hand, the damage any formal Saudi alliance with the US or the granting of permission for US troops to be stationed on its soil would do for both internal and regional security. However, this did not deter the Defense Secretary from calling for a more 'explicit military arrangement'.[4]

The continuing Saudi ambivalence toward the US is very clear. The US is often a source of embarrassment. Lacking discretion it tends to overwhelm its partners rather than the threats to them. Its embrace is still considered almost as dangerous as its withdrawal. The linkage between the security of the Gulf and the issue of Palestine has been

---

1 Libya's severance of ties with Riyadh because of the Kingdom's acceptance of the AWACs is illustrative of the types of pressures that could be concerted in the event of a permanent presence.

2 In the words of one Saudi official, quoted in the *Wall Street Journal*, 25 November 1980.

3 *International Herald Tribune*, 19 January 1981.

4 See *New York Times*, 7 December 1980.

weakened by the war but that linkage persists. The importance of the US connection for Gulf security has not weakened the pressures on the US to produce a settlement on Palestine. The risks that Saudi Arabia is prepared to run depends on both issues:

1  The relevance of the US to its needs in the Gulf and further afield.
2  One of those needs is the pressure the issue of Palestine continues to exert on its policies.

The risks of departure from the Arab consensus, of isolation and vulnerability to terrorism inhibit any change in Saudi policy on this issue. While greater Saudi activism in shaping that consensus is possible, withdrawal from it, as Egypt has done, is unthinkable for the security of the Kingdom is partly sanctioned by it and, dependent as it is on inter-Arab politics, it cannot afford the risks of its alienation.

### Arms diversification

Despite the preponderant role of the US in its defence programme, Saudi Arabia has not sought to obtain all its defence needs from one source. Diversification of sources of supply has been a feature of its arms purchases in recent years. France, in particular, has become a major supplier responsible especially for much of the Kingdom's armour and air defence. Total purchases from this source had reached by the Autumn of 1980 some 12 billion francs, a quarter of which is attributable to training and technical services. Included in the equipment transferred have been some 450 *Panhard* APCs, 250 AMX-30 tanks, 150 AMX-10P Infantry Combat Vehicles, *Gazelle* anti-tank helicopters, *Crotale* (Shahine) air-defence missiles and 155 mm howitzers. In addition an electronics industry is being set up with aid from Thomson-CSF for the manufacture of radar and radio equipment.

In October 1980 Saudi Arabia signed a major new defence purchase agreement with France. Totalling 14.4 billion francs ($3.5 billion), a third of which comprised services and training systems, this agreement extended the French role to the expansion and modernization of the Saudi Navy. The package included the supply of six ships (four frigates of 2,000 tons plus two tankers) together with *Otomat* anti-ship missiles and 24 *Dauphin* helicopters together with the AS-15-TT anti-ship missile. In addition France is to provide logistic and support services and extensive training for the Saudi Navy. France is to send 45 officers and 125 petty officers for temporary service in the Royal Saudi Navy. This training, which is to be extended to hundreds of Saudis, will be done in Saudi Arabia. Reportedly a major consideration for the Saudis in favouring France (over Italy which also competed for the order) was the training component offered.[1] The agreement was understandably seen in France as a sign that Saudi Arabia wanted to intensify its military relationship.

Another indication of the Saudis' new interest in European arms suppliers was their indirect approach to the Federal Republic of Germany in late 1980 for *Leopard II* tanks and *Tornado* aircraft. The numbers discussed were respectively 300 and between 75 and 100. The implications of the approach were more profound than the numbers. There were suggestions that requests for other systems would follow — up to 10 billion marks in value — and there were hints of a possible 'special relationship' developing. As the principal supplier of oil to the Federal Republic (25 per cent of its needs), the reported Saudi offer of linking the arms purchases with the guaranteed supply of oil for ten years to cover the costs may have been especially attractive. The Federal Republic had strong economic incentives to examine the request seriously, including a large trade deficit with Saudi Arabia (together with a $2–3 billion loan from the Kingdom) and cost overruns on its weapons systems which could be reduced by exports extending their production run and so lowering their unit costs. Against this the Republic had political constraints both in the form of an established policy against the export of arms to 'areas of tension' and in the shape of a vocal faction of the SPD opposed to such sales.[2] Prime Minister Begin was not slow to play on memories of the 'holocaust' and Germany's moral obligations to Israel.

The Saudi overture may well have been timed for political reasons to pressure Washington to lift the restrictions on the F-15s but there were practical considerations as well. The *Tornado* aircraft, in which Italy and the United Kingdom are partners with the FRG, could be absorbed more easily than French aircraft given the continuing training programme provided by the UK in Saudi Arabia. A maintenance and logistics base was therefore already in place and diversification would thus create fewer practical problems.[3] The German answer to the Saudi request had not been given by April 1981 and may be postponed for some time but, in the context of a Western policy toward assuring Gulf security and given the Federal Republic's reluctance to commit

---

1   For sources on this transaction see, *Aviation Week and Space Technology*, 3 November 1980, p. 33; *Le Monde*, 14 May 1980, 15 October 1980; *Middle East Economic Digest*, 24 October 1980, pp. 3–5, 23 January 1981, p. 31.

2   See *inter alia Le Monde*, 10 January 1981; *Financial Times*, 13 January 1981; *The Times*, 13 February 1981; *International Herald Tribune*, 23 February 1981.

3   See *Aviation Week and Space Technology*, 9 February 1981, p. 30.

armed forces or ships to the area, the provision of arms has a certain logic. It would entail the supply of some advisers and technicians as well. Bonn's interest in the political dimension of security with an emphasis on economic assistance to the region may well continue but it may be supplemented in the future by a discriminating policy of arms supply to important states.

## Dependence and leverage

The Saudi relationship with the United States has undergone a marked change in recent years. Difficulties in obtaining advanced armaments like the F-15 and AWACs have been embarrassing for the Saudi leadership, while America's continuing alignment with Israel has made a close relationship a growing political liability for them. Furthermore the trend toward non-alignment, so prevalent in the rhetoric of the Gulf, has created its own pressures against a tight exclusive relationship with either superpower. Nor has the extensive military relationship with the US been totally satisfactory for some in the Saudi leadership who attribute the Kingdom's still weak military capability, after massive expenditures, less to the inherent problems of modernization than to a purposeful US policy of stretching out this dependency. An intention to reduce both this dependence and the political exposure attendant on such a close relationship has served as a strong incentive for diversifying arms suppliers. The European states are natural candidates as additional suppliers. They are usually more forthcoming in supplying sophisticated equipment, motivated largely by commercial incentives, and they are less inhibited by hostile domestic interest groups. Above all they are less politically controversial as suppliers within the Arab world.

The diversification of sources of supply does not, and is not intended, to reduce the dependence of Saudi Arabia on the US as an ultimate guarantor, or to substitute for US equipment and training in, for example, its air force, but it does act as a means of spreading the risks of dependence on one source. It is also a way of asserting independence and of achieving political distance from the US. To be sure there are problems and risks. Diversification complicates logistics, maintenance and training[1] and may, in introducing a strong element of commercialism, dilute the essentially political feature of commitment that the supply of arms has meant to the recipient state. Against this has to be balanced the advantages which enable the recipient to

---

1 Furthermore the after-sales service of countries such as France have in the past been criticised.

threaten to go elsewhere for equipment denied by its principal supplier, as Saudi Arabia has done in the case of the F-15 and AWACs. The strengthening of links with other Western suppliers, while it may mean a reduced dependence on the US, does not entail a reduction in aggregate Western influence in Saudi Arabia. Moreover this sharing of influence, if it is not *politically* competitive, need not be unwelcome to Washington. Indeed to the extent that it 'spreads the load' and implies a multilateral Western approach to the question of Gulf security, it may well serve Washington's interest to have its own potential influence somewhat reduced. The conclusion of an agreement between Saudi Arabia and France on the training of police and in internal security affairs[1] is an example. The Saudis, doubtless encouraged by France's prompt and discreet assistance during the disturbances at Mecca in November 1979, decided to extend this relationship. From the US' viewpoint such agreements could only be beneficial, for equivalent American assistance would be controversial domestically and more disruptive politically within the region. In the context of the Gulf, the Saudis' diversification of sources of arms supply need not be unduly worrying to the United States. The basis for the relationship is far broader than that of arms supply alone, and the basis for influence will survive its diminution.

*Perspective and style*

It would be surprising, given their cultural differences and the dissimilarity of their political systems, if US—Saudi relations were without problems of communication. There is foremost on the US side the problem of stereotyping which arises largely from ignorance.[2] This colours the US perception of the Arabs — especially of the oil-rich states. Oil is seen as 'unearned income' or a 'windfall' and sheikhs are associated with 'blackmail', with 'extortion' and with camels. There has been a recurrent political temptation — as in the Eisenstadt memorandum of mid-1978 — to place the blame of the energy crisis on OPEC and specifically on the Arabs. Inadequate knowledge and a low level of US attention combined with the fantastic wealth of the otherwise backward Kingdom with its archaic institutions makes Saudi Arabia an ideal subject for simplistic commentary. Public opinion in the United States is ill-informed, and the 'partnership' with Saudi Arabia is often seen with a mixture of derision and envy. How durable

1  Concluded on a visit by the French Interior Minister in November 1980. See *Le Monde*, 2—3, 4 November 1980.

2  On the persistence of this see Malcolm Peck, 'The Saudi—American Relationship and King Faisal', in Willard A. Beling (ed.), *King Faisal and the Modernization of Saudi Arabia*, Cröom Helm, London, 1980, pp. 230—45.

such a partnership can be under these conditions is a question for the longer term. In the short term it contributes to misunderstandings. These are compounded by differences in style and emphasis. The United States sees Saudi Arabia as too reticent and as demanding security assurances from the West while refusing to help make these possible or credible. It tends to attribute the Saudis' unwillingness to accept an explicit defence arrangement as motivated more by cowardice than by sensitive intra-Arab considerations, and Americans tend to interpret the Saudis' security problems largely in terms of external dangers and in the East—West framework. Saudi reticence, and a style of indirection and allusion which refuses to confront problems head-on, is often seen as being motivated by maddening pusillanimity rather than by political constraints. Saudi caution is rarely viewed with reference to the Kingdom's military weakness and its need to remain within the Arab consensus. Consequently the Saudis are sometimes seen as insufficiently active in substantively pursuing a Middle East peace and given to flights of empty rhetoric.[1] Eager to see its friends stand up and be counted, American public opinion tends to ignore the undercurrent of anti-Westernism and xenophobia latent in the Arab world, including Saudi Arabia, which can be mobilized against its regional friends unless they are careful.

The Saudis have similar problems with the Americans. The trust and dependency that have characterized the relationship in the past have already been noted. Disappointment may provide the basis for more realistic expectations and consequently for a more stable relationship in the future. It is as much the image and the style as the policies of the United States that have complicated relations in recent years. Washington has consistently leaked embarrassing information to the press[2] which has undermined the Kingdom's security. By holding up arms transfers, by placing restrictive conditions on them or by allowing them to be subject to pro-Israeli pressure groups, successive United States' governments have undermined the Saudi position in the Arab world. The inability in Washington to co-ordinate the activity of various agencies often leads to contradictory emphases and pressures on the Kingdom. These are usually questions of style rather than policy. For example the Kingdom cannot afford politically to be seen to be increasing its own oil production beyond its official ceiling while the US uses this to fill up its strategic stockpile, the better to undermine

---

1 The continuing role of rhetoric as an inexpensive functional substitute for action in Arab politics is underestimated.

2 Examples abound the most prominent being reports of feuds in the royal family, corruption, and the instability of the regime.

any future use of the 'Arab oil weapon'. Public pressure on the Kingdom to fall in line with preferred US policy positions is usually counterproductive as it exposes the Saudi leadership to the criticism from factions within the royal family and from enemies abroad of being a 'puppet regime'.

Apart from poor co-ordination of its government agencies and a tendency to indulge in excessive leaking and publicity in its policies, the policies themselves are, from the Saudi view, often ill-conceived. The problem of inconsistency and fluctuation in US policies in recent years is well-known and requires little amplification here. It has created the impression of bad judgement, insensitivity and over-reaction which will take time to efface. This is not a new problem. King Faisal in the 1960s told a US Ambassador: 'You Americans do not make things easier for your friends. You disregard their concerns and thereby weaken their (political) influence in the area'.[1] What is new is the promotion of policies which the Saudis view as positively harmful to them, for example the Camp David agreement. The impatience of the United States with the Saudis' passivity is often understandable but any inclination to believe that 'they have nowhere else to go' and that therefore they can be taken for granted, is dangerously misconceived. At any other time the Camp David process might have stood some chance of Saudi support but, with the slow-motion collapse of pro-Western Iran and with all the pressures that unleashed in the region, it was folly to expect Riyadh to take the risk of identification with the West in 1978-80.

From the Saudi perspective American policy tends to be too one dimensional. Riyadh sees threats emanating from every quarter; internal, on its borders, within the politics of the Arab world, from the USSR and its proxies, and even from the ill-considered policies of its putative protector, the United States. The Saudis want reassurance against these threats but are unwilling to choose any one instrument to meet all of them. Hence they seek security guarantees but are loathe to admit it publicly and want a military relationship but are unwilling to pay the political costs such a relationship would entail. Much of Saudi security policy is therefore one of damage limitation, of alleviating pressures that may create problems rather than meeting them head-on. In this context an issue such as Palestine is directly important — partly because it is a litmus test of the Kingdom's Arab and (because of Jerusalem) Islamic, credentials, and partly because, as it festers, it

---

1 Herman Eilts, 'Security Considerations in the Persian Gulf', *International Security*, vol. 5, no. 2, Fall 1980, p. 96.

creates pressures within the Arab world which *inter alia* inhibit the development of the Kingdom's relationship with the United States — a relationship which is essential if Saudi Arabia is to meet the other threats to its security.

*Leverage or interdependence?*

Each party brings certain expectations and requirements to the relationship. Although each has important assets which the other requires, it is essential to differentiate the possession of these assets from their conversion into leverage or influence. To do this one should distinguish between (a) the leverage to achieve specific goals, and (b) the general influence that permeates the relationship. The latter leads to such general notions as 'sensitivity' or responsiveness to an ally's concerns or to an 'anticipated reaction' by one party before the other even articulates its preference. The value attached to a relationship may increase for both parties at the same time hence presumably increasing their assets (and potential leverage) simultaneously. For example, as Saudi Arabia's importance as an oil producer has increased for the US, so also has the saliency of the US security relationship to the Kingdom.

The quality and style of the relationship determines the manner in which influence is, or is not, exerted. Acknowledged differences in priorities, 'reasonable' expectations and the constraints operating on respective policies can avoid clashes and futile exercises in leverage. The time-frame of mutual expectations governs the quality of the relationship. Are trade-offs issue-specific and immediate or do they reflect part of a much more complex stable, institutionalized, relationship?[1] The emphasis placed here on the arms relationship reflects the pronounced concentration on this visible component of relations. As a functional substitute for formal treaty relations, they have also become a palliative for problem areas. It is easier, though still not easy, to grind out arms agreements than to achieve a Middle East settlement or to devise a strict energy policy.

We have already noted that within the relationship there have sometimes emerged differences as to precisely what is linked with what. On occasion the United States has sought to imply a link between supplying arms and support for the Camp David peace process and to hint that a defence commitment is dependent on access to bases on Saudi soil. At the same time the US has expected Saudi Arabia to moderate

---

1 As noted in Iran's case, the Shah tended to widen differences on a single issue to threaten the entire relationship. This conferred short-term advantages to Iran on issues but also made the entire relationship precarious. It also created resentment in the US bureaucracy. This accumulated resentment was evident in Iran's crisis.

71

oil price rises and maintain the level of production necessary to do this, while ignoring the (admittedly rather slow) build-up of the US strategic petroleum reserve. Moderating the price of oil has been a prime Saudi responsibility — both for the West and its own longer-term interests — and has been acknowledged as such by Saudi leaders. Occasionally Western leaders have made the connection explicit by arguing that oil price increases by the Gulf states 'undermine our very ability to defend them'.[1] Sometimes the linkage is more indirectly evoked as in the case of a notification to Congress of an arms package in mid-1979. The administration had held this up arguing that the circumstances were inappropriate. After Saudi Arabia made a decision to sell its crude oil at $18 a barrel (against the prevailing OPEC price of $23.50) in June 1979 and later increased its production by 1 million b/d, relations were reported to have 'eased'. The arms request followed.[2] Sometimes the American press has baulked at the very ambiguity of the linkages involved in the US—Saudi relationship and has sought, pre-emptively, to sever them. One newspaper editorial argued that any Saudi offer

' . . . to trade off dropping resistance to partial filling of the [strategic] reserves for the sale of the offensive [i.e. enhanced F-15s] military equipment should be rejected. . . . It would be dangerous to concede to Saudi Arabia . . . the right to determine the rate at which the US will fill its reserves and it would be wrong to go back on a written commitment [i.e. that of May 1978]'.[3]

In practice issues are rarely so directly or crudely linked. The relationship is not analagous to the bazaar. It embraces a range of mutual interests and cannot be a single issue arrangement.

It is mistaken to see the 'manipulation of levers' or instruments in the service of a specified goal. The overall relationship is important and this consists of clearly identifiable short-term mutual interests together with less tangible long-term mutual interests. The relationship resembles therefore a sophisticated dialogue rather than a simple trading relationship.[4]

---

1   Defense Secretary Harold Brown, *International Herald Tribune*, 21 June 1980.

2   A US official referred to this as 'negative linkage' that is a case of 'not penalizing' them for what OPEC does because the Saudis had not 'put the squeeze on us' like the others. In fact this distinction is artificial. The Saudis used their resources against policies harmful to the West, and the US acknowledged this by maintaining a close military supply relationship. See the *Washington Star*, 13 July 1979.

3   *International Herald Tribune*, 18 June 1980.

4   I am indebted to Joe Twineam of the State Department for his observations on the relationship.

This is not to deny that either state entertains certain expectations of the other in the relationship. But it does suggest a resistance to the identification of specific levers exercised for carefully defined short-term results which are explicitly set out. More commonly decisions are made in the knowledge that the other party will recognize their meaning. For example, after December 1976, in the OPEC meeting at Qatar, Saudi Arabian leaders indirectly referred to their stand against oil price increases as a 'present' to the new United States President. The implication of this was that it ought to be 'appreciated'. Similarly in 1978-81 Saudi Arabia continued to extend the deadline for the production of oil at 1-2 million b/d in excess of its own formal ceiling on production. The implication of this was that Riyadh, in assisting the US, also expected the United States to implement a rigorous domestic energy policy without any further delay. Since the totality of the relationship is more than merely one of *quid pro quo* and is based on trust, atmosphere matters. This means that declaratory policy, protocol considerations and the symbolic dimension of relations are extremely important, requiring a sensitivity and co-ordination within the US bureaucracy that may be difficult to achieve.[1] Reference has already been made to the 'psychological dependency' that exists (balancing in part the real dependency of the West on Saudi oil). The West is trusted because it is not intent on imposing its system of government on others and can provide security against those who do. A broad co-operative multi-levelled relationship covering a wide range of issues has thus been fashioned — including oil, arms, investment, trade, technology, training, and education. Such a broad-based relationship gives the West multiple sources of entrée into the government and increases the prospects for general influence.

Due to criticisms of the connection with the United States, the Saudis have in recent years been on the defensive, with a drift toward disassociation and an emphasis on the Arab dimension of security policy, best seen in Saudi support for Gulf security arrangements. Within the Kingdom some have pointed to the problems associated with the American link and by no means all of the Saudi leadership are equally in favour of its maintenance, leave alone its intensification. It is not always clear that the mutually advantageous partnership is always equally advantageous. Therefore, in the words of a veteran observer of Saudi affairs 'it may be necessary once in a while to demonstrate its

---

1  This requires careful tuning of policy statements for the effect it can have on various audiences, including a general Arab audience.

value'.[1] Due partly to Congressional criticism and delay, the Saudi leadership has moved to diversify the sources of its military equipment. This need not mean a corresponding dilution of US influence. The supply of military equipment and services has not been a tool for fine-tuning the relationship. United States' influence in the Kingdom antedates the establishment of a large-scale military tie. It will therefore survive it. But whether the relationship matures to become a durable one depends largely on greater sensitivity on the part of the United States to the priorities and constraints of its vulnerable partner.

## USSR—Iraq 1968-80

### The Soviet Union as arms supplier

As a supplier of arms to states in the Third World, the Soviet Union has not been exempt from the generic problems associated with the conversion of arms assistance into continuing political influence. The same problems exist for Moscow as for Washington — arms are a blunt instrument for leverage which cannot be fine-tuned through supply and denial. Too generous a supply for reassurance of the recipient risks reducing its dependency; too much denial will alienate the recipient, driving it toward diversification. Once supplied little influence can be brought to bear on how the arms are used and the pressures for maintaining the supply relationship limit the possibilities of frequent denials. While the nature of the supply relationship is dependent on overall political ties that will fluctuate, erratic supply will accelerate the pressures for diversification. Thus, even in periods of strain and tension, the supplier will have a continuing incentive to provide arms for the decline of supplies will tend to go hand in hand with that of the supplier's influence. Even if arms are used for purposes different from those originally contemplated, to retain future influence the supplier will tend to seek to demonstrate its reliability and responsiveness by maintaining supplies.[2]

There is abundant evidence that the Soviet Union regards military assistance as an integral part of its foreign policy and as one component of its strategic posture in the Third World. Its concentration on its border on South-West Asia and on the Middle East is especially notable.

---

1 Eilts, 'Security Considerations in the Persian Gulf', pp. 79-113.

2 The umbilical cord is therefore two-way. The examples of the US and revolutionary Iran in 1979, and the USSR and the Iraq—Iran war are illustrative.

Equally remarkable is the growth of Soviet military aid which in recent years has overtaken that of the US. Military assistance has been used to achieve a number of ends:

1  Preclusively, to deny the dominance of the West or to erode its position by siding with an anti-Western regime.
2  Intrusively, as an opening wedge for subsequent agreements.
3  As an entrée into society through the armed forces.
4  As a deterrent, to balance against and warn hostile states.
5  As a market, for oil or hard currency.
6  As a hedge or buffer against possible setbacks elsewhere in the region or as a bargaining card *vis-à-vis* pro-Western regimes and the West.

Soviet aims are often more concrete than this, seeking to use arms assistance as a *quid pro quo* for strategic access[1] (staging facilities, overflight rights, prepositioning of equipment, etc.). Arms transfers have often been an opening wedge leading to grants of strategic access. The example of Berbera in Somalia is illustrative. Concessions on overflight rights (even for civilian aircraft), servicing agreements (including personnel and technicians) rarely have primarily commercial connotations, being part of an overall programme of political penetration and area familiarization less typical of the United States.

Generally Soviet policy has shown a willingness to offer attractive discounts in the opening phases of a relationship or to grant aid exclusively to needy countries (such as the PDRY and Somalia) and at the same time to restrict high technology and an abundant supply of parts. The Soviets have shown a high degree of continuity of supply, flexibility regarding the ideology of the recipient and an unwillingness to use their supply relationship to enforce an outcome when their interests have not been clear-cut.[2] When forced, however, they have been prepared to take or to change sides (as with Ethiopia and Somalia). Like the US, the Soviet Union has little control over how its arms are ultimately used and even less in ordering local antagonisms to suit Soviet strategic needs.

In addition, Soviet military aid to the Third World contrasts with that of the West in a different way. The USSR does not compete in the provision of economic assistance, high technology or the produc-

---

1  See the discussion by Robert Harkavy, 'Strategic Access, Bases and Arms Transfers' in *Great Power Competition in the Middle East*, Milton Leitenberg and Gabriel Sheffer (eds.), Pergamon, New York, 1979, pp. 173-75.

2  Contrast the US which has been prepared to alienate one or both allies in the India—Pakistan, Turkey—Greece conflicts.

tion of sophisticated consumer goods. Its military industry is by far its most efficient and it enjoys a comparative advantage in arms production.[1] Marginal costs are often low and, in many cases, arms withdrawn from Soviet front-line service are sold from stockpiles. There are thus stronger Soviet incentives to use arms sales for strictly commercial reasons. This is especially true where the recipient has a large hard-currency income and where it is potentially possible to turn soft currency goods like arms into hard currency. Thus economic considerations strengthen incentives to supply arms to oil-producing states.[2] It is thus not surprising that Iraq and Libya have been two of the major recipients of Soviet arms since 1973.

Soviet economic motives in Iraq are clear. Iraq constitutes a lucrative market and Iraq's repayment record has been excellent. Its oil revenues have doubled in the past five years (1976-81) to over $30 billion. Between 1970 and 1976, Iraq's share of Soviet trade with the Third World grew from 2.2 to 10.9 per cent. In 1978 Iraq was still the USSR's most important trading partner in the Arab world. Contracts in 1977 were double those of 1973 (two-way trade equalling $3 billion) but a declining percentage of Iraq's overall trade.[3] This was due to Iraq's increased trade with the West. Even with the US trade was doubling every year after 1977. Nevertheless, even despite the USSR's reduced importance as a trading partner by 1980, it is significant that the number of Soviet and Eastern bloc economic technicians in Iraq doubled in the period 1977-79.[4]

The Soviet Union has earned hard currency from the sale of arms and of machinery and equipment. Originally these were paid for by Iraq in oil. Iraq's crude oil exports to the USSR in 1972-73, for example, grew from 4 to 11 million metric tons. After that year barter arrangements were revised and payments were made in hard currency, leading in 1974 to a drop to less than 4 million tons in oil exports to the USSR in that year.

1 See Gur Ofer, 'Soviet Military Aid to the Middle East — an Economic Balance Sheet' in II. 'Soviet Economy in New Perspective' (A Compendium of Papers), Joint Economic Committee, Congress, October 1976, pp. 216-39.

2 'As the economic function of arms sales becomes more vital to Soviet interests, the Soviets are likely to become proportionately more avid in seeking customers possessing hard currency or its oil equivalent'. CIA, *USSR: Soviet Economic Problems and Prospects*, CIA, July 1977, p. 28.

3 The Communist share of Iraq's trade was halved between 1973 and 1977 to 11.5 per cent. The USSR fell from first to fourth place as a trading partner.

4 To 12,900 if 1,350 Cuban, and 275 Chinese are included. *Contrast*, CIA, 1977 (November 1978), p. 9; and (October 1980), p. 21.

The development of Iraqi—USSR trade is illustrative of the (increasing) role of commerce as a factor in Soviet military sales to the Third World. A major component of Soviet trade with the less-developed countries (LDCs) is arms sales which are accounted for only as 'residuals' in Soviet statistics. The Middle East is a unique market place where Soviet arms have been turned into either oil or directly into hard currency: 'Almost all of Iraq's oil shipments to the USSR either as barter or repayment for past debts are resold for hard currency'.[1] The fact that an otherwise strategically important target state is solvent and able to pay for its arms in convertible currency reinforces the attractiveness of Iraq as a market for Soviet arms and diminishes any tendency toward denial.

Iraq, of course, has not always been wealthy. In the aftermath of the revolution of 1958, it found its choice of arms suppliers severely constrained by financial as well as by political considerations. It was in this period (1958-74) that Iraq—Soviet relations were potentially at their most rewarding for Soviet influence. The grant component in Soviet aid was high, and alternative suppliers limited for both financial and political reasons. Soviet leverage should have been at its zenith at this juncture, particularly since a tacit anti-Westernism brought the two countries into a marriage of convenience. Overlapping interests and the lack of Iraqi options were certainly responsible for the development of relations. The USSR was able to dispose of a large surplus inventory and to deliver arms more quickly and secretly than other potential suppliers. Soviet arms aid, in addition, consisted largely of weapons and ammunition rather than infrastructure. Moreover the simplicity and ease of operation of Soviet weapons facilitated their assimilation and maintenance. In this area, lack of sophistication is not necessarily a handicap.

But even in this period of maximum convergence, Soviet influence was by no means decisive — for reasons we shall discuss. The subsequent period was initially one of growing intimacy (1972-74) to be followed by a loosening of bonds (1975-81) when, although Iraq's strategic importance to the USSR increased, Soviet influence declined. This was due in large part to the nature of the Iraqi government, and to shifts in the regional environment affecting its perceptions and priorities, as well as to the widening options provided it both by oil wealth and a less doctrinaire and more pragmatic approach to its

---

1 *Communist Aid Activities in Non-Communist Less Developed Countries 1978* (CIA, 1979), p. 34. The Soviets' sale of Iraqi oil at higher prices on the world market was a contentious issue in the relationship in the early 1970s. This was reminiscent of a similar problem with Egyptian cotton and world cotton prices in the 1960s.

interests. In this second period therefore, divergences between Moscow and Baghdad increased despite the existence of a strong military relationship.

The scope of this relationship merits an abbreviated discussion here. Iraq was the Soviet Union's largest arms customer in the Third World from 1974 to 1978. Some $3.6 billion-worth of arms were delivered by 1978 (as against $2.7 billion for Syria, and $3.4 billion for Libya) and, in contrast to Syria and Egypt, it should be noted the equipment provided was not resupply for arms lost in combat. In the opinion of a US government agency: 'Deliveries since the 1977 war have brought in the most modern military equipment ever supplied to an LDC'. The value of Soviet military aid to Iraq outran the economic by 15 to 1. The magnitude of this aid is indicated by noting that in the past nine years Iraq has tripled the size of its armed forces while simultaneously modernizing them. The Soviet Union has assisted this growth, providing, in 1974-78, over 70 per cent of the $5.3 billion spent on imported arms (compared to less than 10 per cent from France).[1] Until the mid-1970s, Soviet arms constituted 75 per cent of the Iraqi inventory.

In addition to the commercial motivation noted earlier, Iraq was becoming increasingly important for strategic reasons — as an ally in the Arab world, as an access point into the Gulf and as a counterweight to Iran. By maintaining a militantly anti-Western tone in its foreign relations, the Iraqi regime could increase the inhibitions of the smaller Gulf Arab states from co-operating with the West. Iraq's rejection of Western formulae for peace in the Middle East — though occasionally embarrassing — could still serve Soviet interests. Iraq's growing power in the 1970s was thus a factor that held promise from the Soviet viewpoint. Yet the course of relations in the past few years has highlighted some of the problems of maintaining influence even in states where the military links are strong.

A number of basic differences have interacted with existing irritants to reduce the margin of Soviet influence appreciably. A basic change (besides Iraq's reordering of priorities and growing options) is the perception within Iraq that Soviet intentions are malign and suspect. This has accelerated a move toward a diversification of suppliers and to an 'even-handedness' toward the two superpowers. This in turn has reduced Iraq's utility to the USSR as an anti-Western ally in the region. Baghdad appears from this perspective to be a political rather than military rejectionist, creating problems for Moscow's regional allies (Syria and

1 The opinion and figures quoted in the above paragraph are taken from *Communist Aid Activities in Non-Communist LDCs in 1979 and 1954-1979*, CIA, Washington, 1980, pp. 156, 160-61.

the PDRY) and complicating the extension of Soviet influence in other states (for example Iran). The fact of arms dependency which remains real (though declining) has not noticeably inhibited Iraq in its policies in the region even where these conflict with the USSR. The Soviet Union for its part has been reluctant to terminate the relationship — not least (one suspects) because it is too entangled in it after over twenty years and would prefer not to jeopardize the relationship until it became absolutely hopeless. It also needs the hard currency. As in the US case with Iran, the supplier's influence is dependent on the overall political relationship which, even if overturned, provides an additional and independent argument for maintaining the arms supply relationship, this time as a possible means of restoring the political tie. Whether the Soviet Union (or the US) can tolerate arms relationships with states whose regional policies regularly clash with their interests appears doubtful. But the arguments against terminating those ties are likely to remain strong as long as the relationships are not confined solely to *quid pro quos*.

## The evolution and scope of the military relationship

*The background: 1958-72.* After the July 1958 Revolution, republican Iraq looked to the USSR for military assistance. In part this was due to the absence of any other major supplier prepared to subsidize sales or able to deliver equipment quickly.[1] Anxious to encourage Iraq's move towards non-alignment, Moscow responded with military assistance — a squadron of MiG-15s plus a military mission. By the early 1960s, Iraq was the first Gulf state to receive supersonic aircraft — the MiG-21. Despite some hesitation about Iraq's repression of communists, and its uncertain political orientation, Moscow maintained the arms link. Henceforth anti-Westernism would be the touchstone for relations and not ideological purity. By mid-1965 any Soviet reluctance to arm a regime engaged in full-scale operations against its Kurdish population had evaporated. An encouraging sign for Moscow was Iraq's growing militance and its severance of diplomatic relations with the United States in 1967.

---

1 France was unwilling to depart from commercial terms. Only the USSR could provide adequate supplies quickly. For a recent affirmation of this see Major-General Fursdon's report in *Daily Telegraph*, 17 November 1980. This capacity distinguishes the superpower from other suppliers. In this connection see Mohammed Haikal's observations on Soviet versus French capabilities. Irritated at Soviet policy, Egypt arranged a 10-year agreement for the supply of *Mirages* from France. Once relations with Moscow improved, supplies were resumed. ' . . . in one month more *MiGs* arrived from the Soviet Union than *Mirages* were due to arrive from France in three years'. Haikal, *Sphinx and Commissar*, Collins, 1978, p. 285.

Baghdad's losses in the 1967 war were quickly more than made up. Between 1967 and 1971 the USSR provided some 110 MiG-21s and SU-7s, 20 helicopters and trainers, 150 tanks, 300 APCs, and 500 field guns and artillery. Soviet economic credits and grants between 1969 and 1971 were nearly double the total in the preceding decade.[1] East European credits and grants from 1969 to 1972 totalled $415 million as against $14 million for the entire decade after the Revolution.

The intensified but still low-level military relationship reflected a convergence of political interests. With the return of the Ba'ath party to power in 1969 and in its hard-line approach to the question of Palestine, Iraq became more strongly anti-Western. The USSR came to be seen as an important power essential for the achievement of Arab interests and as a source of support to balance the conservative states being built up by the West in the Gulf. Iraq's political weakness (the Kurdish issue remained unresolved) and its revolutionary rhetoric, which isolated it regionally, led it toward a dependence on the USSR which the latter welcomed.[2] For the USSR, Iraq would always be important in the Arab world as a hedge against reverses in relations with other Arab states (such as occurred in Egypt in 1971 and in Syria in 1976). Iraq's importance as a Gulf state was daily growing for the USSR which lacked any other friendly littoral state. Furthermore throughout the 1970s, Iraq's good repayment record and growing oil income consolidated the relationship. There was thus a solid commercial incentive lacking in the case of Syria or Egypt.

These ties were further cemented as the Iraqi Ba'ath sought to consolidate their power domestically, to reduce Western influence and to compete with Iran in the Gulf. In February 1972 Saddam Hussein visited the USSR and called for a 'solid strategic alliance'. Responding to this Iraqi initiative, despite some reservations about providing open-ended support, the USSR agreed and concluded a Treaty of Friendship and Cooperation on 7 April 1972. This agreement contained two Articles (7 and 8) relating to consultations in the event of a threat and to defence co-operation. For Iraq it was a way out of regional isolation and domestic disorder. For the USSR it compensated for setbacks in Egypt without providing unconditional support or entanglement. Indeed Moscow was quick to reassure Iran on this point. The Treaty was signed at a time when oil production in the North Rumaila oilfields (developed with Soviet assistance) was inaugurated. It coincided too

1 $365 million versus $184 million (1954-68). See *Communist States and Developing Countries: Aid and Trade in 1972*. Washington DC: State Department, Bureau of Intelligence and Research, June 1973, Tables 2, 10.

2 In 1968 Iraq sought French *Mirages-III* aircraft but an agreement was not reached due to Iraq's inability to pay.

with the visit of a Russian naval flotilla to the Gulf. Finally it formalized the military relationship by providing the basis for a growing pattern of sales, consultations and visits between the two states.

An immediate result of the agreement was the construction of SAM-3 sites in Iraq. In the summer of 1973 a dozen TU-22 (*Blinder*) supersonic medium-bombers were delivered to Iraq, the first such delivery outside the Warsaw Pact.[1] By October 1974 Iraq had received 12 MiG-23s (*Flogger*). Since there were no Iraqis trained to fly these aircraft, Soviet pilots and maintenance personnel accompanied them. As relations between the Ba'athists and the Kurds and neighbouring Iran deteriorated throughout 1974, sporadic clashes grew fiercer in the border areas. There were reports of the use of TU-22s (flown by Soviet pilots) and Soviet ground advisers against the Kurds.[2] Though hardly decisive, this limited involvement, the first use of Soviet personnel since the 1970 Canal War, signified the degree to which USSR—Iraq relations had developed.

Iraq however was dissatisfied both with the level of material and diplomatic support provided by Moscow. After 1974 it sought to order its priorities in such a way as to avoid excessive dependency on any one country. Accordingly 1974 saw its first move to diversify its sources of arms. It concluded a $70 million agreement with France for thirty-one *Alouette* helicopters, (with SS-11 anti-tank missiles) plus mortars and ammunition.

*The move toward a balance: 1974-81*. With hindsight it is clear that 1974 was the high-point of the Soviet—Iraqi military relationship, although both a growing demand for arms and the assimilation of arms previously ordered would require a continuing flow of spare parts, training and technical assistance. Military dependence would persist for the foreseeable future but the nature of dependency would change. The order for French arms in 1974 was one indication. In April 1975 Saddam Hussein pointedly observed that Iraq would diversify its sources of arms if the national interest so dictated.[3] The settlement of the border conflict with Iran and the pacification of the Kurds

---

1 In speed and range the *Blinder* was superior to aircraft provided to any other Arab state at that time. See Roger F. Pajak, 'Soviet Arms Aid to the Middle East since the October War' in *The Political Economy of the Middle East 1973-1978. A Compendium of Papers*, Joint Economic Committee, Congress of the US, 96th Cong; 2nd Sess, 21 April 1980, pp. 445-85.

2 Officially Soviet pilots were seconded to Iraq for training its pilots. In practice operational activities seem to have been included in a team of 'advisers' under a Colonel Vasilev. See *The Times*, 19 June 1974; *Daily Telegraph*, 11 September 1974; *Le Monde*, 12 September 1974; *New York Times*, 29 September 1974 and *International Herald Tribune*, 7 October 1974.

3 *Washington Post*, 25 April 1975.

reduced the immediate security threats to Iraq.

After 1975 a declining proportion of Iraqi military purchases came from the Eastern bloc. Although Eastern bloc arms accounted for $1,443 millions of a total of $1,721 millions transferred to Iraq between 1966 and 1976, this share was reduced thereafter. By 1976 Eastern arms accounted for only $2,710 million of $3,740 million and by 1978 for $3.6 billion of the $5.3 billion of arms cumulatively transferred to Iraq.[1] The value of Soviet bloc arms thus accounted for two-thirds of Iraq's inventory rather than the three-quarters earlier in the decade. Even these figures understate the degree of diversification as they refer to weapons actually delivered rather than to orders yet to be filled. If orders are included the virtual Soviet monopoly has been truly lost. The value has been reduced to perhaps 60 per cent of Iraq's inventory and is declining. The trend in this direction has benefited France, starting with an order for 36 *Mirage* F-1 aircraft in 1977 (with twenty-four more added in 1979). In addition to medium tanks and missiles from France there have followed large orders for APCs from Brazil, for eleven naval vessels from Italy (1981) and for forty-eight trainer aircraft from Switzerland.[2] While actual *deliveries* from non-Communist bloc countries between 1974 and 1978 totalled only $1,524 million, if *orders* were counted the figure would be greater than $3 billion since 1974 — a more impressive testimony to diversification.

The trend however should not be exaggerated. Iraq's military relationship with the USSR is solidly based. Diversification is costly, lengthy and often a risky enterprise for states with imminent security problems. The incentives for a cautious partnership — perhaps shorn of illusions on either side — remain intact. Despite a coolness in relations arising from Iraq's rapid (and unheralded) border settlement with Iran in 1975, which affected Soviet–Iraqi military relations in 1975 and 1976, Soviet problems with Syria in the Lebanon swung Moscow back toward Iraq. The Soviet Union made a conscious effort to restore and consolidate these ties.[3] An agreement was concluded in mid-1976 on a record $1,000 million arms package involving aircraft, ships, tanks and artillery, placing Iraq first among recipients of Soviet

1 See *World Military Expenditures and Arms Transfers*, ACDA, Washington: 1977, 1978, 1979, pp. 78, 156 and 160-61 respectively.

2 Consult *The Military Balance* 1978-79, 1979-80, 1980-81. See also *Le Monde*, 21 December 1979; 8 February 1980 and the section in the text below on diversification.

3 On Alexei Kosygin's visit to Iraq see *Le Monde*, 2 June 1976.

arms.[1] In 1977 Iraq purchased long-range jet transport aircraft (Il -76s) never before exported by the USSR. At the same time Iraq received nearly $600 million of arms previously ordered, accounting for 20 per cent of the Soviet Union's shipments to the Third World. In 1978 the delivery of aircraft to Iraq accounted for 60 per cent of Soviet aircraft deliveries to the Third World.[2] A visit to Moscow by Saddam Hussein in later 1978 appeared to reflect continued dissatisfaction with the manner in which Soviet deliveries were being implemented. Equally important however were the political differences that had emerged between the two states and which had begun to be reflected in the overall relationship. In Iraq this could be seen by more pointed comments about the need for diversification and relationships which lack 'strings', followed by new orders from European states,[3] and in the USSR by a continued willingness to deliver arms but to try to regulate the flow to extract concessions or to register disapproval. In 1979 the USSR concluded a major new arms agreement with Iraq for additional T-72 tanks and MiG-25 fighter aircraft. Even so Moscow appears to have found it easier to continue to deliver arms in the wake of its invasion of Afghanistan in the hope of neutralizing Iraq's opposition to it, rather than to deny her arms until her response was clearly non-critical.[4]

With the vast scale of deliveries of equipment Iraq's dependence on the Soviet Union for training and spares grew apace. Soviet military advisers in Iraq doubled between 1972 and 1979.[5] One hundred Iraqi military personnel were in the USSR for training in 1978 bringing a total of 3,710 military officers trained there in the past twenty-five years.[6] Iraq's aircraft and tanks will, for the foreseeable future, be dependent on the Soviet Union for spare parts and equipment. While the Soviet Union is no longer the sole supplier, it remains the principal supplier of arms and equipment and reports that it will lose that position are, as of early 1981, at the least premature.

1   *Communist Aid Activities*, CIA, 1977.

2   See *Communist Aid Activities 1978*, pp. 2, 34.

3   On the occasion of the French Defence Minister's visit, senior Iraqi officials made pointed references along these lines. See *Military Aviation News*, June 1978, p. 16.

4   Large-scale deliveries of Soviet arms to Iraq were reported in early 1980. See *Baltimore Sun*, 7 February 1980.

5   From 500 to 1,100 in 1978, 1,069 in 1979. Compare *Communist Aid and Trade 1973* and *Communist Aid Activities 1979*.

6   *Communist Aid Activities 1979.*

With the Revolution, Iraq moved to replace the UK with the Soviet Union as its principal supplier of arms. It might have been expected that the new and vulnerable Iraqi regime would be susceptible to the wishes and priorities of its new foreign patron and that the dependency generated by its needs and regional isolation would result in tangible influence for the Soviet Union. The record of relations is however somewhat more complex. Although there have been discernible attempts by Moscow to use its arms supplies as leverage, the evidence for success in this is scanty indeed. This section looks at a few examples while sketching the political divergences between the two states that continue to exist.

In the 1960s Iraq became the USSR's third largest arms customer, and a valuable ally in the volatile politics of the Arab world. But involvement with regimes like that of Iraq (and Syria) in the 1960s was demanding. It potentially strained Moscow's relations with Egypt and raised issues such as Moscow's appropriate policy in applying doctrinal dictates to the under-developed world. In Iraq's case for example, should the USSR acquiesce in the suppression of Iraq's Communist Party? Or should it try to use its role as arms supplier to pressure Baghdad on its policies in this respect? In February 1963 the Ba'ath party ousted Abd'l Karim Qasim's regime and followed this with an extensive purge of the Iraqi Communist Party and subsequently with a military campaign against Iraq's Kurdish population (traditionally a source of support for the Iraqi Communist Party). After initial warnings about reprisals, the Soviet Union in mid-1963 cut off its military assistance and training programmes. Only after the repression eased and the extreme Ba'ath members were dismissed did the USSR make new military aid credit available. This was the Soviet Union's first use of arms transfers as leverage against a recipient,[1] and appears to have had some success. Soviet sensitivity about Iraq's treatment of its communists is illustrated by Khruschev's refusal to shake the hand of Iraq's President Abd al-Salam Aref in Cairo in 1964: 'I'm not going to shake hands with people whose hands are stained with the blood of Communists'.[2] However when the Iraqi regime resumed its offensive against the Kurds in 1965, Moscow did not again resort to the manipulation of the arms relationship to induce restraint. Indeed Soviet

---

1 For a discussion and citations see Wynfred Joshua and Stephen P. Gibert, *Arms for the Third World: Soviet Military and Diplomacy*, Johns Hopkins Press, London, 1969, p. 17; and *The Economist*, 29 June 1963, p. 1,344.

2 Haykal, *The Sphinx and the Commissar*, p. 21.

appeals to Baghdad for tolerance toward the Communist Party were becoming muffled. By 1967 the USSR had accepted that as a matter of pragmatism state-to-state relations must take precedence over ideological preferences. Illustrative both of the Soviet view of the political uses of military assistance and of the benefits it could provide its clients were two episodes relating to Iran. The Shah of Iran negotiated with Moscow for the purchase of arms at a time when Iranian–Egyptian relations were poor. President Nasir objected to this. The Soviet response was to stress the pragmatic benefits to the Arabs of Soviet influence in Iran: 'We must have a presence in Iran . . . we must have our plan to neutralize the Shah . . . Tell me . . . should we leave Iran alone or try to take care of it? Which is better for you — Soviet arms in Iran or American arms?'[1] In fact it was Soviet influence on Iran (in part a result of improved relations) that elicited reassurances from the Shah that Iran would not take advantage of any redeployment of Iraqi troops away from their joint frontier during the 1973 war.[2]

The return of the Ba'ath to power in 1969, with their uncompromising stand on Palestine and their resultant hostility toward the West, inaugurated a new closer phase in Soviet–Iraqi relations. The new Iraqi leadership, harsh with its domestic opponents and militant vis-à-vis all its neighbours, swiftly became politically isolated within the Arab world and excluded from Persian Gulf affairs. Ba'athist ambitions outpaced its capabilities which were largely consumed by the need to consolidate itself domestically. The revival of border conflict with Iran in 1969 accounted for the balance of its energies. The combination of domestic problems, regional isolation, military entanglement with a neighbour, and a strident revolutionary rhetoric, necessitated greater means than were available to Baghdad. The USSR for its part found the combination tempting but dangerous. Baghdad served as an alternative to reliance on an Egypt whose course appeared uncertain with the death of Nasir. Iraq could at least pay for Soviet assistance and did not constitute a bottomless charity case. Moreover Iraq's militant anti-Western posture was attractive.

But there were some debits. The unscrupulousness and unpredictability of the Ba'ath and the prospect of entanglement with them in an open-ended commitment, either domestically or vis-à-vis other

---

1  The conversation between Sadat — representing Nasir — and Kosygin is reported by Haykal in *Sphinx and Commissar*, p. 174.

2  *Ibid.*, p. 267.

states, served to impart a measure of caution. Involvement would increase the opportunities for influence while caution would limit them. Soviet policy toward Iraq after 1969 was an attempt to balance the two.

The April 1972 Treaty with Iraq was illustrative of this dilemma. It increased Soviet involvement in Iraq especially under Article 9 in the defence area and yielded concrete benefits. As a result of the Treaty, the USSR was reportedly granted access to Iraqi naval facilities and the use of her military airfields.[1] A more conspicuous result of the Treaty was in domestic politics. In June the Iraq Petroleum Company (IPC) was nationalized, ending Western dominance in the oil industry. Eager to stabilize their client's hold on the country, Moscow promoted a coalition arrangement among the Kurdish leadership (the Kurdish Democratic Party (KDP)), the Communists and the Ba'ath. The Communists agreed to this proposal in July 1973, were legalized, and joined the Progressive National Front with two cabinet posts. The KDP however refused. The Communist decision split the party. The group refusing to co-operate with the Ba'athists became known as the Iraq Communist Party Central Command, comprised mainly of Shi'a from southern Iraq who threw in their lot with the Kurds.[2]

The Soviet promotion of a largely fictitious power-sharing formula in which the Communist Party accepted the Ba'ath's primacy, reflected an important shift in the Soviet commitment. By promoting co-operation between these groups, the Soviets sought to strengthen the Baghdad regime, even at the expense of the Communist Party. The Soviets thus withdrew support from the Kurds when the KDP refused to join this arrangement. The Soviets hoped that the consolidation of Ba'ath rule in Iraq might make it a more reliable and less impulsive ally in foreign affairs.

The Soviet Union nevertheless trod a fine line between reassurance of an unstable regime and encouragement of its wilder impulses. Soviet arms sold to Baghdad could impair relations with the US or antagonize Iran if they were used impetuously by the Iraqi leadership. The supplier

---

1 Periodically exaggerated reports about a Soviet naval 'base' at Umm Qasr have surfaced. There is no evidence of any base as such. Iraqi naval facilities are poor. The coastline is only *forty-seven kilometres* in length and access to it is further limited by the commanding position of two islands, Warba and Bubiyan disputed with Kuwait. In addition the Shatt al-Arab Estuary leading to Iraqi ports at Basrah and Umm Qasr is marshy and shallow and needs dredging. Work has been going on in improving facilities at Fao, a port near Basrah.

2 For discussion see Abbas Kelidar, 'Iraq: The Search for Stability', *Institute for the Study of Conflict*, no. 59, July 1975.

has always certain residual responsibilities for the ultimate use of the product supplied. The revival of Iraq's claim to Kuwait buttressed by a border incident in March 1973 was illustrative. A Soviet naval visit that coincided with this episode may have been intended as Soviet support for the claim,[1] although the case can equally be made that its timing with the reassertion of the claim was fortuitous and even counter-productive politically in that it further isolated Iraq.

Soviet involvement in Iraq necessitated commitments. The Soviet transfer of twelve TU-22s in mid-1973 was doubtless a form of political reassurance to the Baghdad government that the USSR remained a reliable supplier of advanced weapon systems to match those of the US. The same can be said for the twelve MiG-23s sent in the following year. If these aircraft were in fact used in the offensive against the Kurds in 1974-75, they had no decisive effect. Nevertheless they sent a political signal to Iran while giving the USSR limited operational experience. It did not mean that the USSR fully supported Iraq in its war.

The Soviet Union urged a political settlement with the refractory Kurds on a more liberal basis than that offered by the Ba'athists in their 'Draft Law of the Progressive National Front for the autonomy of the Kurdish Region'.[2] Only after a full-scale military offensive was launched did Moscow side with the Baghdad government. Even then Moscow continued to manipulate the arms supply relationship. Saddam Hussein was reported to have told President Sadat in Rabat in October 1974 that arms deliveries were slow: 'We are suffering from our Soviet friends the same things which you are suffering'.[3] As the war intensified, Iraq's requests for long-range artillery, to match those in Iran's inventory, became more pressing. It was partly this that precipitated the sudden decision by Iraq in March 1975 to settle her border conflict with Iran which came as a surprise to the USSR. The terms of the agreement represented concessions by Iraq. Most significant was the acceptance of the principle not to export subversion throughout the region. This was followed by an approach more favourable to regional co-operation in the Gulf to exclude the superpowers.

1 See Anne Kelly CNA paper and Cottrell-Burrell article. Anne M. Kelly, 'The Soviet Naval Presence during the Iran—Kuwaiti Border Disputes' March-April 1973, Centre for Naval Analysis, Professional Paper 122, June 1974 .

2 This document, unlike its 1970 predecessor, did not recognize two separate nationalities.

3 Al-Nahar (Arab Report) 21 April 1975, pp. 3-4. See also Washington Post, 9 February 1975.

The turn in Baghdad's policy reflected a shift in priorities.[1] Domestic instability and regional hostility had necessitated dependence on the USSR which was now considered onerous and potentially dangerous. The Ba'athists now therefore energetically sought to isolate and suppress the Kurds and to defuse this problem even at the price of a settlement in Iran. Such a settlement was in turn made possible by Iraq's decision to reduce its militantly revolutionary policies in the Gulf. Iraq's dependence on the USSR for security had greatly increased with the growth of hostilities with the Kurds and Iran, and the Ba'athists had stepped back from its implications. To reverse this loss of autonomy the Ba'athists now sought first to defuse some of the threats and then to diversify their sources of arms and to establish their uncontested predominance in national politics without being beholden to an outside power. The pragmatic Iraqi leadership had made a decision to keep its options open. If dependency was a matter of degree and unavoidable, loss of control was not. Iraq stepped up trade relations with the West and sought assistance in marketing its oil. To escape domination by an underground Communist Party, Iraq instituted strong measures to ensure that they were kept under control. With the border settlement with Iran in 1975 dependence did not end but it was reduced materially.

After 1976 antipathy to the West because of its relationship with Israel and with the conservative Arab states did not mean an indiscriminate reliance on the USSR. The settlement of issues with Iran and the consequent weakening of the Kurdish cause gave Iraq greater freedom from domestic pressures. A less militant regional diplomacy made Iraq more acceptable in Persian Gulf politics. Rising oil revenues also increased Baghdad's options for acquiring arms, technology and training. This did not lead to a rapid integration of Iraq into Persian Gulf politics after 1975 but it did start a slow process toward rebuilding trust with the other littoral states. Iraq's decision in 1975 to drop support for Liberation Fronts in the Gulf was followed by a settlement of her border disputes with Saudi Arabia in July 1975. Iraq also played down her claim to Kuwait and to the islands of Warba and Bubiyan and joined discussions about regional approaches to security in the Gulf.

Iraq's attitude toward the Palestine question also underwent a significant change. From a militant ultra-rejectionist position at the

---

1 The Soviet connection had not brought the Ba'athist regime adequate tangible results in their rivalry with Syria, conflict with Iran or hostility toward Israel. Soviet refusal to provide full support on these issues limited its attractiveness to Iraq. Caution and a reluctance to take sides had weakened the potential for Soviet influence.

beginning of the decade, the Ba'ath had moved by November 1978 to a tacit acceptance of General Assembly Resolution 242 combined with a political interpretation of 'Rejectionism'. This movement was not necessarily against Soviet interests. Indeed Moscow had long been more moderate than the Iraqi regime on this Middle East question [1] but it symbolized Baghdad's reintegration into Arab politics particularly as the meeting in November 1978 reflected a new (albeit short) reconciliation with Syria which lasted until mid-1979.

Baghdad's regional option was not necessarily in tension with reliance on the USSR, but there were indications that in practice it was seen more as a substitute than a complement to the latter. The conclusion of agreements on internal security with Iran and Saudi Arabia in 1978 and 1979 symbolized this. Certainly Iraq's involvement in regional security discussions was not well received by the USSR who resists any tendency by its partners to be even-handed *vis-à-vis* the superpowers.[2] There were plausible reports that the USSR held up arms deliveries to Iraq in 1975 to signal its displeasure with its involvement in these discussions. The Iraqi Communist Party also criticized these talks.

Dependency has continued and the scope for truly independent positions is limited. Illustrative of this was the continued Soviet use of Iraq for strategic purposes. Even when the Soviet Union supported the opposing side in the Ethiopian—Eritrean conflict 1977-78, Iraq did not refuse it permission to use its facilities. The most it could extract was an agreement from Moscow not to ferry supplies *directly* from Iraqi soil to Ethiopia.[3] Nevertheless Iraq publicly opposed Soviet[4] support for Ethiopia against the (Muslim) Eritrean separatists. This opposition extended to providing military assistance to the Eritreans and later to supplying oil to Somalia. The conjunction of the pro-Soviet coup in Afghanistan in April 1978 and in the PDRY in July 1978 also evoked an Iraqi reaction that was less than receptive to the change in the political environment.[5]

---

1  Differences between the two states on this issue had been a source of aggravation, e.g. the 1970 Rogers Plan.

2  In fact however 'exclusion' of the superpowers from the Gulf would have consequences more serious for the West than for the USSR given the latter's geographical propinquity.

3  Soviet transports therefore touched down in the PDRY en route to Ethiopia. See S. Hussein interview, *International Herald Tribune*, 10 July 1978.

4  *Ath -Thawra* criticism see issue of 16 August 1978 and report in *Arab Report and Record* 16-31 August 1978, p. 675.

5  Saddam Hussein noted that the USSR will not be satisfied until the entire world is Communist. *International Herald Tribune*, 10 July 1978.

In Iraq the Ba'aths' relations with the Iraqi Communist Party has been a barometer of its relations with the Soviet Union. Iraq's opposition to Soviet advances in the region after 1978 therefore had domestic political ramifications. In April 1978 the Iraqi Communist Party, at that time still in a (nominal) coalition with the ruling Ba'ath, criticized the government's domestic and foreign policies.[1] The Ba'ath responded by asking how, as members, the Communists could be critical of the government, and accused them of being Soviet satellites.[2] Subsequently extensive purges of Iraqi communists were carried out and two dozen were executed for organizing illegally within the armed forces. The Ba'athists were acutely sensitive to such dangers in the light of a similar development in Afghanistan before the coup. A senior official referred to the strain this had caused with the USSR and observed: 'Our differences are with the Soviet Union. Why does the Communist Party take an unfriendly attitude toward us?'[3] Another official observed, 'As far as we are concerned our strategic alliance with the USSR will not change . . . as long as there is no interference in our internal affairs'.[4]

Certainly the strategic relationship with the USSR persisted, but its nature had changed. As the Soviet Union has made inroads into the region — in Ethiopia, in the PDRY and in Afghanistan — so the Ba'athist regime has seen a power originally enlisted to balance the West creeping closer to the 'Arab homeland'. The geopolitical implications of this Soviet presence and its potential political utility within Iraqi politics itself were not lost on the Ba'ath leadership. Furthermore they now found the Soviet Union somewhat reluctant to tolerate these divergences with good grace. Syria — Iraq's Ba'athist rival — appeared to be favoured by Moscow. Soviet arms supplies were manipulated to chasten the Iraqi leadership. Saddam Hussein's visit to Moscow in December 1978 reportedly involved complaints over delays in shipments of spare parts, and over Soviet attempts to co-ordinate and standardize arms supplies to both Iraq and Syria to avoid duplication.[5]

1  *Tarikh al-Shab*, April 1978.

2  *Al-Rasid* (29 April–12 May, 1978).

3  *The Times*, 1 June 1978.

4  Naim Haddad (Member of the Revolutionary Command Council and Secretary General of the Ruling Progressive Front.) *The Middle East*, July 1978, p.30.

5  See *Military Aviation News*, December 1978, pp. 14-15 as cited in *Pajak loc.cit.*, 1980.

Ba'athist suspicions about covert Soviet contacts with the opposition within Iraq sharpened. In 1979 two Communist Ministers were dismissed and another purge of the Iraq Communist Party was ordered. The alienation of the communists from the Ba'ath regime became total, the senior leadership fled into exile, and from there maintained a constant stream of criticism directed at the Ba'ath. Iraq was clearly concerned that the Communist Party, working as a fifth column for the USSR, could provide the conduit for Soviet intervention in the country and, possibly through its strength in the Shi'a and Kurdish areas, provide a link with both of Iraq's hostile neighbours, Iran and Syria. The Ba'ath therefore continued their campaign to depict the Communists as agents under the control of a foreign non-Arab power.[1] They were quick to observe that the existence of a Friendship Treaty with Iraq does '. . . not give the Soviet Union any right to interfere in our internal affairs in any way'.[2] Their interpretation of Soviet policy was straightforward: 'The Soviet Union is now seriously working through its communist parties to penetrate and take over Pakistan and other countries'.[3] To prevent any such possibility, the purge of the Communists was intensified. On 25 April 1980, the offices of Georges Habbash's Marxist Popular Front for the Liberation of Palestine were closed. By November 1980 seven opposition groups within Iraq, consisting *inter alia* of Iraqi communists and a Kurdish faction, joined forces against the Ba'ath with the aim of forging closer ties with both the USSR and Iran.[4] Lastly the Iraqi Communist Party, using the platform of the 26th Party Congress in Moscow in March 1981, denounced the Ba'ath regime both for the continued suppression of the Communists and for its war with Iran.[5] Soviet policy during the war suggested parallel reservations about Baghdad's behaviour.

The Ba'ath have always regarded the Communist Party both as an alien threat to Arab culture and a tool of a foreign power. The agreement to form a coalition in 1972 had been demonstrably tactical, necessitated by multiple simultaneous pressures on the regime. This 'Progressive National Front' had come under severe strain as the Com-

---

1 See especially two *Ath-Thawra* editorials in 1980–81. As broadcast by Baghdad Home Service, 10 February 1980 in ME/6344/A/2, 13 February 1980; and *INA*, 8 February 1981 in ME/6645/A/4, 10 February 1981.

2 Saddoun Hammadi interview with *Newsweek*, 25 February 1980, p.56.

3 Naim Haddad, quoted by *As-Siyasah*, broadcast by KUNA, 7 May 1980 in ME/6414/A/4, 8 May 1980.

4 *The Guardian*, 14 November 1980. See also *The Observer*, 5 April 1981.

5 *International Herald Tribune*, 3 March 1981. (No mention was made at Party Congress of Iraq or of the Iraq–Soviet Treaty.)

munists sought to expand their influence within it, and as the Soviet shadow in the region began to grow, sensitizing the Ba'ath to the implications for their own political survival. The Iraqi leadership, however, sought to separate the issue of its treatment of the communists and its relations with the USSR: 'We will not allow our relations with you to pass through the channel of the ICP'.[1] Moscow was repeatedly advised, 'Our relationship with Moscow is constantly improving . . . while our differences with the ICP are related to security'.[2] The Soviet press was highly critical of Ba'athist attempts to depict the Communist Party as 'anti-Arab' in their efforts to discredit it.[3]

In the aftermath of the Iranian revolution and the Soviet invasion of Afghanistan, Iraq's divergences from the USSR grew wider. Iraq was far from enthusiastic about Iran's revolution, fearing its potential turn to the left more than it was impressed by its 'progressive' credentials. Unsurprizingly the Iraqi Communist Party (and indirectly the USSR) criticized this attitude.[4] Sensitivity about the potential role of the ICP within Iraq was undoubtedly increased as much by events in the region as by its members' (alleged) intervention and recruitment in the armed forces. Nevertheless the fact that the arbiters of change in both Afghanistan and the PDRY had been the military, which had been Soviet-trained and advised, suggested parallels to the Ba'athist leaders of their own potential condition. The military relationship could become the vehicle for Soviet influence and for regime transformation. The subsequent purges in 1978–79 were doubtless to cleanse the armed forces of non-Ba'athists and to serve notice on Moscow as to the limits of the Ba'athists' tolerance for this type of activity. Yet it is doubtful that the principal threat from the ICP came from its potential for organizing coups so much as from its capacity to organize and make common cause with other opposition elements. ICP co-operation with foreign opponents was another possibility, perhaps with the Iranian *Tudeh* (Communist Party) or perhaps with the Syrian regime increasingly aligned to Moscow.

The Ba'ath's understandable sensitivity about their political survival and the threat they saw in the combination of Soviet proximity and its

1  Naim Haddad interview in *Al-Dostour* (London), no.425, 2-8 April 1979, pp.6-7.

2  Saddoun Hammadi (Foreign Minister), *The Middle East Economic Digest*, 18 May 1979, p.3.

3  See for example the *Tass* commentary of 19 December 1979 in SWB SU/6303/A4/1-2, 21 December 1979.

4  See *Financial Times*, 11 April 1980; *Washington Star*, 17 April 1980.

proclivity for domestic interference was sufficient to make any other issue secondary. Sporadic and unconvincing attempts to separate domestic policies from relations with Moscow were made only ritualistically. It was clear that the Iraqi regime was prepared to risk its military relationship with the USSR if its political control was at stake. For its part the USSR found Iraq an increasingly troublesome partner following divergent policies and progressively less susceptible to influence through the medium of arms supply manipulation. Rather than risk rupture Moscow continued the flow of supplies erratically, and one suspects with little expectation that leverage would accrue thereby.

*Regional divergences*

Increasingly after 1978, Iraqi and Soviet policies in the Gulf region diverged. The PDRY—YAR border conflict in February 1979 saw not Iraqi support for the former but rather intensive efforts (which proved successful) to limit and terminate the clashes. The Iraqi government forthrightly condemned the Soviet invasion of Afghanistan[1] and voted against the Soviet Union in the UN and in Islamic *fora* in 1980. Yet the limits to these divergences were still evident. In their criticism of the Soviet invasion, Iraq's leadership appeared equally worried by the prospect of other states moving toward the US for protection or allowing the West a military presence. Furthermore, Iraq's leaders explicitly confirmed that Iraq would not change its relations with the USSR as a result of the invasion. This was despite the acknowledgement that: 'We think the Soviet Union is trying to expand its sphere of influence via the old game of power politics'.[2] Iraq's expectations were thus realistic in that they accepted that differences with Moscow might arise: '. . . while the Soviet Union is Iraq's friend still we may differ with it politically . . . because our policy derives from National and Pan-Arab interests'.[3]

Iraq's political response was twofold: first an attempt to limit both superpowers' presence in the region, and second to provide a regional alternative to that presence. In February 1980 Saddam Hussein announced an eight point Pan-Arab declaration proposing the rejection of foreign forces or bases anywhere in the Arab world, but linking this with agreement on the renunciation of force in disputes among Arab

1  See Saddam Hussein's comments, Press Release, Iraq, 11 February 1980.

2  Saddoun Hammadi, *Newsweek,* 25 February 1980, p.56. See S. Hussein interview, *Al-Watan al-Arabi*, Paris, Weekly, 4 February 1980.

3  Naim Haddad, Iraqi News Agency, 13 July 1980.

states and with their neighbours. Iraq and Saudi Arabia had indeed gradually since 1978 shifted their positions *vis-a-vis* their respective superpower partners and moved toward a non-aligned centre between the two blocs. The Pan-Arab declaration was intended to reinforce the regional option of the Gulf states.

The other component of Iraq's response was related: to limit Soviet influence in the region and to weaken that of its allies. In one sense the competition had become an internecine one among contending radical forces. The Iraqi Ba'ath, highly sensitive to the question of national independence, increasingly saw some leftist groupings, such as the government of the PDRY, as Soviet puppets. In addition the PDRY had granted sanctuary to members of the ICP and had repressed the Ba'ath. On 26 March 1980, Baghdad announced its support for the opposition groups seeking to overthrow the regime in Aden. It did so as an affirmation of its support for the independence of the region. The Iraqi Foreign Minister was quite clear as to the reasons for Iraq's position: 'Every Arab country is free to do anything provided it remains independent, but to bring the physical presence of a superpower to the region is something that causes us concern'.[1] Three months later he referred to the PDRY as being 'under the influence of a foreign power'.[2]

Iraq's sensitivity to competitive intervention by the superpowers in the region did not extend only against the USSR. It was genuinely even-handed to the extent of putting pressure on Oman, but the very fact of even-handedness demonstrates the shift in Iraq's priorities over the past decade. The divergences noted above reflect a shift away from pronounced alignment with the USSR. This can be accounted for in part by increased capabilities and in part by reduced commitments. Increased domestic stability, greater regional acceptance and higher oil revenues freed Baghdad from a dependence on the USSR which had been the consequence of multiple problems, frozen regional relations and a militant foreign orientation. In the process a re-ordering of priorities had also taken place. While this reflected the preference for self-reliance of a regime more sure of itself, more capable of choosing its priorities and less keen on spending itself in diffuse evangelical crusades overseas, it also reflected a changed perception of the USSR and the threat that the USSR poses to Iraq's independence.

---

1 See *Le Monde*, 28 March 1980; *Financial Times*, 28 March 1980; and Saddoun Hammadi's comments in *Al Jambour*, quoted in *Arab Oil* (Kuwait), March 1980.

2 See his *Press Conference* INA, 15 June 1980 in ME/6447/A/7, 18 June 1980.

The war between Iraq and Iran which erupted in the autumn of 1980 had longstanding causes but its immediate antecedents lay in the threat posed to secular Iraq by the militant Shi'ism of revolutionary Iran. Sporadic border hostilities throughout 1979—80 finally escalated into large-scale clashes that consumed quite large amounts of military equipment and ammunition and caused serious human and financial losses. As the war progressed it might have been expected that the war-weary contestants with their equipment spent would be daily becoming more dependent on their major arms suppliers for fresh equipment, ammunition and spares and that this would accordingly increase the leverage of their chief supplier — the more so since the combatants in wartime had few of the options open to a recipient able to move at a more leisurely or measured pace. Therefore it would be reasonable to have expected that, with the outbreak of war, the role and influence of the supplying powers would increase.

This logic was complicated in the real world. First, what may at first glance have looked like a case of a regional conflict reflecting an East—West polarization, with the superpowers as the major suppliers of the two contestants, was deceptive. Iran, since the revolution and especially after autumn 1979, could scarcely be considered a pro-Western power, while Iraq in the same period had drifted away from the USSR toward a truer non-alignment. The result was that the outbreak of the war occurred at a time when the regional states had moved substantially to what amounted to a *de facto* reversal of alignments; Iraq to the West, Iran to the East. The arms-supply relationship to be sure still reflected an East—West division but this was mainly due to the lead-times necessary for supply (and the inertia this was bound to give to acquisition policies) and to the impracticality of rapid or frequent shifts in sources of supply. The superpowers, and in particular the USSR, thus found its interests in the war to be complex and cross-cutting and by no means susceptible to a clear-cut decision for or against either combatant. Soviet attempts to reconcile these interests militated against an unequivocal alignment which in turn reduced its capacity to influence the war — an issue to which we return after we examine Soviet Policy and Iraq's reactions.

As noted above, the strain in Iraq's relations with the USSR had been discernible before the war. Differences in approach to issues in the region's politics had been compounded by mutual distrust. The coldness in the Soviet attitude had been reflected in the virtual silence on the eighth anniversary of the Friendship Treaty and the scanty references to Iraq in the Soviet press. An indicator of the Soviet position was the Iraqi Communist Party's condemnation of Iraq in the April preceding the war. Nevertheless the Soviet Union had to balance a number of considerations in formulating a policy toward the conflict and the continuing rivalry:

1  The exclusion of US influence from the region.
2  The preservation of the possibility of extending influence in Iran.
3  The non-repudiation of an 'ally' which could damage Soviet reputation both as a 'friend' and as a supplier of military equipment.

The outbreak of the war was itself an embarrassment for it demonstrated the suppliers' inability to prevent the recipients' initiation of hostilities. More importantly it increased the pressure on the USSR to choose among the three principal considerations in its overall policy. Under pressure from both belligerents to take sides, the USSR was undoubtedly annoyed by the situation which it saw as a diversion from the principal struggle against the West, and as a pretext which the West would use to increase its military presence in the region. Moscow wanted to balance between keeping its relations with Iraq while not losing its opportunities in Iran for as long as it could. The USSR preferred not to make a choice. Yet the war posed the possibility that a refusal to take sides might risk the alienation of both. Consequently Soviet policy sought to balance these considerations. By declaring its 'neutrality' it sought to avoid antagonizing either State (which in the circumstances implied a tilt toward Iran). But the fear of losing influence over both led the Soviet Union to sanction supplies on a low level and sometimes indirectly to both sides. At worst genuine Soviet neutrality could result in the loss of Soviet influence in both countries and bring about a consolidated Western presence and expanded Western opportunities in the region. It was therefore important for the Soviet Union to retain ties with both states. Assistance had therefore to be provided at a level sufficient to keep the USSR 'in the game'. This assessment reflected a shift in Soviet interests towards Iraq which was no longer the most intimate Soviet ally. As a consequence Soviet policy was not to maximize its influence on Baghdad during the war but to salvage a residual influence there, while pursuing its broader interests in the region.

Before the war Moscow had already found its attempt to cultivate the two neighbouring states under strain. In April and again in August 1980 Iran had asked the USSR to cut off arms supplies to Iraq, depicting it as an unfriendly act toward 'The Revolution'.[1] The Soviets were not willing to comply with this but reportedly offered in August and

1  See *Le Monde*, 13-14 April 1980.

again in October to provide Iran with arms if it so requested.[1] Shortly after the hostilities intensified, Moscow rejected Iran's demand that it condemn 'Iraq's aggression' but it tilted toward Iran by declaring its 'neutrality',[2] even so this elicited it no thanks from the Iranians. Moscow however persisted in wooing Iran — judging that Iraq in the short term had fewer options. A public reference to Soviet enthusiasm for Iran's 'historic' revolution and to its support 'for Iran's right to decide her own future without foreign interference' was contained in a joint communiqué with Syria — Iraq's rival and Iran's ally.[3]

The Soviet tilt toward Iran was not merely verbal. It provided Tehran with jet fuel by air-tanker[4] and agreed to a transit arrangement for Iranian commerce. It granted permission to Syria, Libya and North Korea to use Soviet airspace in providing supplies and ammunition to Iran[5] and may indeed have encouraged this flow of arms as an indirect way of gaining favour with Iran without courting confrontation with Iraq. There were no reports of the direct supply of arms by the USSR to Iran but, if Moscow were interested in doing so, it could provide some useful equipment duplicating that already contained in the Iranian inventory such as SAM-7s and -9s, ZSU-23-4s and ZSU-57-2s, and the 85 mm. anti-tank gun.

Initially Moscow was fearful that the war might lead to a reversal of the revolutionary regime and its replacement by a conservative, more Western oriented government. The enhancement of the armed forces' prestige in Iran was therefore viewed with disquiet. But, as the war continued, this threat receded and so did the prospect of a rapprochement with the United States, its principal potential source of arms. The Soviet press was however emphatic in its denials of support for Iraq.[6] Reports of the transport of Soviet tanks for example were quickly and repeatedly denied.[7] When challenged by Iran's Prime Minister to show

1 See *The Baltimore Sun*, 23 August 1980; *Washington Post*, 24 September 1980; *The Times*, 6 October 1980; *Le Monde*, 9, 14, October 1980.

2 *Le Monde*, 25 September 1980, and *New York Times*, 24 September 1980.

3 *Le Monde*, 12-13 October 1980.

4 *Aviation Week and Space Technology*, 3 November 1980, p.27.

5 There were numerous reports of this originating mainly in Washington. For example, see *International Herald Tribune*, 11-12 October 1980, and 6 November 1980.

6 See for example *Pravda*, 11 January 1981; *Izvestia*, 10 January 1981 and *Krasnaya Zvezda*, 15 January 1981.

7 See *Tass*, 14 January 1981 in SU/6624/A4/1, 16 January 1981, and Leonid Ponomayov in *Soviet News* (London), 10 February 1981, p.44.

its true colours — imperialist or revolutionary — with reference to its position *vis-à-vis* Iraq (and Israel) 'the regional aggressors', the Soviet official press was quick to respond: 'The reality is that from the beginning of the fratricidal Iran—Iraq war, the Soviet Union has not delivered, and will not deliver, arms to either side in the conflict'.[1]

Soviet reiteration of its neutrality amounted to reassurance of Iran which was unlikely to gain the Soviet Union many thanks in Baghdad. But what was Soviet policy toward its erstwhile client and how did Iraq react? In July 1980 Saddam Hussein, the Iraqi President, observed that Iraq had not been subservient to Moscow nor had it entertained excessive expectations of the Soviet Union: 'We have been and are still friends. But when the Soviet Union fails to give us certain kinds of arms, we will go to any other country in the world to obtain those weapons . . . In fact we have done this . . . But our arms are still basically Soviet'.[2] It was precisely this fact that necessitated two visits to Moscow by Tariq Aziz, the Iraqi Deputy Prime Minister, in September and November after the outbreak of the war. Neither trip was successful in obtaining new arms and the Soviet reaction to the visits was pointedly low-key.[3] The Iraqi attitude was also guarded. Tariq Aziz observed that Iraq had not requested more arms: 'Besides we have the arms to support a long war'[4] while Saddam Hussein argued that the USSR had fulfilled its obligations under the 1972 Treaty and Iraq considered it a friend.[5] Occasionally, however, an undertone of concern was also detectable. In October Saddam Hussein referred to Iran's Western armaments and training in glowing terms when contrasting them with those of Iraq.[6] Criticism of Soviet arms not performing well was made more directly by Iraq's Defence Minister.[7] By the end of the year Iraq admitted that the USSR had interrupted its

1  For Rajai's challenge see *Le Monde*, 17 February 1981 and for Moscow's reply see Radio Moscow, 16 February 1981 in SU/6653/A4/3-4, 19 February 1981.

2  Saddam Hussein Press Conference, Baghdad TV, 22 July 1980, in ME/6479/A/13, 24 July 1980. For press reports see *The Times*, and *Le Monde*, 22 July 1980.

3  For a discussion of Soviet policy toward Iraq at this time see Karen Dawisha's two articles: 'Moscow and the Gulf War', *The World Today*, January 1981, pp. 8-14, and 'Soviet Decision-Making in the Middle East', *International Affairs*, London, vol.57, no.1, Winter 1980-81, pp. 43-59.

4  *Le Monde*, 22 October 1980.

5  Saddam Hussein Press Conference, 10 November 1980. Complete text from Embassy of Republic of Iraq, Press Office, London. (See also *Le Monde*, 12 November 1980.)

6  See *International Herald Tribune*, 19 October 1980.

7  Adnan Khairallah, *The New York Times*, 12 November 1980.

supply of arms from the start of the war — arguing nevertheless that this would have no effect on either Iraq's capabilities or its relations with Moscow.[1] By February 1981 the Soviet cut-off appeared to be biting. In welcoming the continuing supply of French weapons, Iraqi officials contrasted the willingness of France to honour agreements with those who sought pretexts to avoid them.[2] The Iraqi First Deputy Premier reported that Moscow had 'stopped implementing pre-war [arms] contracts signed with Iran' adding that Iraq would not forget this.[3] Saddam Hussein claimed that Iraq had concluded arms agreements since the start of the war amounting to several billion dollars, which would allow her arms 'superior to that which it possessed before the start of the war' including aircraft, tanks and artillery.[4] A month later both the Defence and Foreign Ministers acknowledged the Soviet cut-off and pointedly emphasized that Iraq would buy arms from any other source 'with the sole exception of Israel[5]' . . .'including the United States'.[6]

There were indeed signs that Iraq was obtaining supplies from other sources. France delivered four *Mirage* fighters (ordered in 1979) in January 1981 and promised to continue deliveries until the order for twenty-four was completed. In addition France, Italy and Germany were reported to be the source of spare parts and some missile reloads for Iraq. France in particular could play an important role for the supply of the HOT anti-tank missiles, helicopter (*Puma, Gazelle* and *Alouette*) replacements and spares, light tanks (AMX) and artillery shells already in Iraq's inventory (Spain and Brazil were also potential suppliers). The delivery of the *Mirage* though was unlikely to have any practical effect on Iraq's capabilities (*inter alia* because pilot training had not been completed) although it provided a psychological boost to the Iraqi armed forces and served as a contrast to the Soviets' denial.

To what extent the Soviet Union in fact cut off Iraq from supplies is not demonstrable with any precision. It is clear that Moscow could not acquiesce in a major defeat of its arms client but this was not yet a real risk. At the other extreme it was equally clear that the USSR did not

1 Tariq Aziz, *Le Monde*, 24 December 1980.

2 *Le Monde* 4 February 1981.

3 Taha Yazzin Ramadin, *International Herald Tribune*, 5 February 1981.

4 *Le Monde*, 17 February 1981.

5 Saddoun Hammadi, *The Times*, 12 March 1981.

6 Adnan Khairallah interview *Al-Hawedess*, in *Le Monde*, 15-16 March 1980, *International Herald Tribune*, 14-15 March 1980.

wish to identify with or encourage Iraq's prosecution of a war which held risks for Soviet interests in the region. Within these parameters Soviet interests were to retain some influence in Iraq while currying favour with Iran. This might place it in a position to act as peace-maker − or in any case in a position superior to the US which lacked diplomatic relations with either combatant.[1] This still gave Moscow considerable latitude in its supply policy. The definition of 'resupply' was itself subject to considerable debate. It could perhaps be argued that the provision of ammunition and spare parts did not meet the definition of 'resupply' and was merely a 'normal' flow.[2] Semantic distinctions apart, the issue was subject to elastic interpretation. The replacement of arms and equipment lost in the conflict on a one-for-one basis (with no quantitative or qualitative increase) might well be argued to constitute a policy of restraint falling between the extremes of a dramatic air-bridge ferrying in more and better equipment, and its opposite, a complete denial of any equipment whatsoever. There were reports that Moscow had indeed settled for this one-for-one replace-ment.[3]

The impact of Moscow's policy on Iraq's war effort is equally diffi-cult to pinpoint with precision. What had been Iraqi expectations with respect to the length of the war, the attrition of equipment and Soviet resupply policy? How much stockpiling of ammunition and spare parts had it been allowed to complete by a USSR notorious for the short leash it holds over its recipients? What other sources of supply existed that could make a material difference to Iraq's war effort?

Iraq had entered into its 'strategic' partnership with the USSR under the pragmatic Ba'ath with few illusions. Its movement toward the diversification of arms supplies had accelerated after 1978 as it found its interests less congruent with that of the USSR. The result had been the placement of large-scale orders with France especially, but also with Italy and Brazil. Its determination to diversify its sources of supplies had been constantly reiterated before the war, most recently in the summer of 1980.[4] As a consequence its dependence on the USSR was

1 High-level American acknowledgement of 'no irreconcilable differences' with Iraq in January 1980 which hinted at renewed relations were rebuffed by Iraq. See *Wall Street Journal*, 15 January 1980 and 8 February 1980. Some new movement was evident in April 1981, see *International Herald Tribune*, 8 April 1981.

2 *Daily Telegraph*, 9 October 1980, and *Financial Times*, 3 October 1980.

3 *The Times*, 20 March 1981.

4 See the Iraq Information Minister's comment in June 1980, *Al-Nahar* (Beirut), 21 June 1980.

in the process of being appreciably reduced when the war started.[1] However it was inevitable that Iraq should rely on material already in its inventory and this meant Soviet material. Iraq has thus remained dependent on the USSR — potentially vitally so — for spare parts, ammunition and re-equipment during the war. This dependence could be modified by the course and nature of the conflict and by the availability of alternative suppliers.

It was evident from Iraq's official comments that there was disappointment at the Soviets' resupply policy although there was little sign of panic in Baghdad. As long as the war remained spasmodic and prolonged, alternative sources of supply could be found — from an unnamed East European country[2] (doubtless with full Soviet acquiescence), from the international arms market, and from former recipients of Soviet arms.[3] Iraq had wealthy allies in the Gulf and healthy foreign exchange reserves and could afford premium prices. Furthermore Iran's difficulties in locating sources of supply suggested that the pattern of low-level and desultory exchanges of fire might continue, thus reducing the pressure on Iraq to pay the political price that Moscow might wish to extract from a renewed commitment.

Moscow's price for the opening up of the arms tap would (in all probability) be an Iraqi withdrawal from Iranian territory. Depending on its terms, this might be considered as a considerable defeat for Saddam Hussein in his *Qadissiyah* against the Persians, which would jeopardize his political standing in Iraq and in the Arab world in general. Furthermore acquiescence in such terms as a result of Soviet pressure would be a humiliation for Iraq's aspirations for independence and non-alignment. It therefore appeared unlikely that Soviet influence, deriving from its role as principal arms supplier, could be converted into the kind of leverage that would impel Iraq toward a settlement. If the war revived in its intensity, Iraq could be expected to seek and find other sources of supply while, if it continued to sputter sporadically, both belligerents might tacitly allow it to die down without a formal agreement. In either case it is clear that, even in the case of (some) inter-state wars, the supplier of arms is by no means assured of influence.

---

1 Many orders had yet to be delivered let alone absorbed into the armed forces. Consequently Iraq's reliance on the USSR remained a major consideration during the war.

2 Probably Poland.

3 Egypt's Agreement to provide 4,000 tons of ammunition and spares in March 1981 was illustrative.

The onset of a war which consumed military equipment but which yielded no decisive result and promised further rounds of fighting might well have been expected to maximize the influence of the arms-supplying power with regard to its more desperate dependent partner. In some respects the war was in fact a test case of such assumptions. It could for example be argued that the outside powers as arms suppliers were unable to prevent the initiation of the war, to limit its consequences, or to influence its termination or outcome. This was largely though not completely accurate. Limits on 'influence' came in part because of the shift in the political relationships between supplier and recipient, which had not yet been reflected in the military side, and in part because the suppliers' own relationship was under strain and could not have survived a clash in the Persian Gulf.

Furthermore the nature of the war itself limited the influence of the supplier. Neither intense nor short, the recipient was accordingly under less direct pressure to seek resupply rapidly. The actual hostilities did not concentrate on the sustained use of air power — an area where the supplier would have a virtual monopoly and hence maximal leverage. Alternate sources existed for most other material. Iraq was thus less beholden to the USSR than might have been anticipated. This was even more the case because Iraq's adversary — Iran — was in even worse condition in respect to organization, morale and the acquisition of spare parts and replacements. The decline in the tempo of the fighting after the first few weeks testified to this and reduced any likelihood that Iraq would be irreversibly locked into dependence on the USSR as a result of the war.

Soviet influence as a result of the war might have been increased if it had been used to achieve something more compatible with Iraq's war aims — but Moscow's preferred outcome — a reversion to the *status quo ante bellum* — was for the Iraqi leadership a recipe for regional humiliation and possibly domestic political instability. The price of Soviet military assistance — a compromise peace — would leave Iraq 'with nothing to show for its efforts'. Iraq's willingness to accept the USSR's conditions would increase only if the alternatives to it — outright military defeat or an imminent overriding need for resupply due to an expanded war — were the immediate prospect. So long as its leaders felt that it could salvage something better than the unpalatable terms the Soviet Union was offering for assistance, Iraq's leaders would persist in the war and remain oblivious to the incipient dependency on the USSR that only a full-scale war would make manifest. The likelihood in the future, however, was for a winding-down of the war by tacit consent without agreement on a formal settlement. After the hostilities, Iraq's policy of arms diversification can be expected to accelerate further the erosion of Moscow's potential influence in that country.

*The conditions for, and scope of, influence*

Soviet interests in Iraq are best served by a responsive government sensitive to its wishes, while optimally this 'sensitivity' would extend to tight co-ordination in the diplomatic realm. Specific goals include access to Iraqi territory (especially to airspace, and to air and naval facilities) and preferential terms of trade, particularly for Iraqi oil. The achievement of these interests is dependent on the acquisition of influence in Baghdad, and Soviet policy in the past two decades has concentrated on this. It has encountered setbacks and achieved some successes as the relationship has evolved. Soviet influence too, though it has ebbed and flowed, still persists in Baghdad. This reflects a continued convergence of interest in opposition to 'Western imperialism'. The USSR has sought to reduce Western influence in the region for its own purposes. Iraq has sought and used Soviet power to achieve its own 'independence' and to assist the Arab cause on the issue of Palestine. Overlapping interests have facilitated the extension of Soviet influence but the durability of the relationship is now more in doubt than before while its scope has been reduced in the past decade. Because of the increasing importance of the Persian Gulf, it is unlikely that the USSR will accept such a reduction in influence passively. Iraq's importance in the region has increased, perhaps particularly so in the aftermath of Iran's instability. In addition, Iraq's oil wealth,[1] relative political stability and reintegration into the mainstream of Arab politics increase her influence and hence her value as a regional ally. Yet it may well be that the qualities making a state a valuable regional ally (stability, cohesion and wealth) also make it less likely to need the USSR. The search for influence when its target has choices and exhibits flexibility may prove to be expensive.

The record of Soviet–Iraqi relations to date sheds light on the conditions tending to increase or decrease the scope of external power influence. In a nutshell Soviet influence has depended essentially on its value to Iraq (in terms of the latter state's priorities and alternatives) and on Iraq's strength or weakness. When the Iraqi leadership was domestically challenged, regionally isolated and financially weak in 1969–74 (and in earlier periods) dependence on the Soviet Union increased. Ideological militance at this time further precluded a search for

---

1 Her oil reserves may be as high as 90 billion barrels, second only to those of Saudi Arabia.

alternative sources of arms supply or diplomatic support. A common hostility to the West then cemented a relationship which was already bound by arms supply and commercial links.

All of these elements changed in the late 1970s as Iraq's leaders consolidated their control domestically. They mended their fences regionally, diversified their arms purchases and entered into pragmatic commercial relations with the West.[1] The shift in international orientation which was symbolized by a de-emphasis on spreading revolution and by less intransigence on the Palestine issue, though marked, was by no means a reversal. It permitted a corresponding shift in emphasis from almost exclusive dependence on the USSR to a wider arena where Iraqi interests might be served.

Soviet influence in Iraq in the late 1970s was thus diluted and Western technology, French arms, regional co-operation and more diplomatic activity gave Iraq more options. France appeared keen to further this co-operation by offering arms and technology, including in the nuclear field.[2] Furthermore France shrewdly played on the Ba'athists' attraction to Gaullism; they appeared to share assertive nationalism which judged the two blocs solely in terms of their contributions to national interests. Yet whatever these other sources could offer, they were not yet in a position to replace the USSR as a source of diplomatic support on Palestine. As long as Iraq had Palestine as a priority in its foreign policy and judged other states by their positions on this issue, the Soviet position remained a privileged one. This remains true despite the growing realization in Iraq that the Soviet Union's growing presence on the periphery of the Gulf constitutes a threat to Arab interests. With a priority on Gulf issues, Iraq now judges the USSR by different criteria. Saddam Hussein put this well:

> Our relationship with the USSR . . . is not linked to any special time, but to an understanding of the extent and nature of the Arab struggle, as well as to what the Soviet Union can do to help the Arab nation through agreement on strategies, mutual interests or both.[3]

That the Soviet–Iraqi 'strategic' partnership is solidly based has not meant that it is static or immutable. Its durability could be affected by Western policies. The West could soften Iraqi hostility by modifying its

1 Contrast direction of trade in late 1970s with that in late 1960s. Note especially that from 1972 when USSR was leading supplier of non-military products; by 1980 USSR was fourteenth. (*International Herald Tribune*, 5 February 1980.)

2 Iraq is France's largest supplier of Middle East oil.

3 Quoted in Claudia Wright, 'Iraq: New Power in the Middle East', *Foreign Affairs*, vol.58, no.2, Winter 1979-80, pp. 257-77.

policy toward Israel. A European initiative on this issue may well increase Iraq's disposition to strengthen its ties with states such as France, Italy, Germany and Spain. Similarly, a change in Soviet policy could also affect the partnership. Greater Soviet militance and an increased supply of arms and support for the Palestinians and the Rejectionist Front could see a revival of intimacy in the relationship. Alternatively, continued stalemate and the inability of the USSR to influence events or produce results could accentuate the trend toward a diminished Iraqi reliance on the USSR.

In its relations with Iraq, the USSR has suffered from considerable constraints. Allied with a militant state to which it has supplied arms, it has inevitably been identified with the policies of the recipient. Yet the supply of arms has not given the Soviet Union any control over their use. Failure to support fully and unconditionally the recipient in its regional quarrels (with Syria and Iran) has brought only resentment, weakening any influence the supply of arms might have been expected to bring. At the same time support for the Ba'ath regime has entailed the sacrifice of domestic allies (the Iraq Communist Party) and a switch of support away from erstwhile friends (the Kurds). Finally, as the recipient has become stabilized and more confident, it has sought to loosen the 'unnatural' closeness of the earlier relationship, to diversify relations, and even to be critical of Soviet policies in other areas.

To a considerable extent the consolidation of the Ba'ath's power has meant the diminution of Soviet influence in Iraq. In terms of regional politics the relationship with the USSR has been a liability for Iraq, raising the suspicion of the other littoral states and slowing Baghdad's quest for influence. It may be accurate to suggest that Soviet leverage at present is less positive than negative, conferring the power to cause a nuisance rather than the power to distribute rewards. In a sense it has 'relevant' power through the capacity to meet the Iraqis' principal concern, their maintenance of political control within Iraq. Soviet influence within the Communist Party and the potential use of Kurdish dissidence provide important reminders of the leverage that can be exerted against a recalcitrant Ba'athist leadership. It is not necessary to accept fully the reports of a communist plot for a coup against the regime in 1978–79 (or of Soviet sponsorship of this on the PDRY–Afghanistan models) to remark that the Soviet Union's retention of these levers provides a powerful incentive for Iraq's leadership to remain minimally pliable to Soviet concerns, or risk domestic troubles. If the Soviets can offer the Iraqi leadership a means of staying in power (by not causing them any trouble) their leverage is likely to remain

105

considerable. This is an asset that the West does not possess.

*The arms relationship*

The supplier's influence is clearly increased if it is the sole (or even primary) source of arms to a state that has both a pressing security problem and few alternative means of meeting it. In the 1960s and early 1970s Iraq faced security problems inside the country and on its borders while dependent on the USSR for military aid. Iraq had neither the luxury of time nor the economic means to diversify her sources of supply. The Soviet position as primary and practically sole supplier carried with it undoubted influence. It enabled the USSR to pressure the Ba'ath into a National Front coalition with the Communist party in 1972–73. It had earlier, in the mid-1960s, used the manipulation of arms to prevent attacks on the Kurds. This was less effective in 1974 when denial of arms contributed to the Ba'ath decision to settle their differences with Iran and no more effective in 1975 or in 1976 when the USSR had agreed to a major new sales agreement. This experience suggests that while supplier-influence varies largely with the imminence of the security threat perceived by the recipient and the feasible alternative sources of arms, it is also dependent on the political context. The overall relationship of the recipient to the regional environment is a conditioner of its dependence. When isolated, Iraq's dependence on the USSR increased; when in tune with the region, the Soviet connection assumed less salience. At times the USSR has provided the means for the fulfilment of the Iraqi leadership's priorities *vis-à-vis* Israel and the Arab world; at other times, these have been best pursued by other means. Relations with the supplier state need not be brittle: Iraq's 'strategic alliance' has allowed for divergences and strains without a total disruption in relations. This is due largely to the make-up of the recipient state which, in the case of Iraq since 1969, has been characterized by both flexibility and idealism.[1] A lack of illusions both about the nature of the supplying state[2] and the recipient—supplier relationship has made for fewer disappointments and shocks than might otherwise have been the case. The Iraqi leadership has started from the premise that 'no country with serious problems which relies on importing its weapons can claim to be absolutely independent with regard to

1 Saddam Hussein clearly considers these virtues: 'We are pragmatists. If confrontation doesn't work we change. We haven't closed any doors'. *Los Angeles Times*, 12 November 1978.

2 Saddam Hussein refers to the immobility of Soviet bureaucracy as the 'Siberian mentality', see Haykal, *Sphinx and Commissar*, p.279.

106

many calculations of politics . . . '.[1] It has seen its relationship with the Soviet Union as essentially one of *quid pro quos* wherein the latter expects returns on its investments:

> . . . we consequently must not expect the Soviets to support us without assuring them of our friendship in the form which they consider would serve the objectives of their international strategy through joint action.[2]

The corollary to these assumptions is that a strategic relationship is also a partnership, the terms of which can be revised by either partner.

There is considerable evidence that the USSR views military aid as an instrument of influence and not merely a commercial commodity. In the 1970s it used this aid both as a punishment and as a reward for its clients.[3] The manipulation of arms supplies is clearly a risky business for both recipient and supplier but the balance of risk varies with the imminence of the threat to the supplier, its choices, and the supplier's own degree of interest in the state. A sustained interruption of the process of supplying arms (rather than a temporary curtailment to signal displeasure) may unnerve the recipient. This would tend to re-inforce the permanent incentive that exists for maximizing sources of supply and reducing dependence on a sole supplier. Iraq's move in this direction in the mid-1970s was doubtless accelerated by the Soviet reluctance to provide the arms Baghdad wanted, and to Soviet manipulation of supplies. Nevertheless, to a considerable extent the incentives for diversifying already existed. Once the economic means became available this became possible. The result was to reduce dependency on any one power and hence to forestall or dilute pressure if it were applied. In addition the move toward diversification after a period of near total reliance on one supplier acted as a lever with which to exert pressure on that supplier for more or better arms. If it was to retain influence, the supplier would have to deliver.

For the Soviet Union the military component has undoubtedly been the core of the relationship with Iraq. Arms have been a currency that

1 Saddam Hussein Statement to Iraqi Ambassadors in West Europe and Japan, 12 June 1975, reprinted in *Saddam Hussein on Social and Foreign Affairs*, Croom Helm, London, 1979, p.72.

2 Interview given to Egyptian journalist, 19 January 1977 in *Saddam Hussein on Social and Foreign Affairs*, p.101.

3 It increased its supplies to Syria when that state refused to co-operate with the US in 1975, and withheld supplies when Syria refused to end its involvement in the Lebanese civil war in 1976. The Soviet Union used the curtailment of arms supplies as a weapon in its debt negotiations with Egypt after 1974. This contributed to the deterioration of relations, the Egyptian abrogation of the Friendship Treaty and the loss of the largest customer for Soviet arms.

the USSR could provide relatively easily. They provided a tangible bond, an indication of Soviet constancy and goodwill. In the 1970s, as the relationship evolved, the trade and aid pattern of exchanging commodities for arms gave way to payments in hard currency. No longer a favour, the arms were subjected to more critical assessment by the recipient. They became more 'commercial' in nature, particularly as the USSR was known to be less competitive with the West in areas of non-military technology.[1] If the supplier had strong incentives for sales, its capacity to manipulate them for other purposes correspondingly decreased. If they were the one area in which the Soviet Union met Iraq's needs, jeopardizing it would end the only channel of Soviet influence. For, unlike the US in Iran and in Saudi Arabia, the military link was likely to be the only significant link as Iraq's foreign trade expanded in the 1980s. The Soviet ability to use arms as a means of influence is therefore likely to be further circumscribed in the decade ahead. 'Influence' would be derived less from extreme and tangible Iraqi dependence than from a parallelism of view and a convergence of interest. The belief in the importance of the relationship and the indispensability of ties would ensure continuity but the pattern of interactions would be businesslike involving the exchange of favours, *quid pro quos* and bargaining with the reciprocal use of levers. Soviet influence from the military supply relationship would persist but only if it was uninterrupted. Entanglement and loss of 'control' were inevitably the price of supplying arms, an essential by-product of the Soviet quest for influence.

This analysis holds only if the Iraqi leadership remains the same, pursues its pragmatic policy of contacts with its neighbours and is presented with no major and urgent security problem. In a crisis, the importance and the influence of the military supplier tends to increase. The transition from virtually total dependence on one supplier to a more balanced mix of suppliers, consistent with political demands and logistic efficiency, takes time and is costly. Whether it is also risky depends upon the threat environment. The length of the transition, particularly in terms of training, language skills and the like to assure full assimilation of the new arms, may be more than the military as an interest group will tolerate. Whether the USSR or their supporters in Iraq's armed forces are in a position to arrest the move toward diversification seems doubtful. Nevertheless, as a potential interest group they are a powerful reminder of the umbilical cord that binds nations in

---

1  Note Saddam Hussein's comment that the Soviet Union 'believe(s) that their most effective means for changing the world to their advantage is with arms. . . . The Soviets cannot compete with US technology'. *International Herald Tribune*, 10 July 1978.

major military relationships. This cord can only be rapidly severed (as in Iran) if the consequences for the nation's military preparedness are deemed to be tolerable, or if (again as in Iran) the supply link itself is seen as the greatest security threat. There are no reasons to expect Iraq to end its military relationship with the USSR but a reduction in its scope will give Iraq's leaders greater latitude in their approach to their interests. For the USSR the transformed relationship will mean fewer risks of involvement but the cost in influence may well be sorely missed and encourage the promotion of other, more pliable groups in Iraqi politics.[1]

---

1  The best work on the USSR and Iraq is Francis Fukuyama, *The Soviet Union and Iraq Since 1968*, Rand (N-1524-AF), July 1980. This monograph appeared after the initial draft of this chapter was completed in May 1980. Many of the interpretations of issues are parallel and I have found it instructive and stimulating.

# 2 The Superpower Contribution to Conflict Management

## The record of outside powers

The modern history of the Gulf as it relates to the management of conflict may be divided into three distinct phases. The first was the era of British paramountcy and protection which saw an outside power playing the role of manager, guardian and arbiter of the region. Intervention by other outside powers was deterred, piracy and smuggling were suppressed, interstate conflicts were frozen, and coups were either vetoed or encouraged pre-emptively. As a result of the UK's presence, disruptive forces were contained and their manipulation by outside forces prevented. Saudi Arabia was prevented from acquiring the Buraimi oasis: and Iran was denied Bahrain. Iraq's claim to Kuwait (1961) was balked first by a British military response and subsequently by use of the Arab League machinery. Territorial claims between Iran and Arab states were likewise shelved. Not only in inter-state rivalry, but also in the thwarting of unfavourable internal developments, the British exercised a veto. Sheikh Shakhbut in 1966 and Sultan Taimur in 1970 were ousted to forestall internal discontent.[1] The British role as protector thus guaranteed internal and external security in a region largely insulated from other inter-Arab pressures. But as these pressures grew in the 1960s and the region became politicized, the UK's presence

---

1 However, the revolution in Iraq in 1958 showed the limits of British power in the non-protected states.

became more difficult to justify in narrow political-economic terms.

Paradoxically the British withdrawal from the Gulf came at a time when growing Western dependence on the region was becoming evident, with projections that it would become acute in the next decade. The financial cost of the UK's presence was negligible (£12 million) and, although the smaller littoral states offered to pay that cost, the UK's imperial era was terminated with a minimum of attention to future policy interests.

The second phase was characterized by an indirect superpower role in conflict management, confined to the supply of arms and the provision of training and occasional joint exercises (mainly in CENTO and with the US naval detachment MIDEASTFOR stationed in Bahrain). These exercises involved the use by *P-3 Orion* maritime reconnaissance planes of Bandar Abbas in Iran and Masirah in Oman. Besides showing an interest in maintaining some access to friendly states, little was done to maintain an efficient base structure near the Gulf region. Within the region the US ruled out any new or direct physical presence. It was recognized that formal pacts would be targets for criticism and that bases would be vulnerable to subversion and might increase political instability. From this it was concluded that the assumption of primary responsibility for conflict management in the region lay with the local states. The major friendly states, Iran and Saudi Arabia, were encouraged to improve their relations and to assume greater defence tasks for the security of the region. For its part, the USSR also lacked a direct presence while cultivating its ties with Iraq and securing a Treaty of Friendship with Baghdad in April 1972. Relations between the two superpowers throughout most of this period (1969–78) improved and their rivalry in the Gulf remained muted and indirect.

It was domestic not regional tensions which undid the principal pillar of Gulf security – Iran. The Iranian revolution not only undermined the notion that local states could play important roles in the maintenance of regional security, it also unleashed new and very destabilizing pressures which themselves required containment.

The third (and current) phase of conflict management in the Gulf is visible only in outline. With growing interests in the region and a more hostile and competitive relationship, the superpowers' role will be more direct. This is especially clear from the Western perpective where acute dependence and Soviet proximity to the region are even more stark in the aftermath of Iran's upheaval. Past structures have broken down and, without regional states as buffers, the prospect for direct East–West confrontation arising from local instabilities has increased. Unlike the preceding era, the pressures on the superpowers in assuming a greater role in conflict management have intensified. Their interests are greater and no obvious substitute exists. The issue in this phase is not whether but how the superpowers can usefully play this role and what role exists for regional structures.

In the Persian Gulf (more than elsewhere in the Third World), outside powers are confronted by a strong dependence on a region whose stability is precarious. The sources of this instability are multiple and interactive. Limitations on the capacity of outside powers to maintain order exist both because of the nature of the instabilities (modernization and rapid change) which are impervious to traditional instruments of influence and because of political competition within the region itself and between outside powers. The margin for influence, though narrow, is real and requires clear definition if it is not to be further eroded.

The nature of some of the threats to stability are resistant to easy manipulation but they are not immune to some influence. Modernization may be inherently unpredictable and open-ended but it is not thereby incvitably disruptive. Other factors acting as constraints on outside power influence are not immutable either. The regional context which conditions the exercise of influence (unanimity, fragmentation, polarization) can alter as can the cultural historical-legacy (real or fancied slights), the political popularity of a given elite, or even the nature of the interests of outside powers (which may tend to define stability statically or alternatively to promote change indiscriminately to undermine the other bloc's interests). Moreover, all of these can be affected by outside powers' policies. This is most obvious in the military arena where the power balance can sharply affect the range of choice open to either bloc. A pre-condition for any influence is military power. It can balance or deter the other bloc and reassure local allies. By deterring threats to allies, it can prevent the exploitation of local disputes and, by providing reassurance, it can discourage the accommodation or appeasement of threatening forces by local friends. It can therefore affect policy choices as well as constrain military threats. If a necessary instrument, military power is not sufficient by itself. Much depends on its availability, its relevance, its flexibility, how it is used, and how it is perceived.

The region is still recovering from two recent shocks, the revolution in Iran and the Soviet invasion of Afghanistan. After the first, many analysts argued that 'internal' instabilities were the greatest threat to security in the Gulf. The 'lesson' of Iran was therefore to reduce arms sales and to loosen ties with 'unstable' regimes and to play down the military instrument. Within a year the invasion of a nearby state by the Soviet Union served as a reminder that 'lessons' ought not to be

113

digested too quickly or mechanically. Just as there are multiple threats to regional stability (internal, regional and external), a variety of instruments are necessary for managing and containing them. The interesting questions are the priorities and their mix. Threats to regional stability are varied and reinforcing. Although some originate in domestic tensions (for example sectarian or ethnic differences, disagreements on the pace or goal of state policy, income or status inequalities, low levels of institutionalization and highly politicized populaces) these are not purely domestic issues. Moreover they are often harnessed by states (regional or external) for their own parallel or quite different purposes such as support for a secessionist movement to weaken an adversary (Iran/Iraq, Kurds, Arabistan or the USSR/PDRY in Oman). It is then that they become dangerous. 'Simple' interstate or boundary disputes rarely remain self-contained. The search for the 'clear' case of external aggression calling forth a direct military response is chimerical. The military balance (which embraces notions of both reliability and relevant power) overhangs the politics of the region[1] and has an effect on perceptions of the range of choice. It can constrain or widen the margins of choice for both outside and local powers. It can psychologically inhibit and so affect the opportunities and the costs of local aggression. Military power cannot (and is not designed to) prevent social dislocations but it can influence their direction and specifically the degree to which outside forces use it for their own purposes. It may not guarantee political settlements but it can provide the context to make them possible. Military power is one of several complementary instruments in conflict management. That it does not by itself suffice is not an argument for its renunciation. The alleged inadequacy of any one remedy to settle all the region's problems is hardly an argument against that remedy. The choice is not between doing nothing and doing something risky, but between the costs and consequences of two different types of risk.

With the fall of the Shah the Nixon doctrine was buried. With it was interred the attempt to decouple local instability from direct superpower competition. In its place has arisen a highly unstable system to which the linkage between local and global stability is stronger and more direct than anywhere in the Third World. The end of the twin-pillar security era in which local powers insulated local tremors from global rivalry[2] has thus meant a greater potential for direct confron-

---

1   See Albert Wohlstetter, 'Half wars and half policies in the Persian Gulf' in Scott Thompson (ed.), *National Security in the 1980s: From Weakness to Strength*, Institute for Contemporary Studies, San Francisco, 1980.

2   See next section.

114

tation between the blocs in a region where there are no rules defined by experience as there are in other conflict-prone regions (such as the Arab—Israel zone). It has also entailed a correspondingly greater pressure on regional states. With Iran in turmoil, the margin of tolerance for further instability is diminished. Saudi Arabia has come under intense scrutiny as interests and pressures have focused on her. The Western states' dependence in the region means a vulnerability not just to cataclysmic revolutions but also to minor tremors, such as the balance of power within factions in the Saudi leadership which might result in policy reversals.

Yet it would be erroneous to conclude that this vulnerability too is not susceptible to influence. The 'assurance of oil supplies' also requires balancing the USSR, although that is not sufficient in itself as a policy for oil. If the issue were merely one of indigenous instabilities and the social strains generated by rapid growth, the West's task of assuring oil supplies would be radically different. It is the prospect of these instabilities being exploited by hostile powers in ways harmful to Western interests that makes the military instrument relevant. The distinction between deterring the USSR and assuring the flow of oil is not always as clear as it may appear to some.[1]

Western interests are by their nature more difficult to pursue. It is harder to stabilize a region undergoing multiple crises with many regional antagonisms than it is to accentuate and to seek to benefit from them. It is harder to support orderly change without risking either open-ended support of existing regimes than it is to flirt with opposition elements (as a hedge) and hence hasten the shift. It is inherently risky to attempt to assist in fine-tuning social change so as to conserve interests but to accommodate 'reasonable' demands. Mass democracies are rarely equipped with the means to calibrate and subtly sustain that involvement over time whilst eschewing dependence on simple panaceas, be they military—technical fixes or isolationist impulses.[2]

Nevertheless there remains, as asserted earlier, scope for influence. The maintenance of a military balance in the region is a precondition for other forms of influence — it must be credible, relevant and disposable in a timely fashion. The US is unique as the only outside power able at once to deter the Soviet Union and to bring about a Middle East settlement. Nevertheless it is generally recognized that the military instrument can be sufficiently obtrusive to weaken the regime it is

1  See Leonard Binder, 'Iran', *Current History*, January 1980.

2  Another set of opposites to be avoided is the alternation between the beliefs that either telescoped, compressed democracy, or the reinforcement of traditional structures, will bring stability to the region.

designed to protect. Yet the reassurance which it provides should not become a license whereby the local powers' concerns come to drive the suppliers' policies. It is also true that a Western policy that concentrates only on 'access to oil' or 'denial of the USSR', invites failure with the populace of the region. An equitable bargain across a much broader agenda needs to be struck for the establishment of more durable relations.

## The range of security problems in the Gulf: actual and potential

Although the priorities and vulnerabilities of the local and outside powers to specific threats may differ, the gap between their perceptions of these threats has narrowed. Whereas in the past decade 'local' threats would have been considered a responsibility of the regional powers, this may no longer be the case in the 1980s. The revolution in Iran has at once weakened the basis for a regional response and intensified the threats to Gulf stability. As a result Saudi Arabia (in particular) has become most important for Western interests yet has been weakened at the same time. The critical importance of Saudi stability and the narrower tolerance for (further) disruption has concentrated attention on Saudi security. Although many of the threats to Saudi security could properly be considered local and internal, because of that country's military weakness there is now a clear recognition that outside power assistance may be needed even in meeting some of these low-level threats. The question is how can this be done without weakening the state that is being protected? Because of the extreme dependency of Western states on Gulf oil and hence their interest in stability and access to the region, in an era of uncertainty even the smallest tremors have the potential for escalation into confrontation between the two blocs. This much closer coupling between regional conflicts and global competition is inevitable in an arena where the interests of the two blocs increasingly overlap and where no indigenous 'buffers' yet exist capable of substantially decoupling local from global disturbance.

There is nevertheless no automaticity about this connection; dependence may argue for it but policy decisions still have to be taken. The contrast between Iran's revolution and the probable Western reaction to a coup in Saudi Arabia demonstrates a 'learning process' at work. It also highlights the fact that there is no exact 'fit' between Western notions of 'threats' and those of the indigenous states.

For the latter, threats to regime stability are at least as important as threats to national security. In a state such as Saudi Arabia the two would be considered identical — as indeed the name of the country implies. In all the states the counter-elite or opposition are considered a primary potential threat. Where in this context the maintenance of regime power is the objective, for the *outside* power the assurance of stability which allows the uninterrupted supply of oil is the primary consideration. At least theoretically the outside power may prefer to accept a regime change as a means of preserving its major interest. In the Iranian revolution the West's acquiescence in the change of regime did little to reassure the other monarchical oil producers about their indispensability under similar circumstances.

From these differences in priority and emphasis — on the maintenance of power for the one, and on the continued flow of oil for the other — stem different approaches to conflict management.

1    Starting from the domestic sources of threat, security as defined by the littoral states starts with regime security. Factionalism and divisions within the ruling elite (whether Royal family or Revolutionary Command Council) are urgent matters. For outside powers a principal concern is that a change in leadership will result in differing policies (for example, over oil production) or shifts in orientation.

2    A second threat to security arises in the possibility of political strife such as military coups and revolutions. In the Middle East, coups not revolutions have been the norm. This has meant a continuity in institutions and administrative structures with replacement occurring at the top — usually without much disruption. Revolutions on the Iranian model — or prolonged unrest — threaten not just the loss of an ally but the prolonged loss of oil.

3    In most states the ruling elite do not represent the entire population, and national integration is not far advanced. Ethnic or linguistic minorities, sectarian schisms, and large numbers of foreign immigrants give these states the appearance of a mosaic. Overlapping populations also constitute potential problems as cores for secessionist movements, or as objects of political *irredenta* by neighbouring states, or as sources of domestic opposition.

4    Given the inadequate assimilation of most minorities and the prevalence of existing sources of tension between neighbours, the next category of security threats is external aggression. These are rarely clear-cut and often interact with domestic vulnerabilities. For example assistance by a neighbouring state to armed dissidents within a country (Iraq in Iran; Iran in Iraq; the PDRY in Dhofar) may constitute an unfriendly act, but is it the source or instigator of these dissidents?

The line between internal dissidence and external support (aggression) will be difficult to pinpoint with precision. The provision of arms, sanctuary and diplomatic support still falls short of actual armed aggression. *Irredenta* if periodically revived but not physically pursued (as in Iraq's past claims to Kuwait) are illustrative of a source of tension and threat falling short of actual armed aggression.

A clearer distinction exists between two types of aggression, (a) regional — by a state within the area (such as Iraq or the PDRY), or (b) extra-regional by a state from outside (perhaps Cuba or Libya). These are more clearly identifiable when the aggression is overt. When limited to training and advisory functions, it becomes equally difficult to weigh.

Overlapping the concretely identifiable sources of threat to the security of the region (such as coups, fragmentation and external aggression) are more diffuse sources of instability — rapid, disruptive and unequal growth, radicalism, crises of legitimacy and identity.

Few of the sources of instability and of threat to Gulf security will be susceptible to easy categorization. Internal vulnerabilities and external alignments and opportunities will interact and mutually reinforce each other. Threats will not come clearly and conveniently labelled. The important consideration will have to be what contribution the outside power can make to meeting it. The list below is an attempt to match threats to *appropriate* response from external actors.

*Categories of contingency and the range of superpower instruments*

| | |
|---|---|
| Coups, revolutions, domestic unrest: | prior warning; intelligence; political adaptation; accommodation; pre-emption; arms; coup reversal. |
| Civil Wars; secessionist movements: | Conciliation; recognition or non-; agreement on non-intervention; arms; sanctuary; transport; intervention. |
| Inter-state conflicts (neighbours): | arms supply/cut-off; tactical intelligence; deterrence of outside intervention; conciliation; good offices; provision of peacekeeping forces. |
| Extra-regional power involvement: | Military-naval presence; provision of transport; advisers; arms; rapid deployment force; nuclear deterrence. |

It is by no means clear that the outside powers have similar interests in the Gulf region. On the contrary, differences exist in their degree of dependence on the region (and hence in their interest in its stability) and the range of instruments for influence at their disposal. The following discussion will first emphasize the issues from the Western perspective, that is with the assumption that orderly change is a goal sought by the outside power, followed by that of the USSR.

First it is necessary to identify again a range of contingencies, political and military which the outside power may be called upon to influence:

1  Coups, internal unrest, revolution, secessionist movements, civil war, subversion.
2  Inter-state conflict, local or regional.
3  Superpower intervention.

As already noted none of these are likely to be clearcut. In the first two categories there may be varying degrees of foreign involvement, instigation, and exploitation. The upshot of such crises could be a reversal in policy in a (friendly) oil producing country leading to a shift in its alignment and interruption in the flow of its oil. Specific military threats could involve its oil installations or access to the Gulf itself in the Straits of Hormuz. In terms of East—West competition the threats identified could take various forms:

1  Accession to power of an anti-Western regime (either supportive of, or supported by the USSR), with an alliance of convenience with the USSR.
2  Subversive support for internal dissidents, secessionists or revolutionary groups.
3  Aggression by a pro-Soviet regime (or client) such as the PDRY.
4  Outright intimidation, aggression or invasion by the USSR.

The instruments for meeting these contingencies though limited are by no means negligible. The constraints on them are pronounced and require identification to point to the need for a variegated and multifaceted policy to address them. The constraints would appear to be:

1  The fluidity of politics in the region. The US cannot guarantee the *status quo*. It cannot stop shifts in alignment. As a resolute, powerful and dependable ally it can increase its attractiveness as a partner. It can defuse the pressures that may encourage defections from its camp (for example, over Palestine).
2  The intractability of many contingencies to clear-cut labelling or to the neat application of influence. US military power is no

panacea against threats of subversion. In some cases it may invite them.

In both these cases the value of the Western commitment must be seen to outweigh its costs. This means it must be credible and it must address the needs and priorities of the regional state. This need has two components: *relevance* to the military threats they face, and *appropriateness* to the political environment in which they exist. In brief, Western military power (and policy) must be capable of defending these states without at the same time undermining them. This requires, for example, a Western policy with respect to Palestine in tune with the aspirations of the moderate Arab states. This would insulate them from the pressures of inter-Arab politics that otherwise make a pro-Western connection a political liability.

There are three further constraints:

3   The fluidity of regional politics and the intractability of many regional problems to clear-cut solutions has tended in the past to encourage approaches to regional security which are formal. In part this is due to the technical necessities of military supply, access and rapid deployment. In practice such pressure tends to exacerbate regional political differences, and increase polarization by inviting states to make the USSR (rather than Israel) the priority issue.[1]

4   A further constraint is the very ambiguity of the military instrument in the Persian Gulf. Is it intended to reassure the oil-producing states and to deter attacks on them or to warn them against certain policies ('blackmail', etc.)? The US has specifically declined to rule the latter possibility out. As a two-edged sword ambiguity is useful to the West but it does tend to add to the disquiet of the local states.[2]

5   Finally, practical political-military necessities are an obstacle to the exercise of influence. To be effective the military instrument has to be either in place or able to respond rapidly to sudden threats. Without an extremely rapid response[3] the outside power may be met by a *fait accompli*. The current ability of the US to match the USSR in air and sea lift into the Gulf region in a timely fashion to influence events on the ground early is in

1   See the discussion of regional security below.

2   The possibility that facilities granted to the US might be used for purposes other than defending the Gulf or oil is highlighted by Washington's use of Oman (to that state's embarrassment) to mount the abortive Tabas mission to free US hostages in April 1980.

3   The premium on rapid response, for deployment on warning, also raises the risks of false alarms. Interventions triggered by false claims may politically undermine the protected state, exposing it as a 'puppet'.

some doubt. Yet attempts to improve this capability by a presence within the region runs into the reluctance of the Gulf states to accept the political risks entailed.

The constraints on the exercise of influence in the region should not obscure the fact that these constraints are only partly immutable and that they exist for both superpowers (though not necessarily equally). As stated at the outset, a necessary (but not sufficient) condition for influence is military power, and without it an outside power is likely to be a spectator. Military power affects the perceptions and the policies of regional and external powers. It affects their calculations of the balance of risks to be run in supporting or opposing that power. And it affects the incentives and choices of regional state. It is therefore a precondition for other measures that will stabilize the region. The military power must be real rather than theoretical. It must be relevant to the most plausible threats faced by the regional states, it must be flexible and it must be dependable. If it is all of these, the costs of association with it will rarely be higher than its gains.

Defining conflict management in the broadest terms it may be useful to divide it into three categories: (a) prevention, (b) containment, and (c) settlement.

*Prevention*

1   This includes the *deterrence* of aggression, whether by a regional state or a superpower, and the maintenance of a *regional balance of power* (through arms, training, advisers). It also includes *reassurance* of regional allies, through a policy of steadfastness, a military presence through occasional naval deployments, joint exercises, and diplomatic support.

2   In addition, outside powers can help by *forestalling* political strains by the provision of advice or political intelligence to preempt pressures likely to weaken friendly regimes, by the encouragement of adaptable political institutions and safety valves, and by assistance in anticipating assassinations or terrorism.

3   Third, outside powers can undertake the amelioration (or non-exacerbation) of political pressures on the regimes. This would include, for example, efforts to settle the Palestinian issue as a means of *defusing* it as a contributory tension and as an instrument used against the pro-Western regimes. It would also include paying careful attention to the longer-run implications of indiscriminate commercialism for Saudi Arabia's security and willingness to forego pressure on Saudi Arabia to increase oil production in recognition of the political exposure it entails for

121

the Kingdom. Being sensitive to measures which increase Oman's isolation from her neighbours is another example. In the same category would come the avoidance of sudden withdrawal of support or fluctuations in policy that leave the regional partner politically exposed and unprepared.

### Containment

This includes a willingness to defend and, if need be, to reverse unwelcome developments and to limit their consequences. It could include, for example, a guarantee of territorial integrity, protection of specific areas (such as oil installations), the provision of air defence or minesweepers, the reversal of a coup, and assistance in counter-insurgency.

### Settlement

This may include the freezing of conflicts as opposed to their settlement, through the maintenance of a stable regional balance. The specific contributions of outside powers tend to be limited but they can, for example, seek reciprocal restraints, provide compromise solutions, offer good offices or a channel of communications and assist in setting up an international peacekeeping force. The most important contribution of the outside power is in providing the setting where peaceful settlement is possible. This involves the entire range of activities discussed under these three headings.

### The Rapid Deployment Force (RDF)

A dawning recognition of the importance of military power in influencing Gulf politics saw Washington quicken its plans for a quick-reaction force in 1979. If the revolution in Iran suggested that instabilities were primarily internal in origin, the invasion of Afghanistan underscored the interaction between domestic instabilities and external power exploitation. In combination the two events undermined the US military position in the region. The former removed a potentially strong buffer with the USSR and replaced it with a state veering between disintegration and the active export of revolution to the Gulf. In either form Iran became an active force for destabilization of the Gulf. The invasion of Afghanistan, in turn, as it becomes permanent, opens up a variety of means for the extension of Soviet influence and perhaps power into the region. Finally the revival of a border conflict between the YAR and PDRY which threatened Saudi Arabia in March 1979 had the unmistakable appearance of Soviet probing of Western responses. It has already become clear that the US might indeed be called upon to defend one local state against another. The means available to do this effectively are being fashioned as the RDF is accelerated. The reasoning behind it was that contingencies in the Persian Gulf (and elsewhere) might require the rapid deployment of US military power. Related to the need for military means to react to crises was an awareness of the political importance of military power — for reassurance, for deterrence, as a symbol of commitment and as a means of defence (whether of US interests or of friendly states). This reflected the necessity after Iran's upheaval (and the end of reliance on regional states for regional order) of a more direct US role in the region to shore up the regional balance of power, which could now be upset by even the smallest infusion of force. Disagreement nonetheless persists as to the best method by which the US could at once shore up its friends and influence events in the region without further destabilizing it. On the need for greater military capability and for a better and quicker air and sealift capability there is no real dispute. Similarly on the need for more over-the-horizon presence there is little disagreement.

Accordingly in mid-1979 the US MIDEASTFOR stationed in Bahrain was augmented by the addition of two destroyers (from three ships to five) and naval deployments into the Indian Ocean were increased (from occasional to permanent). A decision was made to increase port visits and to 'show the flag' in friendly states more regularly. Consideration was given to the creation of a new Middle Eastern Command integrating the land-sea-air components of US military power in the region. A consensus also existed on the need for continued arms supplies — both as a means of strengthening local states and as a demonstration of the importance attached to them by the US. The possibility of joint exercises and contingency planning with local states was also mooted although it was clear that publicity could jeopardize this type of co-operation. There was also substantial agreement on the need to preposition equipment close to the zone (in floating stockpiles or on the territory of friendly states) and to build up the necessary means for transporting material in bulk over long distances with minimum dependence on permission from other states *en route* for refuelling (the CX cargo plane is seen as the answer to this problem). Access agreements for the use of facilities in four states close to the Persian Gulf had been completed by early 1981.

Generally speaking there was no basic divergence on the need for a quick-reaction force, on what that force should comprise, on the urgency for it, and even on the necessity for some agreement with states *en route* to the Gulf for air-staging and access rights in emergencies. Differences emerged, however, on whether this type of capability, which would not be ready until the mid- to late-1980s, would be enough. Those sceptical about alternatives argued strongly against any attempt to negotiate agreements with local states that would permit the stationing of a skeletal staff of US personnel on their territory. Three arguments were used, two of them serious. Firstly, that such agreements would be regionally disruptive, would undermine the host government politically and expose it to criticism while depicting the US as aggressive. Secondly, that these facilities would be useless against Soviet political penetration and internal unrest, which were primarily political problems. Finally, that the creation of such capabilities would generate incentives for their use and make for unnecessary interventions. The proponents of an RDF plus a military presence in the region started from an assumption that military power could demonstrate US interest, reassure allies and deter disruptors of regional order. They accepted the political sensitivity of the question of a US presence in the region but argued that the military balance of power affected the policies of local states and that, by maintaining a credible and resolute commitment, the US could 'redistribute the risks' affecting the calculations of the local states.[1] They saw a need for an obtrusive or local presence and argued that a tacit, informal but visibly capable ground force was essential for sustaining Western (and local) interests. In this view a naval over-the-horizon presence was doubly inadequate in the same way as the RDF was inadequate. Not only could it not affect events early enough to be meaningful but its very merit as a flexible tool in crises made it a less effective instrument than ground forces as a symbol of commitment.[2] A basic assumption of this school was that crises were likely to erupt quickly, giving outside powers little warning or reaction time. Unless it had the means to respond quickly — before the other power — it would face a *fait accompli* and risk a choice between escalation and acquiescence. Given the geopolitics of the region and Soviet access to the airspace of the countries to its south, the USSR's reaction time would be far less than that of the US if the latter started from the continental US or Western Europe. Over short distances (below 1,000 miles) Soviet airlift was superior to that of the US. To match the Soviet ability to project power quickly into the region it was therefore imperative to set up the local infrastructure. This was essential not only technically but to serve notice on US friends that Washington was serious about their defence.

---

1   See especially Albert Wohlstetter, 'Half wars and half policies in the Persian Gulf' in Scott Thompson (ed.), *National Security in the 1980s: From Weakness to Strength*, Institute for Contemporary Studies, San Francisco, 1980.

2   See Barry Blechman and Stephen Kaplan (eds), *Force Without War: US Armed Forces as a Political Instrument* (Washington, DC: Brookings Institution), 1978, had noted this in their studies of the post-war use of force.

A distinction should be made between policies before, during and subsequent to crises. The first would encompass a range of actions intended to prevent the exacerbation of (imminent) local problems, or to anticipate, warn and forestall them. The second would be intended to contain, limit and freeze actual crises by addressing their causes subsequently.

The types of crises have already been identified. It is evident that, in the range of factors tending toward the destabilization of societies undergoing rapid change, the military instrument is limited but not useless. The greater the obtrusive presence of the superpower in the domestic affairs of a state, the greater its identification with the prevailing regime and, if Iran is an indicator, the greater the difficulties caused for the regime thereby. But this is not immutable. Superpowers' reputations are not static. A breakthrough on the Arab—Israel question or clear signs of commitment could change American reputation in the Arab world. The superpowers' role in conflict management may nonetheless be ambiguous. The extension of a security assurance may deter external aggression but it may also embolden the protected party to resist settlement on any but its own terms. The superpower connection, by transforming the stakes of local disputes, may make them more resistant to solution by quiet diplomacy. An overt superpower presence or connection — whether in military bases or through formal alliance ('pacts') — may exacerbate regional tensions (for Saudi Arabia for example) rather than contribute to their reduction. However it may also deter aggression. It is evident, given the range of security problems, that the superpowers' role is one that is complementary to other structures for assuring security.

Some domestic threats in the region cannot be met efficiently by outside powers[1] unless an external element is identified (or manufactured, as in the case of USSR/Afghanistan) but they can be forestalled by intelligence co-operation.

Clear or even cloudy regional threats are different. Aggression by the PDRY in February—March 1979 was met by a strong US response, including arms deliveries and naval deployments. This prompt response served notice as to the limits of US tolerance and warned the USSR of the probable consequences of its continuation. In this setting, the USSR exercised corresponding pressure for restraint on the PDRY. However, the diplomatic defusion of the conflict came through a regional security structure (the Arab League) and through the efforts of

---

1 Partly because a rapid coup in Kuwait would be difficult to prevent. If it were to be reversed it would have to be by a regional not an outside power. A coup in Saudi Arabia though would require an outside power if it were to be reversed.

Syria, Iraq and Kuwait.

In cases of a major inter-state conflict or large-scale aggression, the infrastructure for a military response by superpowers needs to be in place. For example, an Iraqi attack on Saudi Arabia would require a prompt US response. Hence the Rapid Deployment Force with its attendant problems. But this is not an appropriate instrument for lesser contingencies.

The military assistance instrument has already been noted. Here it is only necessary to repeat that the provision of arms for the attainment of influence and to enable the recipient to achieve a measure of self-reliance is a lengthy process with indeterminate results, which is nonetheless essential for the bilateral relationship.

In the case of arms supply, perhaps one can identify an area of potential compromise and harmonization of policies between the super-powers but, in a period of distrust and uncertainty, this is a chimera as regards practical politics. The arms supplier relationship is central to the diplomacy of both superpowers and especially the USSR. Agreement on restraint in this area will come only when the risks of direct confrontation become stark to the suppliers. However, if the Arab—Israeli case is any indicator, even here restraint and caution will compete unfavourably with the impulse for political advantage.

## Soviet interests and policy

As Soviet interests in the Persian Gulf have increased, so have its political and military means of influence in the region. A growing and expansive definition of its security interests (given substance by Eastern Europe's probable incipient dependence on the region's oil), has been strengthened by a military capacity for rapid intervention and the consolidation of a Soviet political presence on the periphery of the Gulf — in Ethiopia, in South Yemen and now in Afghanistan. A permanent presence in the latter country broadens its strategic options and means for exerting pressure on the Gulf states and reinforces the perception of cumulative setbacks for the West in the eyes of the regional states.

Though by no means the primary source of day-to-day influence, the Soviet military relationship with the states on the Gulf periphery has grown. Treaties of Friendship (and Defence Co-operation) now exist with Ethiopia, the PDRY, Afghanistan and Iraq. In the first three states, Soviet power is strongly ensconced and the host state is more dependent and less able to expel Soviet advisers, unlike Egypt and Somalia. At the same time the USSR has since 1979 wooed the YAR back into a military aid relationship and arrested its movement toward the West. Capitalizing on Saudi Arabia's anxiety since the revolution in Iran, the USSR has concluded an agreement allowing it the use of Saudi airspace for its 'Aeroflot' civil aircraft — in practice for its transport and surveillance aircraft. A mixture of threat (military presence and hostile radio propaganda) and reassurance (an alternation between criticism and flattery) is designed to gain changes in the foreign policy alignment of these states. At the same time the USSR has exerted pressure on the Gulf states to oppose Oman's proposal for co-operation on regional security matters, and has been critical of the RDF, underscoring its potential use as an instrument for pressuring them on their oil and Middle East policies. By intensifying regional pressures against the West and by playing on their anxieties regarding the credibility of the West as an ally, the USSR has increased its own relevance as a factor to be reckoned with.

A good example of Soviet capacity for exploiting regional politics is that of the American hostages held in Iran. At the outset Moscow supported the Iranian action but was sensitive to the possibility that, if too overt, this support might jeopardize détente with the US. After December 1979 this inhibition was shed. Iran's position became 'understandable', and the Embassy 'a nest of spies'. The US was accused of using the episode as a pretext for using force and intervention. The US military build-up, it was argued, jeopardized European interests and threatened the entire Gulf. Moscow pointed out that the implication for the Gulf states was clear — the US would not condone their 'independence', and US military forces were designed to intimidate them and to prevent, through intervention, 'unfavourable social changes'.[1] Moscow contrasted US threats against the revolution with its own support for it. A specific feature of Soviet policy in this crisis was the support extended to the most radical elements within Iran and the discrediting of those in favour of ending the impasse through compromise. By radicalizing Iranian politics, the USSR sought to widen the rift with the US and, after the application of economic sanctions, to pose as the saviour of the revolution. Soviet policies in this episode precisely reflected a mixture of insecurity and expansionism so prevalent in its attitude toward events in the region. At once fearful that the hostage issue could serve as a pretext for US intervention in Iran, and that its resolution could serve to normalize ties between Tehran and Washington, Moscow sought to prevent any settlement while blaming the US for its hostility toward the revolution.

1  *Pravda*, February 1980.

## Soviet assets and vulnerabilities

In contrast to the West, the USSR is less dependent on the region's resources for its economic well-being, or on the stability which this requires. It is also better equipped with the instruments for covert political—military operations in this region than is the West. These asymmetries are by no means decisive but they reinforce the prospects for Soviet influence. The primary Soviet interest is to attain sufficient influence in the region to ensure sensitivity to its own security needs. Ideally this would involve denial of the region to the West but, at least in the first instance, it requires a diminution of Western influence (and presence). A secondary interest which is growing daily is in access to the region's petroleum supplies for itself and for its East European allies. A third interest might be to use petroleum politics to split the alliance and put pressure on OECD states. Theoretically the second interest could entail a stake in an orderly region for normal commercial relations. More likely, however, given the high cost of OPEC oil, the Soviet bloc's limited hard currency reserves, and the alternative markets available to the producer states, it will entail an attempt to use political—military influence to gain oil on preferential terms — whether for barter agreements or discounted prices. In this essentially 'colonial' approach to the region's resources, the USSR will dispose of numerous assets.

1   It has relevant power and the means to ensure that regimes stay in power, and to threaten them with mischief-making and instability if they are 'unhelpful'. Vulnerabilities in the Kurdish areas or in Saudi Arabia's Eastern province serve as reminders of this.
2   It has a major means of influence through the provision of arms (a sector of her economy which is relatively efficient).
3   It can apply pressure in many ways — through communist parties, secessionist groups and through covert operations.
4   It has political and military staying power, a willingness to invest, hedge, and to persist in the quest for influence, despite setbacks.
5   It has shown a (new) marked preference for satellites over more independent clients and hence a willingness to consolidate control over states.

The USSR is a beneficiary of anti-Western sentiments. Cultural backlashes or reactions to an obtrusive presence, to the extent that they weaken the West, assist the USSR. Political alienation of regional states by the West's policies in, for example, Israel, serve the same function, creating the basis for an alliance as in Iraq. Finally in a region in which the *status quo* regimes are identified with the West, those elements

128

opposed to it look to the USSR. In a region witnessing rapid change this is a not inconsiderable asset.

Against these are arrayed a number of liabilities:

1 The USSR is an atheistic regime in a region where religion is not solely personal or spiritual in connotation.
2 Soviet power and proximity cause unease among even its tactical supporters.
3 The Soviet Union is not an attractive partner as a supplier of technology, in a region where states can afford to choose what they purchase.
4 The Soviet tendency to hedge its bets by supporting several states — often in competition with one another (Iraq–Syria; Iran–Iraq) — and its refusal to choose between them, has limited its appeal as a dependable ally.
5 The USSR has shown itself to be of only marginal relevance to the Palestine issue.

On balance Soviet interests have been pursued relentlessly but with reference to the risks involved. In the Iran–Iraq hostilities of the 1969–75, and in the Dhofar insurgency between 1973 and 1975, Soviet investments were limited and its policy was averse to risk. With the growth of its military power, its incipient oil dependency and the disarray in the West after the upheaval in Iran, Soviet probing increased. With the revolution in Iran and the invasion of Afghanistan, the prospects for the extension of Soviet influence have improved but so too has the prospect of military confrontation with the West which has reacted with sudden alarm. The resultant deterioration in East–West relations in 1980 (which was aggravated by the US diplomats-held-as-hostages issue) has raised the spectre of inadvertent conflict through uncontrolled escalation or miscalculation. In this setting, with the growth of Soviet influence and the volatility of the West's reaction, the risks have grown. The incentives for superpower management of conflicts in this arena — in which both have stakes — have risen proportionately. The Iran–Iraq war thus demonstrated a willingness on the part of the superpowers to forego opportunities for gaining influence through greater involvement. Admittedly the political context in this case was mixed and not conducive to a clear polarization between the superpowers, yet their restraint was due in part at least to the risks of competitive involvement and escalation.

## Superpower relations and conflict management

The superpowers are more directly involved in regional politics because of their growing interests, yet this involvement has not been matched by any sustained experience of interaction in this area. No tacit agreements on the scope and legitimacy of their respective positions has been reached. Without any such tacit agreement, or experience of crisis management (as in the Arab—Israeli zone), the attendant risks of confrontation and miscalculation are high — particularly given the nature of the stakes and the volatility of the political environment. The state of the superpowers' overall relationship clearly conditions the scope and nature of their policies in particular regions. When the co-operative dimension is dominant, it affects the incentives for risk-taking in specific areas. When the competitive element prevails, the potential gains in particular regions may look more attractive than the overall relationship. The superpower relationship also affects the regional political context. Extreme superpower competition tends to focus pressures on the local states to stand up and be counted and accentuates pressures toward regional polarization. This may have the effect of either freezing regional disputes or imbuing them with much greater importance, thereby transforming them from a local to a global stake and into a test of power and resolve.

When superpower relations are characterized by muted competition, regional priorities emerge with cross-currents that militate against polarization. Issues are damped down and become significant in terms that can be contained with fewer risks.

### The current situation

Politics in the Persian Gulf today are especially volatile and fluid with the local states looking afresh at their alignments. The Iranian revolution and the invasion of Afghanistan have changed the balance of power in the region against the West. The new Iranian regime now acts as an additional and major source of disruption and insecurity in the region. This has had the effect of modifying past orientations and in bringing together the secular Ba'athist Iraqi Republic and the Kingdom of Saudi Arabia. With intensified and growing superpower competition throughout South-West Asia (and continued arms supplies reflecting this interest), the prospect of an unregulated superpower competition subject to fewer constraints and seen in zero-sum terms, has encouraged most of the littoral states to seek security by loosening links with either bloc and by emphasizing their independence. Thus, as the risks of superpower confrontation have risen, so have the incentives for the littoral states to lie low and call down a plague on either side. Differences still exist among the Arab littoral states but they have been reduced. Iraq is now more conscious of the Soviet threat which has moved nearer and which may increase if Iran disintegrates or its clerics stumble. At the same time US credibility has shrunk to a new low in the Gulf as a result of the cumulative impact of the upheaval in Iran, the 'loss' of Afghanistan and the debacle in Tabas over the hostages. If the Soviet threat has increased, the attractiveness of the US as a countervailing power has not correspondingly increased.

Even if developments in the region have so far been adverse to the West, from the point of view of the superpowers the risks in this new era are apparent. Intensified competition in an uncharted area where interests intersect and no learning process has been undergone, threatens inadvertent war or conflict through miscalculation as much as offering the prospect of unilateral advantage. It is still too soon to see what course superpower relations will take but a summary of the choices is merited.

*Unregulated competition.* This characterizes the current situation in the region and its periphery where the stakes are high, tensions in the overall relationship feed into assessments of policies within the region, and the politics of the region are volatile and sufficiently murky to provide few indicators as to the origin of specific events. In this context each has a stake in the region itself, one (or both) see a means of weakening the other (by denial or by exploiting and redirecting events), and the region is not only the stake but the symbol of a wider value. There is no agreement on 'legitimate interests' and each sees the other as aggressive. No regional buffers exist to insulate or moderate this competition. After several crises the seriousness of the situation may dispose the superpowers to work out some ground-rules. Alternatively the region may continue as the focus of competition with consequent militarization and pressures for alignment.

*Regulated competition.* A prerequisite to the identification of rules governing competition will be the need to agree on a definition of stability. Current Soviet policy does not see support for revolutions or national liberation wars as incompatible with détente. It argues that repression breeds revolution, that people must be free to choose, and that détente was never intended to consecrate the *status quo*. Whether this attitude toward change and its exploitation can be reconciled with Western views of the necessity of restraint by outside powers in regional affairs seems doubtful. A common interest in a specific access area such as in the 'Free Transit'[1] of ships through the International Straits of Hormuz has resulted in co-operation between the two blocs at the Law

---

1 or 'Straits Passage'.

of the Sea Conferences. But asymmetrical interests, dependencies, and hence opportunities for extending influence, block other avenues of co-operation. For example the fundamentally misconceived notion of Naval Arms Limitation Talks (NALT) in the Indian Ocean overlooked both these asymmetries and the proximity of the region to Soviet land-based airpower which would be unchecked if US carrier-based aircraft were limited.[1] Superpower agreement on limiting arms supplies to the region, potentially a common interest, is unlikely to be effective even if agreed as the oil-rich states can choose their supplier. Nevertheless a situation could arise when even the prospect of unilateral gain *vis-à-vis* the other superpower comes to appear less attractive. This could come about not only if there is a heightened risk of conflict but also if one or both come to see that there is nothing to gain by unregulated competition and that they may lose ground to third parties (Europe, China, or the regional states themselves).

*Towards co-management?*

The incentives for an accommodation between the superpowers over the Persian Gulf involving tacit recognition of their mutual interests could gradually develop. In theory their interests overlap as each shares an interest in avoiding war through loss of control, and in maintaining its influence in, and preserving access to, the region. OPEC could to some extent be seen as a common adversary. To eliminate the risk of manipulation by local states and to minimize uncertainty about each other's reactions in crises, the prospect of a tacit superpower agreement may in future look more appealing. If détente were to be revived and given substance, the Persian Gulf, where interests overlap, could serve as an important test-case for restraint and for negotiations. Co-management is not of course the only possibility. One can imagine in abstract varying degrees of superpower co-operation and involvement varying from a 'hands-off' agreement to a partition arrangement embodied in a formal division of spheres of influence and working as a condominium. An agreement on reciprocal abstention from the region appears at present less likely than its opposite, but the movement toward an intermediate formula such as co-management appears more likely than either.

The arguments in favour of co-management and especially of Western acceptance of the USSR's 'legitimate interests' in the Gulf region, are

---

1 See Richard Haass, 'Naval Arms Limitation in the Indian Ocean', *Survival* XX, no.2, March–April 1978, pp. 50-8. For background see Joel Larus, 'The End of Naval Détente in the Indian Ocean', *The World Today*, April 1980, pp. 126-32.

seductive. Essentially they revolve around several propositions:

1 That the Soviet Union (and Eastern bloc) have equal interests in the Gulf that must be accepted by the West.
2 That formal acknowledgement of these interests by the West in its security policies in the Gulf will elicit a 'responsible' Soviet policy, whereas attempts at its 'exclusion' through unilateralism will encourage Moscow to play the 'spoiler'.
3 That the current Western policy in respect to the Gulf is doomed to failure. This is so both because of Soviet geographical advantages in power projection and the intrinsic limitations of military force as an instrument of influence in a region of political instability.

Many in the West who make these arguments are not persuaded that Soviet partnership in the region has been truly sought. They believe that the region's problems do not emanate solely or even principally from Soviet activities. Furthermore they do not believe that the 'militarization' of Western policy is a useful or necessary response to issues relating to Gulf security.[1] Others, who are convinced both of the nature of the Soviet threat and the utility of military force, argue for co-management from the allegedly 'realistic' grounds that some parts of the Gulf are militarily indefensible[2] and need to be conceded, the better to defend more vital areas. An underlying assumption of these varied views is that the current Western military build-up is costly and either counterproductive or useless, and that there exists an independent path to Gulf security (seemingly divorced from the military balance) namely a 'diplomatic' solution. The most prominent exponent of this is Selig Harrison who has argued that anxiety about its security was the primary motive for the Soviet invasion of Afghanistan. To allay these anxieties and to facilitate the withdrawal of Soviet troops, he argues for the permanent neutralization of Iran, Pakistan and Afghanistan.[3] He appears to recognize that in this context 'neutralization' would be tantamount to conceding predominant Soviet influence in all three countries, but finds this acceptable.

Still another stream of thought in favour of co-management originates in Europe and prefers this route to the assurance of

---

1 For a discussion of this and citations see my 'US Security Interests in the Persian Gulf in the 1980s', *Daedalus*, (Fall 1980).

2 For example, Northern Iran.

3 Selig Harrison, *Foreign Policy*, no.41, 'Exit through Finland'. Harrison earlier argued that it was Iran's attempts to reduce Afghan dependence on the USSR that prompted the Soviet invasion, see 'After the Afghan Coup: Nightmare in Baluchistan', *Foreign Policy*, no.32, 1978, and *New York Times*, 22 December 1980.

unimpeded oil supplies, primarily because it foresees no security conceivably resulting from an open-ended competition. In this view European powers have as much to fear from a reckless and precipitate military response by the United States as from Soviet expansionism. Here co-management is interpreted not as a superpower arrangement — which is sometimes labelled as a 'Yalta'[1] — but by a more general formula involving European consumers and possibly producers.

The various arguments adduced in favour of 'co-management' (specifically those regulating superpower competition) often tend to be propounded as an alternative to a policy that seeks to restore the military balance in the region. As an inexpensive short-cut to meeting the security needs of the region, co-management is rarely seen in perspective. It is not, for example, asked how a meaningful arrangement between the blocs is to be enforced in the absence of a military balance, or how 'restraint' is to be interpreted when the Soviet Union insists on the right to assist revolutionary forces. Furthermore the notion that the US and USSR have overlapping interests is very far removed from accepting that they have identical interests. The West's dependency on the region is much more acute than that of the Eastern bloc and its involvement in the region has the weight of historical experience. The USSR is a newcomer to Gulf politics, its interests in the region are of recent standing and remain general and diffuse. Acquiescence in the Soviet claim to having 'legitimate interests' in the region would be in itself a considerable concession. Creeping expansionism and extension of claims, though rarely spectacular, require a consistent and predictable Western response if they are to be deterred. The inexorable Soviet push for political predominance in this region, a historic fact accelerated of late, will not be contained when co-management is mooted in the West as a serious solution to the problem of the West's vulnerability. Co-management formulae are only likely to be realistic options where superpower relations are more co-operative and where their overall interests can be defined more compatibly.

To be sure it is in periods of strain that such arrangements are at their most appealing. Spheres of influence would reduce the prospect for confrontation in states that are currently contested and (it is argued) clearly draw the lines of political predominance for both blocs. This would reduce the chance of inadvertent hostilities through the

---

1  M. Jacques Chirac in September 1980 specifically alluded to the need to ensure that there was not 'another Yalta' while proposing that the USSR be excluded from any arrangement to guarantee navigation through the Straits of Hormuz. For the Soviet response see the article in *Sovetskaya Rossiya* as broadcast by Tass, 3 October, in SWB SU/6540/C/2, 4 October 1980, and *The Financial Times*, 4 October 1980.

escalation of local conflicts, and lend to relations an element of predictability. An informal arrangement could not determine oil prices or production policies or prevent shifts in domestic politics leading to a shift in orientations (though these too could be met by a formal condominium or partition of the region), but even so it could reduce even if it could not eliminate regional tensions.

Whether the attractions of predictability weigh equally heavily with the two superpowers is not clear. The extremity of Western vulnerability and the instability of the region combine to make a Western interest in predictability understandable. The Soviet Union, however, may count these as opportunities for exploitation. The risks of unlimited competition which may provide the USSR with an incentive for seeking predictability have not hitherto been self-evident. To be influential on Soviet policy, these risks must be tangible, credible and communicated unmistakably. This requires not only an enhanced presence and improved military capabilities, but also a consistency of practice which will arrest both the erosion in the credibility of American resolve and the decline of its military instrument so evident in recent years.

The search for a regulation of competition between the superpowers must continue but without illusions that the military balance can be divorced from it. Similarly the very process of seeking regulation must be handled with sensitivity by the United States if it is not to create problems with its partners. Conflict-management and co-management may be manipulated by the USSR as a means for weakening the Western alliance. Any hint of a US–USSR condominium in the Gulf would send the West's local partners scurrying to Moscow for protection, and would reinforce tendencies in Europe to seek to mediate between the two superpowers. The risks of 'co-management' need to be assessed as clearly as the risks of less regulated competition.

*Soviet proposals for a 'collective solution'*

More likely than a formal arrangement is the continuation of the pattern of probing and response which over time may make clear to both sides the limit of its competitor's tolerance. The loss of control over even regional conflicts by the superpowers was made strikingly clear by the Iran–Iraq war which erupted in September 1980. Due to its special circumstances (notably the virtual reversal in alignments by the two regional states which still depended on their original patrons for military supplies), the superpowers had no clear incentive to support either side. The first Gulf war thus elicited a tacitly restrained response from the two superpowers who, aware of the risks involved in these uncharted waters, consulted and agreed to refrain from supplying arms. It was notable, however, how each superpower saw the other as better placed to benefit from the war. The United States feared (a) an Iraqi victory which could fragment Iran and drive it into Soviet arms, (b) an Iranian victory with Soviet support that destabilized the Gulf, and (c) lacking diplomatic relations with either combatant, a negotiated settlement on the lines of Tashkent in 1966 managed by the USSR. Soviet worst case perceptions were a mirror image. They feared (a) an Iranian victory which owed nothing to the USSR but depended on US-supplied arms, (b) an Iraqi victory which consolidated Baghdad's anti-Soviet position without affecting Iran's orientation, and (c) a stalemate or settlement in which the USSR was exposed as conservative, risk-averse and unreliable as an ally.

Despite these mutual fears, the agreement held. There was no evidence of significant or direct supply of arms by the superpowers to the belligerents. The USSR, however, saw in the continued deployments of Western naval vessels in the region, and in the dispatch of four US AWACs early warning aircraft to Saudi Arabia, an example of the United States' search for pretexts to justify its 'militarization' of the region.

Since the invasion of Afghanistan the USSR has sought to underline its own interest in a political settlement of the contentious issues centred in South-West Asia. In so doing it has not departed from the basic principles it first enunciated in its Asian Security formula of 1969 which was elaborated upon in the course of the subsequent decade. Nevertheless, in the light of newly enunciated 'Carter Doctrine' of January 1980 which reserved for the US the right to respond with force if necessary to threats in the Persian Gulf which it claimed as a 'vital interest', there was clearly a need for a reiteration of the Soviet position. This was prominently put forward twice in 1980 — in the Portugalov proposal of February and the Brezhnev proposal of December. In between came various commentaries which elaborated upon the Soviet approach.

The Portugalov proposal was essentially an elaboration of a speech made a week earlier (22 February) by Brezhnev in Moscow. It made four points:[1]

1    It emphasized the risks of instability in the Gulf region which made it a 'powder keg' liable to explode as a result of intervention and miscalculation.

1 The full text of Nikolay Portugalov's commentary was carried by Tass, 29 February, in SU/6360/C/1, 3 March 1980. For comments see *Le Monde*, 3 March 1980; *The Sunday Times*, 2 March 1980; *The Christian Science Monitor*, 15 April 1980.

2   It noted that the European states were more dependent on Gulf oil than the US.
3   It affirmed the Soviet Union's own interest 'in the security of oil supply routes in the Persian Gulf area'.
4   It proposed an 'All-European conference on Energy' [comprising the membership of the Helsinki agreements] to discuss guarantees of:
    (a)   The security of the oil supply routes;
    (b)   Equal commercial access for all countries;
    (c)   The territorial integrity of and independence of the producer states.

In time the European context would be expanded into a United Nations framework.

The proposal was evidently framed as a response to the Carter Doctrine. It contrasted its own peaceful approach to 'American militarism'. It also sought to appeal to European anxieties about superpower relations after Afghanistan. It acknowledged the Europeans' interest in Gulf oil (while affirming its own) and offered a 'diplomatic track' to guarantee it. Lest there should be any misunderstandings, the USSR repeatedly asserted that the concentration of US forces in the Gulf area was 'a direct threat to the southern parts of the Soviet Union'.[1] In May 1980, the Warsaw Pact returned to the theme of guaranteeing the sea-routes in the context of their demilitarization making reference *inter alia* to the Persian Gulf. Brezhnev repeated this theme when acting as host to the Ethiopian president in October.[2]

In December, while visiting New Delhi, Brezhnev elaborated upon the Soviet approach in a five-point proposal aimed at guaranteeing military non-intervention in the Gulf area. Both the timing and the formulation of the proposal were shrewd, coming just before a scheduled non-aligned meeting in India whose members formally supported the idea of a 'peace zone' in the Indian Ocean. Its principal components were an agreement by the great powers to neutralize the region, to:

1   Foreswear military 'bases' in the Gulf area or adjacent islands.
2   Renounce the deployment of nuclear weapons in the region.
3   Abstain from the threat or use of force against states in the area or from interference in their internal affairs.

1   For example, the Soviet Ambassador in Paris, Stephan Chervonenko repeated this theme while seeking to accentuate the differences within NATO. See *International Herald Tribune*, 17 April 1980.

2   Declaration of the Warsaw Pact Members' Consultative Committee, 15 May. See *Le Monde*, 29 October 1980.

4  Forego any attempt to draw the Gulf states into 'military group-ings'.

5  Pledge non-interference within states or in the use of the sealanes linking the states of the area with other countries.[1]

In practical terms the 'peace proposal' sought to inhibit Western means of naval deployment and regional security arrangements while leaving unconstrained Soviet land-based power nearby. Soviet commentaries made it plain that the proposal was essentially propagandistic by contrasting the United States military approach with its own more reasonable one. The Soviet proposal was portrayed as a 'barrier against US aggression' while Washington's policy was dedicated to grabbing oil, shoring up reactionary regimes, dictating economic subservience and fighting national liberation forces.[2] Precisely how demilitarization and neutralization of the 'area' could guarantee Western interests while the Soviet Union remained in the immediate vicinity remained pointedly unclear. Equally important the Soviet proposal sought to widen the gap between European and American responses to the task of securing access to oil by playing on doubts in some quarters of the wisdom of Washington's leadership. Representative of such tactics is a report by Anatoliy Gromyko on Brezhnev's proposal which argues that 'the [United States'] policy of militarization of the Indian Ocean and Persian Gulf area creates for the Western European powers and Japan real difficulties on the path of developing broad economic links with the countries of the region'.[3]

The Soviet appeal for a 'collective solution' found a welcome echo among those who remained sceptical about the utility of military power in securing access to the Gulf and those analysts anxious to allay Soviet

---

1  For references to the proposal made on 10 December, *International Herald Tribune*, 11 December, 12 December. For reactions, press and governmental, see *The Times*, 12 December 1980; *The Guardian*, 12 December 1980; *Le Monde*, 13 December 1980; *The Economist*, 13 December 1980. Contrast the press reactions of *The Observer*, 14 December 1980 with *The Daily Telegraph*, 12 December 1980. No Gulf state welcomed the proposal and a number like Oman, Iran and Saudi Arabia were in varying degrees critical of it.

2  For a representative sample containing these themes consult *Radio Moscow*, 12 December, in SU/6601/A4/1, 15 December; Dmitry Volsky, 'Time will not Wait', *New Times*, 51. (80). Pavel Demchenko, 'The Persian Gulf can become a zone of Peace', *Pravda*, 2 January 1981, Tass 2, 3 January 1981 in SWB SU/6614/A4/1, 5 January 1981; Vikentcy Matreyev, *Izvestiya* (commentary), 18 January in Moscow, 18 January SWB SU/6628/A4/1, 21 January 1981. Vladimir Kudryavtsev, *Izvestiya* (commentary), 22 January in Moscow, 22 January in SWB SU/6632/C2/3, 26 January 1981 and Dmitry Volsky, 'Harder to Build than to Destroy', *New Times* 2.(81), pp. 5-7.

3  Report of an article by Anatoliy Gromyko, Director of the African Institute of the USSR Academy of Sciences in *Izvestiya* excerpted by Tass, 12 January in SWB SU/6624/A4/3, 16 January 1981.

security anxieties in their bordering regions. This appeal is likely to grow because, with future instabilities in the region inevitable, Moscow will be keen both to point out its capacity for disruptive behaviour and the price of its restraint. Implicitly (the USSR may argue) with so much indigenous instability would it not make sense to come to an arrangement? Indeed it may condition its good behaviour on joint management − a possibility evidently feared in Washington during the Gulf War.[1] The risks of entering into such an arrangement (rather than agreeing to consult and concert informally during crises) may well be higher for the West given the existing balance of military power.

## The role of other outside powers

### Extra-regional power

The political problems associated with a superpower presence in the form of 'bases', military advisers, and the like have already been elaborated upon. For Saudi Arabia, for example, an American presence to guarantee its security may be counterproductive, attracting nationalist agitation and focusing attention on Riyadh's ties with a government supportive of Israel. It may well be of little practical use in dealing with many security threats. Less disruptive and liable to provoke a counter-reaction by the other bloc, a contribution by European states to regional security is also less politically troublesome because of the European position on the Palestine question. Furthermore, unlike the United States, some European states are able to react militarily to murky situations without loud and anguished debates and selective leaking of information. France's assistance in meeting the Mecca disturbances of November 1979 and her past activities in Africa bear testimony to this. In addition, her proximity in Djibouti with some 6,000 troops provides her with a flexible instrument for meeting lesser contingencies quickly. The development of co-operation between Saudi Arabia and France in the internal security field over the past two years is ample testimony to Saudi recognition of this important role.[2]

Parallel to this has been a Saudi keenness to diversify the source of its armaments. France has agreed to supply a large part of the Saudi Navy. Germany in 1981 has been sounded out about a possible sale of

---

1  See James Reston's report, *International Herald Tribune*, 25 September 1980.

2  The potential role of Taiwan and South Korea in assisting Saudi Arabia in the maintenance of internal security should also be mentioned. Well-organized and motivated, both states maintain good ties with Riyadh and could provide discreet assistance when necessary.

Leopard II tanks. Although reluctant to embark on large-scale arms exports, the Federal Republic has played a distinctive role in regional security in the economic area. It has disbursed large-scale grants and loans to Turkey and Pakistan with the aim of contributing to the social–economic underpinnings of security.

Britain's contribution to Gulf security has also continued to be low-key. It retains particularly close ties with the smaller Arab states of the Gulf where its relationship has historical sanction. It has on secondment or on contract some 800 military personnel in Oman assisting in the maintenance of security in that state. It has discreetly encouraged co-operation among the sheikhdoms under the umbrella of Saudi Arabia and furthered the cause of a regional security arrangement.

From the point of view of the Western Alliance, too, this division of labour in which the allies, according to their respective strengths, assist in the maintenance of security, makes eminent sense. The European contribution provides a 'third-choice', an intermediate connection which is less polarizing than that of either superpower. The informal co-ordination of policies toward the region thus protects both the regional state and the outside powers' interests. A naval presence in the Gulf of Oman exclusively made up of US ships during the Iran–Iraq war would have been less effective as a symbol of Western concern about the security of the flow of oil than was the inter-allied contribution including elements from France, the UK and Australia. The dangers of *loose* co-ordination reside in the temptation among individual allies to improve their bargaining position *vis-à-vis* the regional state by departing from alliance positions and offering greater concessions in exchange for preferential agreements (for example by 'recognizing the PLO' in return for guaranteed oil supplies). This danger can be exaggerated but it is worth emphasizing that allied policies can contribute to Gulf security in a healthy decentralized way only if they are parallel and not competitive.

*Regional power*

Less obtrusive than even the Europeans are other Muslim or Arab states which could contribute to Gulf security. Jordan is the pre-eminent example of a state which has long assisted the Gulf sheikhdoms in military training and with the dispatch of military advisers. Economically less well-off than its oil-rich neighbours, there is reason to expect a growing role in this area for Jordan's security forces. Although not quite as well placed, Pakistan has the Muslim connection to recommend it in addition to considerable experience in providing military assistance to the Gulf sheikhdoms. It too could find the economic incentives of such assistance tempting. In the past year there have been repeated rumours of an agreement between Pakistan and Saudi Arabia whereby the former would provide a military contingent (numbers vary from 600 to 10,000) to act as a form of 'Swiss-Guard' for the Saudi Royal Family.[1] In addition they could, as mercenaries, check disloyal elements within the National Guard and provide oil installation security. Although repeatedly denied, there is no gainsaying the logic of such an arrangement which would provide Pakistan in turn with much needed cash.

There may also be roles for other regional states outside the Gulf. Egypt has offered to assist the Arab states in the event of Iranian aggression and to provide the West with facilities for access to the region for its defence. If relations between the Gulf states and Egypt improve this may become an additional form of security assurance.

## The scope and limits of conflict management

### The superpowers

The Iranian revolution ended any prospect of exclusive or primary reliance on regional states for assuring the security of the area. The indirect role of the outside powers was jettisoned and followed by more intensified involvement. But this had the potential of polarizing the region, exacerbating internal and intra-Arab problems and triggering counter-reactions by the other superpower. Much of the recent tension in the Gulf is due to the over-hasty US response to a situation which — in a broad sense — was susceptible to anticipation. Under the Carter administration, false assumptions and erroneous distinctions bred transitory comfort, followed by ingenuous alarm.

The role of the superpowers in conflict management is primarily to deter one another. This deterrence must cover a broad spectrum from direct aggression through to covert and indirect exploitation of regional vulnerabilities. The West's difficulties in achieving this have already been noted by reference to the debate concerning the merits of presence-on-the-ground versus over-the-horizon, the trip-wire versus the rapid early projection of power. Just as important is the recognition by the West that distinctions between 'outside' and domestic threats may obfuscate problems. The Carter doctrine referred to 'outside' threats

---

1 See *New York Times*, 20 August 1980; *The Economist*, 13 September 1980; *Washington Star*, 10 December 1980; *International Herald Tribune*, 9 February 1981.

while the dispatch of AWACs in October 1980 was designed to contain a local war.

An acknowledgement by the superpowers of each other's interests may in time be forthcoming in concrete terms but it will not in itself constitute a short-cut to conflict management. Co-management with all its attractions cannot be erected out of phase with a balance of power. Even then its effect on allies and partners will need to be gauged before it is embarked upon. More important in the short run is the need for a shared definition of what constitutes permissible behaviour by outside powers in the region. What degree of involvement under what conditions, is mutually acceptable? Is covert activity acceptable? Is the supply of arms the same as the dispatch of advisers, or the latter equatable with military formations? Because the superpowers share an interest in avoiding conflict that arises inadvertently through miscalculation and in reducing their manipulation by local governments, procedures and guidelines for reaction to crises may well evolve. Consultations on the 'hot-line' during regional conflicts are a logical starting point. Agreement, as in the Iran—Iraq war, to supply no arms during hostilities may be a principle that can be extended to future conflicts. Tacit agreement on non-interventions during civil wars or revolutions could also be agreed, provided it was clear that neither side was directly or indirectly involved in instigating these.

Agreement on such principles will be difficult however as long as Moscow believes in its right to 'protect change' that favours it, extending to them a doctrine of irreversibility and equates adverse changes with 'counter-revolution'. Without a convergence between the two superpowers on the question of change and the *status quo*, and on an appropriate code of conduct, superpower competition will evolve *ad hoc* and unregulated.

The conditions for successful conflict management by outside powers are as simple to identify as they are difficult to achieve. They require:

1   A military balance and a perception of commitment that brooks no doubt and reduces the possibility of miscalculation.
2   A recognition that the risks run through opportunistic unilateralism are greater than the rewards and that the risks include the loss of control, an open-ended commitment and the possibility of escalation, and an understanding that restraint may be mutually advantageous.
3   An agreement or understanding on a definition of respective interests.

Superpower agreement on restraint — a tacit form of conflict management — will not be a panacea. It will not reduce locally driven instabilities or end superpower competition. It will however, provide the possibility of decoupling some local conflicts (such as that between Iran and Iraq) and seek to regulate that rivalry. Nor will it be static. Local opportunities will constantly beckon. The temptation to break the Western alliance if it develops cracks may be irresistible. The price of restraint with regional allies which are anti-*status quo* may prove high (as in Egypt and Somalia). The incentives for restraint may revolve around perceptions relating to whose assets are more effective in peacetime and who time favours. Soviet restraint cannot be obtained solely by manipulating the military risks. Positive incentives will also be needed. But equally Soviet restraint and non-disruptive behaviour cannot be encouraged solely by conceding it a 'stake' in the region nor can it be divorced from an effective military balance in the region.

*Regional security*

There are six principal scenarios in which the flow of oil may be jeopardized:

1 The political use of the 'oil weapon', as in the producer's embargo in 1973.
2 Prolonged internal instability affecting oil production in a major producer (as with Iran in 1978).
3 Protracted inter-state conflict reducing exports in one or more states (such as happened in the Iran—Iraq war of 1980—81).
4 The control of the choke-points through which most oil exports pass.
5 Attacks on the sea lines of communication outside the Persian Gulf.
6 Invasion by a hostile outside power of one or more oil producing states.

Of the six contingencies, the first three have already occurred and are liable to recur. In these the role of the superpowers has not been primary. However it must be conceded that their future role in regional conflicts is likely to be important as in the most recent case, if only to communicate their interest in its geographical containment to areas away from other producers and the Straits of Hormuz. In the three other scenarios, which have not yet occurred, the role of the outside powers is critical. In providing for the security of navigation in the Straits and beyond, and in deterring major aggression they are essentially irreplaceable.

It is in the lesser threats to the region that hope is often placed in a regional security arrangement. This approach to conflict management should be seen not as an alternative to security arrangements with outside powers but as a complement. In the past, progress toward regional co-operation was bedevilled by a legacy of distrust and tension attributable less to any Arab—Persian differences than to differences in orientation and disparities in power. These impediments have not disappeared with the Shah, and they remain in the Iraq—Saudi relationship. Nevertheless the twin shocks of the Iranian revolution and the Soviet invasion of Afghanistan have galvanized the Arab states into greater co-operation. In meeting common threats — from Iran, from sectarian disputes, from sabotage to oil installations — the co-operation has been effective.

In addition the shared fear of intensified superpower rivalry has contributed to a growing (rhetorical) emphasis on the exclusive rights of the regional states to manage the security of the region. Apart from erecting norms to complicate the superpowers' quest for facilities in the region, this co-operation has had a substantive value. It contributed, in the case of the YAR—PDRY border war of March 1979, to a search for a regional solution. In the event of future conflicts among the smaller states this type of regional approach can be helpful in decoupling local from outside power competition. Yet it is evident, as in the Iran—Iraq war, that such co-operation will not be effective in the event of a major regional war. And, even in the events of March 1979 just cited, it was necessary (as in October 1980) to call in an outside power patron to signal its concern about the conflict.

There is no reason to expect that the maintenance of Gulf security will be a matter exclusively for outside powers or conversely solely the task of regional states. A variety of elements will be needed, comprising military and economic measures, political and institutional responses, local arrangements (formal and informal), co-operation with states situated nearby, and measures designed to buttress security through relations with European states as well as ultimate reliance upon the United States.

# 3 Regional Co-operation and Conflict Management

The superpowers' most obvious contribution to regional security is in deterring one another while reassuring local allies. But here the problem of asymmetrical interests and assets arises. While Western interests are served by change that is not disruptive of regional order, it is by no means clear that regional forces left to themselves will work in this direction. The West must seek to support the forces of order unobtrusively without suppressing evolutionary change. To do this, as we have seen, it is necessary both to deter outside powers and to reassure and buttress friendly regional states to enable them to meet and to adjust to the varied pressures working on them. This requires the extension of a defence commitment to the region (and especially to Saudi Arabia) that is at once credible and relevant to their needs for such time as is required for each to attain a capability for self-defence against regional threats. This may take a decade. The way in which this commitment itself is made has, however, the potential for destabilizing the recipient. This can be assisted by the USSR which argues that the Western commitment is not to the Arab peoples but to specific 'regimes' and that it is intended not to further orderly change but to suppress 'progressive forces' opposed to Israel.

Given the enormous difficulties for the outside powers in meeting the threats to regional security, and in the light of the problems associated with influencing or channelling rapid social change, it is scarcely surprising that other complementary means of bolstering regional order should be examined. Regional approaches to conflict-

145

limitation and management in particular are especially appealing in abstract. The emergence of harmony in regional politics would dampen the incentives for local conflict, reduce the opportunities for Soviet or radical exploitation, and diminish pressures on the US to assume a 'forward' position in the region's defence.

A regional security arrangement could be an important though partial solution to the problem of Gulf security. To be effective it would ideally be truly regional — in composition as well as inspiration. It would respond to common indigenous needs and in so doing address local priorities. At the present time it is difficult to envisage any but a partial arrangement emerging for Iran, preoccupied by its own problems and disruptive of regional order, cannot be involved. But the very fact of Iran's estrangement from her neighbours may provide the catalyst for greater co-operation among the Arab states.

The idea of a regional security arrangement in the Gulf is not new. Over the past decade it has been much discussed. Initially, after Britain's withdrawal, the US (and the UK) encouraged it as the primary means of meeting threats to the region. With the collapse of a pro-Western Iran and the emergence of a more pronounced Soviet threat, it became evident that a more direct Western military commitment would be necessary. A Gulf security arrangement thus became an adjunct to meet the lesser threats to the region and to provide for greater regional co-operation in general. The contribution that a regional arrangement might make to conflict-management in the Gulf has never been systematically examined. In this section I examine the general assumptions behind such an approach to conflict management — those held by the littoral states, by the US, and USSR, and those theoretically tenable. Second, I trace briefly the evolution of the various ideas involved in such an arrangement and their record over the past decade ending with an analysis of the limitations and potential of this approach to conflict management in the Gulf.

## Assumptions

### The local states

Though Gulf politics have been characterized by division, tension and distrust for much of the period since 1969, a sense of common interests has not been totally absent. This has been due to cross-cutting interests which have until recently prohibited polarization on Iran—Arab, or Republican—Monarchical lines.[1] Even during military hostilities co-

1 See S. Chubin, 'International Politics of the Persian Gulf', British Journal of International Studies, October 1976, pp. 216-30.

operation in certain areas has been maintained.[1] The element transcending the manifold differences among these states has been the perception of shared vulnerability, of diffuse insecurity which has manifested itself in a desire for more autonomy in regard to the superpowers. Despite different alignments, a fear of loss of control has been held in common. This has translated itself into support for the general proposition of a regional security arrangement, and the assertion that regional affairs are the concern of the local powers. The containment of local disputes is essential, in this view, to avoid the intrusion of the superpowers, whose entry would polarize the region. What is viewed by the outside powers as 'decoupling' regional from global disputes is seen from the region as 'not importing global tensions'. The threat posed by the superpowers is both one of unrestrained competition *and* a bilateral accommodation: either could pose a direct threat to the regional states' interests. Competition could spark counter-reactions and serve as a flashpoint for conflict or for sustained pressures on local states for bases, preferential treatment, and public diplomatic support. On the other hand a superpower concert would diminish an already limited margin for manoeuvre. The avoidance of polarization thus has two components: no direct association or alignment with the preferred superpower; and the opening of lines of indirect communication with the other. This does not detract from reliance on a particular superpower ally for ultimate protection, but it militates against the provision of bases or signing of pacts which could facilitate such protection.[2]

In brief, the regional states assume first that limited co-operation among themselves could erect norms to inhibit and reduce the risks of intervention, and second, that the most durable means of defusing conflicts are regionally based rather than through outside power management which creates other risks.

## The United States

Washington's attitude toward a regional security arrangement has undergone considerable change since 1968, in part due to developments in the region itself;[3] and in part due to a better understanding of the region. The initial response to Britain's imminent withdrawal was to

---

1 This was true in the 1969–75 border incidents and the war in 1980 between Iran and Iraq, in OPEC affairs.

2 This may appear somewhat speculative. In my view it explains both Saudi and Iraqi reluctance *vis-à-vis* their respective superpowers, and accounts for the move each has made to meet the other in the centre away from sole reliance.

3 These are sketched below. This section deals with the current US approach, not with how it has evolved.

look to a NATO-type pact — a proposal made by Eugene Rostow in 1968 which was never pursued. By the end of 1980, Washington's conception of a regional arrangement was more subtle.[1] It now envisaged a variety of informal and formal relationships between the Gulf states, their neighbours, the US and Europe. The diversification of ties rather than a unilateral approach and the importance attached to non-military relations is testimony to this. Thus the security framework sought was explicitly not a replica of NATO and it would entail no permanent bases. It would be multi-levelled, seeking to defuse threats to the region in the political—economic as well as the military realms. It would encourage the wealthier regional states to provide their poorer neighbours with the means to resist external subversion, and would encourage the wealthier NATO allies to do the same for the poor but important states located near the Gulf — such as Turkey. As part of a diversification of roles and the sharing of responsibility which would diminish the visibility of any one power, Washington encouraged military co-operation among the states of the region as a whole. Thus Saudi—Pakistan in co-operation, or Jordanian co-operation with the Gulf states, or Egyptian offers of assistance to Oman and the Gulf states would be tacitly encouraged.

In 1979, with the fall of the Shah, the United States' approach to regional security in the Gulf underwent a remarkable transformation in three major respects. First Washington realized that it needed a greater military capability to meet threats in the region quickly and directly. Second, it recognized that threats to the region were not necessarily all military and it therefore looked to other means to shore up the political stability of the region. Third, it understood the political limitations on a direct unilateral presence in the region and sought to encourage a diversification of roles among local and external states interested in Gulf security. None of these detracted from the necessity for a greater military capability to meet threats to the region.

The United States' attitude toward regional security has thus been favourable, though with diminishing expectations. It has encouraged co-operation among pro-Western states as beneficial for regional security. It has seen in this a means for providing security for the smaller Gulf states which is more politically palatable. In the 1970s, in line with the tenet of self-reliance, it encouraged the assumption of defence responsibilities by local states. This was less burdensome in that it allowed the West to provide the means for security (arms and training) without a direct or formal involvement. Such involvement was not, however, excluded in the event of major threats.

1   The most authoritative description was by Z. Brzezinski, 'Building a Security Framework in the Persian Gulf', speech to Canadian Club of Montreal, 5 December 1980.

After 1979 the need for greater US responsibilities for the direct defence of the region became pressing for the regional buffers, the 'twin-pillars' had collapsed. Whereas between 1969 and 1979 the regional states had been assumed to be the first line of local defence, this was no longer tenable in the 1980s. Hereafter regional security arrangements would be encouraged but without illusions. They could meet minor threats, allow the improvement of each other's defence capabilities without the attendant political costs of external powers, and facilitate the co-ordination of policies to diminish local rivalries.

## The USSR

Moscow has consistently opposed the concept of a regional security agreement in the Persian Gulf. In part this may be attributed to the persistent echoes it has had of a (revived) anti-Communist military pact. Eugene Rostow's comments in 1968 and the Shah's comments in Washington in May—June 1975 lent credence to the view that it was to be a substitute for a US military presence, a surrogate arrangement directed against the USSR. More important though is the USSR's refusal to accept a 'partial' arrangement in the Gulf without integrating it into the broader proposals she had herself made, namely the Asian Security plan and Brezhnev's proposal for the neutralization of the Gulf of December 1980. What the USSR seeks to achieve by the Asian Security formula has been discussed elsewhere.[1] It has been elaborated upon in the more recent five-point proposals. One of these is quite explicit in its provisions, namely that major powers should not try to draw Gulf states into 'military groupings'. This prohibition does not apparently refer solely to formal arrangements between local and out-side powers. If Soviet declarations are indicative, it extends to regional arrangements among pro-Western states or bilateral co-operation between local states. Thus the Soviet Union has been exceedingly critical of military co-operation between Saudi Arabia and Pakistan, seeing in it a link in the 'structure of regional security', as part of a 'new aggressive military bloc', 'knocked together' by the US and as a sub-stitute for the defunct CENTO.[2]

The Soviet Union has been equally critical of regional co-operation within the Gulf, which it sees as an old attempt by the US to form 'an aggressive military bloc in the Persian Gulf' to draw some of these

---

1   See S. Chubin, 'Soviet Policy towards Iran and the Gulf', *Adelphi Paper*, no.157, Spring 1980 (and citations therein).

2   See *inter alia*: Tass in Russian, 9 December 1980, SWB SU/6598/A4/1, 11 December 1980; Tass in English, 19 January 1981, SWB SU/6628/A4/3, 21 January 1981; and article in *Sovetskaya Rossiya*, Tass in English, 27 January 1981, in SWB SU/6634/A4/1, 28 January 1981.

states 'into the orbit of its hegemonist policy and to cause a split within the ranks of the Arab countries'.[1] Specifically this regional co-operation (it has argued) is being nurtured by Washington into a mutual security pact directed against the 'national liberation movement'. It has thus criticized plans by the Arab states of the Gulf announced in February 1981 to intensify their co-operation on internal security matters. It sees in this anxiety about the growth of these liberation movements rather than hostility toward the West's militarization of the region. The fact that the participants in this scheme — Saudi Arabia, Kuwait, Bahrain, Qatar, Oman and the UAE — are 'military clients of Western states' has not gone unremarked.[2]

Precisely what sort of regional arrangement would be acceptable to the USSR is as yet unclear. Presumably it would depend on the precise linkage between such attempts at insulating regions from outside rivalries and the broader strategic relationship. Issues such as the nature of the relationship between local and outside powers, in terms of pacts, access to facilities, military aid relationships and 'presence', would be involved. Arrangements between pro-Western states, particularly if they have any security content, are clearly unacceptable. Though silent on Iraq's call for the exclusion of the superpowers from Gulf affairs (February 1980), it is evident that the USSR wants assurances of co-management of the region rather than 'co-exclusion'. However it is also clear that, while rhetorically opposed to any equation with the other superpower, any proposal that gives them equal rights and imposes apparently equal constraints on them is in practice acceptable. This is so for two principal reasons:

1   Soviet geographical proximity facilitates its land based power projection capabilities and lengthens the shadow of its military power in the region. This advantage encourages Soviet officials to look for constraints on naval activities that will asymmetrically inhibit the US and her allies, while appearing 'equal'.

2   The dependency of the East on stability in the Persian Gulf is not yet as acute as that of the West. Disorderly change in the region does not therefore have similar connotations for the two blocs. The prospect is that it will (at least initially) prove disruptive of Western interests and influence, sweeping aside pro-Western regimes. The consequent 'loss of control' will have a quite dif-

---

1   See *Pravda*, 16 December 1980 (Rafail Moseyev). See also Dmitry Volsky, 'Time will not wait', *New Times* (51), 1980, pp. 7-8.

2   See Tass in English, 31 December 1980, in SWB SU/6613/A4/3, 3 January 1981. Moscow in Arabic, 6 February 1981 in SWB SU/6644/A4/2, 9 February 1981 and Vladimir Peresada, *Pravda*, broadcast by Tass, 10 February in SWB SU/6646/A4/2, 11 February 1981.

ferent impact on the two blocs, and it is for this reason that there exists a gap in the incentives of the two blocs to seek stability in the region.

The Soviet Union's attitude toward a regional security arrangement has certainly been consistent. During the Shah's day it sought with some success to frighten the Arab states with Iran's ultimate designs in seeking a collective security arrangement. Now it depicts Arab attempts at co-operation as an aggressive pact aimed *inter alia* at the overthrow of the Iranian Islamic Republic.[1] Since a primary aim of a regional arrangement is co-operation to maintain the stability of the region, Soviet support can only be expected when it is convinced that such stability is indeed in its interests.

## The evolution of regional co-operation

The period prior to the UK's actual withdrawal from the Gulf (December 1971) was marked by increased contacts among the Gulf states and across the shores of the Gulf — in many cases the first contacts between sovereign states. In the Gulf sheikhdoms, Britain left behind security organizations to assist the governments, and Jordanian officers seconded to their armies remained in place. Iran and Saudi Arabia, encouraged by the West, improved their contacts, increased their military appropriations and succeeded in somewhat reducing mutual antipathies. Iran's offer in 1968 of formal military co-operation with the Gulf states was rebuffed. So too was Iraq's proposal in July 1970 for an 'Arab defence organization' but informal progress in concerting policies was achieved. There was general agreement that the peace of the area could best be achieved through regional means, and that co-ordination among local states could reduce the opportunities for external power intervention. There was a general willingness not to pursue territorial claims, even if these were not entirely dropped. Among the Arab states, Saudi Arabia played a leadership role while Iraq remained isolated and in conflict with Iran. It was under Saudi auspices that meetings were held in 1973 and 1974 to discuss co-ordinated action against subversion and the possibilities of joint defence.[2] Practical measures discussed included a plan for Kuwait to use airfields in Bahrain, Saudi Arabia, and Abu Dhabi for the dispersal

1 See National Voice of Iran (*Baku*), 16 January 1981 in SWB ME/6626/A/2, 19 January 1981.

2 See *Financial Times*, 25 June 1973 and *The Times*, 29 November 1974.

of its air force in the event of a threat to Kuwait's military airfield.[1] A measure of tacit co-operation was evident elsewhere. In the UAE, Jordanian officers took over Britain's training role while, in Oman, British officers remained in Salalah and Masirah to assist the government meet a secessionist threat. Iran's military assistance to Oman (1972—76) in combatting the PFLOAG (Patriotic Front for the Liberation of the Arabian Gulf) despite rhetoric to the contrary, 'won the grudging approbation of the Arab states of the Gulf, Iraq excepted'.[2] Iran's and Oman's joint naval patrols of the Straits of Hormuz after 1974 were another indication of limited regional co-operation in the defence area. Saudi leadership and example succeeded in settling several border disputes among the Gulf sheikhdoms, although those between Iraq—Kuwait and Iraq—Iran persisted.

The settlement of the latter in Algiers in March 1975 opened the door for more general regional co-operation. It removed an obstacle precluding co-operation between the Arab States and Iran. It ushered in an era of relative Iraqi moderation, reflected in Baghdad's acceptance of the principle of the non-export of subversion and it was followed by a period of intensified consultations among the Gulf states. For the first time, discussions revolved around a Gulf-wide 'security structure'. In the summer of 1975 and autumn of 1976, in conferences in Jiddah and Riyadh, various approaches were examined. The July 1975 Islamic Foreign Ministers' meeting in Jiddah reiterated the principle of the exclusion of outside powers and the inadmissibility of foreign bases, coupled with an assertion of the local states' responsibility for regional security. Nevertheless there was no unanimity on how to act together to that end, multilaterally or bilaterally, and little consensus on whether to seek an integrated defence arrangement or to settle merely for improved co-ordination among existing forces. The November 1976 conference of Gulf Foreign Ministers in Muscat was specifically convened to consider this issue. Six items were discussed:

1 Limitations on foreign powers' presence in the region.
2 A guarantee of the territorial integrity of states.
3 A non-aggression pact among the states.
4 Mutual assistance against subversion and co-operation in intelligence.
5 Measures to ensure freedom of navigation.
6 A territorial division of Gulf waters and establishment of the limits of the continental shelf.

1  See *The Washington Post*, 17 September 17 October 1974, and James Noyes *The Clouded Lens*, Hoover Institute, 1979, pp. 41, 125.

2  See Herman Eilts, 'Security Considerations in the Persian Gulf', *International Security*, vol.5, no.2, Fall 1980, p.96.

Representative of the difficulties in achieving agreement were the differences between Iran and Iraq on the type of defence arrangement sought and on the issue of navigation. Iran sought a unified, multilateral military force under a joint command to deal with both internal and external defence needs. Iran sought also the more restrictive legal regime of 'innocent passage' to govern transit through the Hormuz Straits. Baghdad preferred informal and bilateral arrangements for defence co-operation and the more permissive concept of 'free navigation' (or 'free transit') to govern access to the Straits. These issues need not detain us except to note that these positions reflected their proponents' assets. As the most powerful state with the longest coastline, Iran's interest was in dominating any defence arrangement and policing any suspicious activities in the Straits. Iran's attempts to proclaim the Gulf a semi-enclosed sea was, correctly, seen by the Arabs as an attempt to control traffic through the Gulf.[1] Less powerful, with only a few dozen miles of coastline on the Gulf and no prospect of naval influence in the southern Gulf, Iraq's position was also understandable. Saudi Arabia refused to be drawn into these differences and Kuwait's attempts at mediation failed.

Despite this set-back, considerable progress was made in less formal settings, especially in bilateral agreements, in the field of internal security. Consultations on this resulted in 1977 in agreements between Iran and Kuwait in June, Iran and Iraq in July—August and Iran and the UAE in November. Meanwhile Saudi Arabia intensified her discussions with the smaller Arab states. This trend toward an emphasis on co-ordination of internal security measures was given further impetus in October 1977 with the assassination of the UAE Minister of State for Foreign Affairs, Said al-Ghobash. Plans to form a Gulf organization to pool intelligence information and co-ordinate measures against sabotage and terrorism, were announced on 8 May, 1978. The principal aim was to share information among Iran, Saudi Arabia, Kuwait, Bahrain, the UAE and Oman.

The fall of the Shah created new problems in the quest for a regional security arrangement. While underscoring the need to buttress security throughout the area, the Iranian revolution set off new pressures making the achievement of an area-wide arrangement well-nigh impossible. At the same time in its militant nationalism it created problems for states in the region with close ties to the United States. By posing an acute security problem for both Iraq and Saudi Arabia, it served to catalyze their co-operation. On 9 February 1979 these two states signed

1 See Herman Eilts, 'Security Considerations in the Persian Gulf', *International Security*, vol.5, no.2, Fall 1980, p.96.

a 'security agreement' covering co-operation on internal security and extradition.[1] In the face of the common danger, both states loosened their ties with their respective superpower partners and moved toward the centre and a non-aligned posture, thus reducing their exposure to charges of being puppets or anti-Islamic.

Despite a reluctance to offend or provoke the new regime in Iran, the Arab states continued their consultations. In July 1979 the rulers and ministers of five states (Bahrain, Qatar, Kuwait, and the UAE under Saudi leadership) pursued their discussions on greater military co-operation, at a meeting in Khamis Mushait. In September 1979 Oman, which had aligned itself closely to the Shah's policies and which now found itself facing an unpredictable but unfriendly neighbour across the Gulf, offered a proposal for the defence of the Hormuz Straits. Aimed specifically at ensuring the freedom of navigation, the Oman proposal envisaged two levels of co-operation. The first, among the littoral states, would be to raise $100 million to purchase mine-sweepers, shore-based radar and patrol boats to protect the Straits. The second, related to outside powers, envisaged a multilateral naval force drawn from US, UK and the Federal Republic of Germany to provide a presence outside of the Gulf. The plan was doomed to failure because it contravened an article of faith of the adherents of regional arrange-ments — it made explicit provision for the inclusion not the exclusion of outside powers. It was interpreted, especially by Iraq, as a Western-inspired bid for a 'bloc' to replace CENTO.

By the Autumn of 1979 it was clear that Iran's revolutionary impulse would not be confined. Large-scale Iranian naval manoeuvres in the Gulf, border clashes with Iraq, and the revival of irredentist claims to Bahrain, combined with inflammatory radio broadcasts beamed to the Gulf, testified to this. Significant Shi'a minorities in Saudi Arabia, Kuwait and Bahrain were becoming restive, while Iraq, with the largest number, came under intense pressure. The common fear of Iran, and particularly of sectarian disturbances encouraged from that quarter, drove Riyadh and Baghdad closer. For Iraq, the gradual movement away from the Soviet bloc which has been taking place since 1975, and towards 'moderation' on Israel as evidenced in the 1978—79 Baghdad conferences, reflected a drive for influence in the Arab world. Saudi acquiescence if not support was essential for the achievement of this wider influence.

For the Saudis, Iraq had become an indispensable regional ally and buffer against Iran. In October both states extended assurances of

1 See *Le Monde*, 16 March; 6 April 1979.

assistance to Bahrain in the event of an Iranian attack.[1] In response to Shi'a disturbances in Bahrain, an Arab Foreign Ministers' conference was convened in Taif. Iraq's failure to attend reflected the now standard practice of Saudi leadership of the smaller states and bilateral co-ordination between Riyadh and Baghdad. The only public announcement was a reassertion that the defence of the Gulf was the responsibility of the littoral states, but the meeting testified to a habit of consultation that was becoming ingrained.

The Soviet invasion of Afghanistan in December 1979, followed by the espousal of the Carter Doctrine the following month, asserting a US vital interest in the Gulf region, together with the hostage crisis, which had stimulated a large US naval deployment in the Gulf of Oman, all testified to the difficulty of compartmentalizing into neat packages issues of security into 'internal' and 'external'. From the Iraqi perspective, these events underscored the danger of foreign interventions which would spark competitive or parallel interventions by the adversary bloc. Iraq's proclamation of an Arab National Charter on 8 February 1980[2] was intended as a counter to the right of foreign powers to intervene. It rejected all 'foreign' military forces or bases in the area, and threatened to boycott and ostracize any Arab regime which failed to adhere to this principle. It eschewed Arab involvement in international conflicts except against Zionism, and called for total neutrality and non-alignment toward any foreign party in the event of conflict. It called for a non-aggression pact among Arab states and, implicitly, for the resolution of all territorial disputes. The specific machinery envisaged for giving substance to common security interests was reminiscent of Iran's proposals of 1976. Its preference was for a collective security agreement encompassing the Arab states. A collective Arab security force,[3] drawn from the littoral states with a joint military command which would be autonomous with an independent budget, would provide the teeth for the arrangement. Financial contributions to the force would be according to resources but manpower commitments would be equal to avoid the domination of the force by any one state. In the event that these proposals were considered too ambitious, Iraq offered a fall-back position — bilateral agreements.

The Iraqi proposal, which essentially offered a third course between alignment with either bloc, obtained the 'endorsement' of the smaller

1  *Financial Times*, 2 October 1979. Egypt also offered its services if they were needed.

2  Text in *Survival*, July/August 1980, XXII, no.4, p.178.

3  This would supplement the Arab League Joint Defence Pact.

Gulf states but elicited no comment from Saudi Arabia. It was indeed an indirect challenge to Riyadh. The convergence of the states politically did not obscure the continuing lack of trust which was in part a reflection of differences of regimes and of alignment but also of disparities in power. A tactical partnership had not yet blossomed into a confident friendship and the Iran—Iraq war of 1980—81 was unlikely to convince the Saudis of the wisdom of exchanging American protection (with all its limitations) for a still more unproven and uncertain Iraqi umbrella.

The clashes between Iran and Iraq that escalated into major conflict in September 1980 increased the solidarity among the Gulf Arab states. Indeed it is possible that Saddam Hussein gained prior Saudi approval for his attack in his unprecedented visit to the Kingdom in the summer before the war. Certainly the Gulf states supported Iraq and intensified their consultations. At the Amman Arab Heads of State meeting in November discussions took place between Saudi Arabia and the other five Arab littoral states[1] and there were indications that, in the light of the war and its possible extension and prolongation, something approaching formal defence arrangements were contemplated. Initially this might take the form of bilateral security agreements between Saudi Arabia and Kuwait, Bahrain, Qatar, the UAE and Oman. While going beyond existing agreements to co-ordinate policies and share intelligence on internal security matters, it would not be intended as a 'defence pact' in the sense of a military alliance. However it would look remarkably like one in that it would be based on the assumption that a threat to one would be a threat to all, and in that it encouraged the attainment of improved defence capabilities.[2] Subsequent meetings in Taif and Riyadh in February 1981 bore testimony to Saudi interest in accelerating the movement toward a comprehensive political—defence arrangement with the other Arab Gulf states. Under the shadow of the continuing Gulf War, the Saudis took the initiative to propose a series of far-reaching measures integrating its neighbours more closely with the Kingdom.

1 Agreement was reached on forming a Council for Gulf Co-operation to pool resources to safeguard the stability of the region.

2 An organization consisting of a Council of Gulf Heads of State and another of Foreign Ministers was to be set up, with a secretariat, for regular meetings.

1 Still excepting Iraq.

2 See especially Patrick Seale's report in *The Observer*, 30 November 1980, and the document on Gulf security printed in *The Middle East*, January 1981; *The Times*, 9 March 1981.

3   A meeting in Abu Dhabi in May announced details of an agreement to get a secretariat and increase consultations but avoided mention of defence co-operation.[1]

The aim of these measures was to improve co-operation politically, economically and in security affairs. A form of loose political confederation appears to be under consideration to increase co-ordination in foreign affairs, to rationalize and streamline economic planning and so avoid wasteful duplication or harmful competition. Means for co-ordinating and eventually unifying military capabilities are also under study. An urgent priority here is co-operation to ensure the safety of oil installations and pipelines. Finally an arrangement encompassing the security of navigation through the Hormuz Straits is reportedly under consideration but, unlike the 1979 Oman proposal, it looks only to the littoral states' participation.[2] The role of outside powers in such a regional arrangement appears to be indirect: to provide the arms and technical assistance required for its realization.

The marked acceleration of movement toward a partial regional security arrangement is directly attributable to the advent of a revolutionary regime in Iran which threatens, in different ways, the security of its Arab neighbours. The deterioration of the international political environment and of relations between the superpowers, together with a marked devaluation of the United States' security connection, has increased Saudi Arabia's incentives to look for a regional substitute. Whether this politically less burdensome path constitutes a practical alternative remains to be seen. While the Gulf War has focused the minds of the sheikhs on security and eroded their reluctance to move quickly to practical measures of co-operation, it has also (with the dispatch of US AWACs aircraft to Saudi Arabia in October) underlined that even in regional conflicts there may still be no substitute for defence links with an outside power.

## The scope and limits of a regional security arrangement

As a contribution to alleviating the security problems of the Gulf states, a regional arrangement — even loosely organized and partial in its composition — has value. Agreement on the proposition that superpower involvement in the region is likely to contribute to instability is widely

1   See *International Herald Tribune*, 26, 27 May 1980.

2   The preceding analysis is based on press reports which may prove inaccurate or at least premature. Useful sources include *Le Monde*, 6 February 1979; and Patrick Seale's reports in *The Observer*, 11 January, 15 February 1981.

shared. Decoupling the Gulf's conflicts from outside power rivalries by providing a modicum of local order has been a shared objective among the littoral states. The rhetorical genuflection accorded this proposition has not been totally without value. It has erected a norm which the local states themselves are bound to consider in their own policies and demonstrated a shared interest in regime survival, an awareness of exploitable domestic political weaknesses, and the exposure and vulnerability of oil installations to sabotage and attack. Therefore it has provided the littoral states with areas of common interest on which co-operation can be built.[1]

This co-operation has taken concrete shape in the past decade in the defusion, for example, of border conflicts and in the suspension of territorial claims especially among the Arab states. Where border disputes have flared into hostilities between Arab states, such as in the YAR–PDRY clashes in March 1979 which threatened to polarize the region between East and West (and to split the consensus of the Baghdad Front), the Iraqis played a major role in producing a cease-fire.[2] Here the Gulf states took advantage of the existence of the Arab League, a forum which can be used as a complement to any institution set up in the Gulf. Vulnerability to sectarian or minority disorders which the littoral states share has led to an agreement not to exacerbate each other's problems, most notably in the Iran–Iraq Accord of 1975. Not merely in defining the impermissible, but in co-ordinating policies in the face of the common threat of Iran's claims in 1979, the Gulf states have testified to their mutual security interests. The growth of co-operation in the security area covering intelligence, extradition and protection of oilfield installations similarly assists in meeting a concern — transnational terrorism — which affects them all. Finally, the Gulf states have real incentives for a regional approach in preventing divisive competition and in co-ordinating approaches to common problems such as pollution in the Gulf or strategies of industrial development. In this respect the harmonization of policies and the more rational distribution of resources and tasks makes political sense. Economic assistance by the richer to the less endowed states (for example from Saudi Arabia to Oman and the YAR and offers to the PDRY, or by Abu Dhabi to Ras al Khaimah) serve a security function in diminishing the incentives for alliances of convenience with outside powers.

---

1 This excludes revolutionary Iran which sees its interests as different from those of its neighbours.

2 In conflicts which can be settled by the provision of funds, the Saudis are usually available chequebook at hand to practice crisis management.

Co-operation among the Gulf states in security affairs has nevertheless been spasmodic. It was slow in the period 1969—75 when Iran—Iraq rivalry and distrust of both states impeded the other littoral states' co-operation. It moved faster in the period 1975—79 when real progress was made bilaterally in the field of internal security and it has moved faster still since the fall of the Shah. Co-operation soon may extend to the harder areas of defence.

The limits to the contribution that *any* regional security arrangement is likely to make to the overall security of the Gulf are clear. It will not be able to meet external threats to the region for the foreseeable future. It will not be able to deal with major inter-state wars within the region: conflicts between Iran, Iraq and Saudi Arabia could not be covered by such an arrangement.[1] As the Iran—Iraq War shows, not merely the Gulf but other *fora* such as the Islamic Conference, the Non-Aligned group, and the Arab League are paralysed in such cases. Only a partial arrangement, excluding Iran but (perhaps) co-ordinating with Iraq, is likely to emerge in the current political context. This has its value in that the threat posed by Iran concentrates the mind wonderfully and increases the prospect of real integration among the smaller states and the suspension of petty differences. But to the extent that it is oriented *solely* against Iran, it runs the risk of institutionalizing what may otherwise be a temporary polarization.

A second set of limits are intrinsic not to any regional arrangement but to the one likely to emerge in the Gulf. With respect to Saudi Arabia and the five countries discussing tighter political integration, there should be no serious problem in achieving substantial progress. Where difficulties will arise is in the precise relationship of such a grouping with Iraq, and especially in the area of establishing a common defence force. Despite Saudi—Iraqi political convergence since 1979, serious differences remain. Disparities in military power, different emphases in foreign orientation and radically contrasting domestic structures are the realities underlying the pious platitudes of Arab solidarity prevalent today. These have hampered the growth of trust and impeded co-operation in sensitive areas such as the exchange of intelligence, which could always be misused by the recipient. If real co-operation in the defence field were sought (such as the stationing of Iraqi troops in the Kingdom, or the establishment of a joint command, with the political contamination that might ensue from fraternization), these professions of solidarity may prove empty. Alternatively, should Saudi leadership of the other Arab Gulf states advance without a

1   This is inherent in the disparity in power among the littoral states.

parallelism in overall policies with Baghdad, the temptations for Iraq to play the spoiler in the unity arrangements may increase. So long as Iraq and Saudi Arabia agree on the overriding threat to the region posed by Iran, and on the importance of maintaining some distance from the two blocs, Iraq—Saudi co-operation in the Gulf will survive. Differences in response to crises in the Arab world, or in approaches to Israel, may however, crack whatever unity has been achieved in the Gulf, with the possible deterioration leading to a three-way split in the Gulf.

# 4 The Scope, Limits and Conditions of Influence

## Arms transfer and influence

Western interests in the Persian Gulf include the traditional components of its denial to the USSR and securing access to the region but to these is added a dependency on the region's oil supplies that imparts to this interest a special dimension. The policies of regional governments and their attitude towards the West become extremely important. To cement a durable bond between the regional states and the West, a mutually advantageous bargain has had to be struck. This has entailed the exchange of oil at reasonable prices and levels of production, in return for assurances regarding security, the provision of technology, and a market for investments. By its very nature this compact is unequal; the commodities and services exchanged are not quantifiable or commensurable. Moreover the relationship is distorted: Western (and especially US) security assurances to Saudi Arabia are vague and hardly cast in concrete. By their very nature the threats to Saudi security are not easily susceptible to military guarantees. Furthermore the relationship with the Western superpower brings with it many problems for the Saudis — identification with the disruptive West (for the traditionalists) and support for the Zionists' ally (for the militant Left) — which give rise to problems both within Saudi Arabia and in the arena of Arab politics.

Western interests nonetheless dictate the cultivation of friendship with the major oil producing states. As we have seen, this has taken concrete form in various projects and particularly in arms sales and military modernization programmes. A narrow focus on arms transfers as a tool for supplier manipulation or leverage is mistaken. But, as one dimension of a broader relationship, the sensitive use of the arms supply component remains important for its symbolic aspect as well as for its practical military utility in the event of inter-state war. The question of the influence conferred by the transfer of arms was examined in depth in the first part of this study but it is worth summarizing the conclusions at this point.

For the supplier state the provision of arms holds several potential benefits: (a) it may serve as an entrée into the recipient's society and provide a key channel for influence; (b) it may serve as a visible symbol of its commitment to the recipient, act as a deterrent, and substitute for its own military involvement by bolstering a regional balance of power; (c) it may serve as a *quid pro quo* in the bilateral relationship creating an entangling dependency for the recipient and binding it closely to the supplier; and (d) it may provide a means for conflict management by restraining the recipient from certain actions and making it dependent on the supplier for new stocks.

Supplier influence derives in the first instance from the relevance of the supply of arms to the major security threats faced by the recipient and to the value attached to these arms by it. But the arms supplied are scarcely divorced from their political context. Influence is derived not from an arms relationship but from a *political* relationship, one tangible manifestation of which may be the supply of arms. This has important implications for the potential for supplier influence. The supplier is as much entangled as the recipient in a situation where arms are the product of a political relationship. For if arms are withheld or denied the political relationship will suffer, hurting both states. As a result of this deterioration, the arms tie will also inevitably be affected. A related issue is the degree to which the supplier can manipulate the arms relationship for influence in other areas. It would appear most difficult in the cases examined to document this. The arms supplied have largely been the reflection of shared interests (for example in the maintenance of a regional balance). Why this parallelism of interest should generate influence for the supplier (by threatening to renege on it) is not clear. In cases where arms are provided not as a 'favour' but for specific purposes, it is not self-evident that a refusal to furnish weapons would strengthen the supplier's influence. On the contrary it would suggest a redefinition of its interest and the recipient would draw the appropriate conclusions therefrom. A further complication surrounding supplier influence is the distinction between dependence and influence. The translation from a state of recipient dependency to one of supplier influence is by no means simple or inevitable. It is at least partially determined by the recipient's range of choice and his (subjective) response to this state of dependency. The record suggests that arms are more effective as inducements in relations than as coercive levers.[1] The Soviet Union has gained little influence from manipulating Iraq's arms supplies, and the US experience before and after Iran's revolution strengthens the proposition. No cases can be found where positions have been adopted (or changed) as a result of (explicit) pressure. More often positions taken can be plausibly explained by a parallelism of policy.

The conditions for maximal supplier influence are therefore:

1   If the recipient has overriding dependence on the supplier for arms and security and faces an imminent security threat.
2   If the recipient state has few options due to regional isolation, inadequate resources, or the absence of alternative suppliers.
3   If the recipient state is united both as to the priority of the security threat and on the appropriate response to it.

The relevance of arms to security requirements naturally affects the influence of the supplier. Where there is an overwhelming or imminent security threat, the value of this component of the relationship increases dramatically. Saudi insecurity regarding the PDRY lends special urgency to its military modernization programme, and the importance to it of the US connection. In Iran, where the US connection itself was a target of hostility, influence became impossible but that situation is not permanent. The perception of an aggressive neighbour or a malign proximate superpower could do much to revive Iran's traditional policy of seeking countervailing power from more distant states. An impending security problem might then well revive interest in Iran in a military connection with Europe and, in the short-run anyway, with the US. The durability of influence depends on the resilience of the political relationship. This requires: (a) a common 'language' (similar strategic perception and common values); (b) institutionalized, broad-based ties which can absorb differences of view and divergences; and (c) a sense that the alternatives for one or both parties are worse.

A related consideration is the weight of the two partners. It may well be the case that the most desirable relations are those involving near-equal or very markedly unequal partners. The oil-rich Gulf states are at neither extreme. Sensitive and insecure, they are acutely vulnerable to

---

1   Cf. Thomas R. Wheelock, 'Arms for Israel: the Limits of Leverage', *International Security*, vol.3, no.2, Fall 1978.

changes in political atmosphere and shifts in tone and nuance. For them the symbolic dimensions of the relationship assume great importance. Reassurance and 'hand-holding' are substantive issues. The denial of advanced aircraft to one but not to another state is seen as a political signal. The political implications of denial, or even delay, are greatly amplified in this setting and reverberate throughout the region. Because they are endowed with potent symbolism, arms are risky to manipulate and even more risky to deny. The desire to decide arms sales on 'specific evaluations of their concrete political and military contexts'[1] is understandable but these decisions cannot be divorced from either their domestic political setting or the overall relationship. When denial is a rebuff and a rejection, and supply is taken to mean approval and support, this reduces the ability of the supplier to manipulate the flow of supplies without risking the impairment of relations.

The utility of arms as a source of influence is further constrained in the following circumstances:

1   When they are no longer relevant to the major problems facing the recipient, as in a period of peacetime, or when arms supplied are marginal to defence capability.
2   When the risks associated with continued supply (or to adapting to the suppliers' pressure) are deemed to be higher than the alternatives (as in Iran after the revolution or in Iraq in 1980–81).
3   If the supplier is as equally entangled as the recipient in that he cannot refuse arms requests without disrupting relations.
4   If the recipient state's leadership is divided in its attitude toward the supplier, pressure may be counterproductive for supplier influence.
5   If the arms are the principal tie divorced from an overall relationship, or simply a commercial proposition, they will generate little influence for the supplier (as, perhaps, with the USSR in Iraq after 1975).

Supplier influence is also limited by considerations unrelated to the recipient. For example the supplier's interest in avoiding a regional arms race or provoking the other superpower may influence his policies. The supplier may also be unwilling to choose unequivocally or definitively between his regional partner and another (competing) regional state, thus setting limits on his influence with his partner.

1   Barry Blechman, *New York Times*, 2 April 1980.

Arms transfers are potentially more effective as levers in conflict than in peacetime. Experience in the Arab–Israeli Wars suggested that, while suppliers cannot prevent conflict, they can control its scope and duration and influence the mode and terms of its termination. This influence derived from the intensity of the conflict and the rapid need for extensive resupply which could be met only by the superpowers. In the Iran–Iraq War the intensity of the hostilities has not been such as to necessitate immediate reliance on the supplier. By limiting or severing supplies, the outside powers have prevented any major escalation of conflict — but even here personnel and other limitations have been equally operative as a constraint. Certainly it was the imbalance of arms in the region, in part a result of the strain in Iran–US relations, that furnished the conditions for the initiation of the conflict by Iraq. It is generally true that the supplier's influence will increase if (a) the protagonists decide to pursue the conflict as a priority and (b) if the war intensifies, requiring major resupply of the belligerents' inventories. While the supply of arms does not guarantee a continuing source of supplier influence, it does furnish the recipient with an incentive to maintain workable relations, unless that country is prepared to accept the consequences of a breakdown in relations. Iran in 1980–81 is illustrative of the proposition that advanced weapons require constant attention and maintenance, skills which recipients generally lack and can only attain gradually. Refusing to acknowledge its continuing need for the United States as a supplier has entailed high political and military costs. Iran in 1980–81 bears striking testimony less to the vulnerability of supplier influence than to the costs to the recipient of seeking to evade it.

## The USSR and Iraq

Studies that focus predominantly on influence relationships in terms of access and leverage tend to ignore variations in the condition of the recipient. This is clearly illustrated in USSR–Iraq relations. Concentration on a range of variables would illustrate the more fluctuating and evolving context in which the supplier–recipient relationship takes place. These variables include:

1  The imminence of the security threat(s).
2  The degree of domestic support (unity, discord).
3  The capacity to otherwise defuse problems.

The latter in turn may be divided into component parts:

(a) Resources: alternative suppliers or means.
(b) Regional environment: the quality of relations with neighbours and the capacity to forge other alliances.

(c) Flexibility: the ability to adjust priorities tactically and to be nimble in the face of multiple challenges.

A focus on these factors would underscore the fact that 'influence', when identifiable, ebbs and flows, varying with many factors other than the supplier–recipient relationship itself.

Iraq's relationship with the USSR has been a function of the degree to which its interests (and priorities) have converged with those of Moscow, and of its capacity to achieve them elsewhere or by other means. The primary goal of Iraqi leadership has been regime security. In the initial period (1958–73), Iraq's alternatives were limited. Her ideology made the West largely unacceptable, her resources limited her choices and the imminence of problems (with the Kurds, Israel, Iran and Western oil companies) gave her little leeway.

In the second phase, (1974 to date) regime survival and independence were still the priorities but pragmatism and money made new choices possible. The willingness to assign priorities and to limit the multiple sources of insecurity, facilitated a reduced reliance. As the Soviet and Communist threat was seen to increase, a willingness to compromise on regional politics became evident. Emphasis on the Gulf replaced militance on Palestine and relations became less subject to doctrinal preferences. Domestically, while communists were suppressed, attempts at compromise with Kurds and Shi'a muslims were pursued and national elections were held in mid-1980. Iraq's aspiration to the role of defender of the Gulf's Arabism was not new but, in its anti-Soviet manifestation, it reflected a new component.

Seen from Soviet perspective, Iraq's evolution since 1974 must be testimony to the inherent unpredictability of ties with the Third World. As it has grown richer Iraq has become more independent and assertive, pursuing policies regionally divergent from the USSR and so posing for the USSR the usual dilemma — to deny arms or to maintain supplies (with caution) in the hope that things will improve?[1] Apart from the parallelism on policy with respect to certain areas (Palestine), Soviet arms have not generated anything resembling tangible or enduring influence. Strategic access has been limited and is unlikely to last in the light of Soviet policy during the 1980–81 War.

Iraq's current positions run counter to those of the USSR. Iraq is co-operating with conservatives in the Gulf, diverting energy away from

---

1 This may be illustrative of the proposition that 'gains in influence may be an illusory goal but anticipation of losses of influence is more compelling'. See the brilliant article by Richard Betts, 'The Tragicomedy of Arms Trade Control', *International Security*, vol.5, no.1, Summer 1980, fn.38.

Palestine, is at odds with Syria, and has suppressed Iraq's Communist Party. In some respects Iraq's continued dependency on the USSR for arms for the immediate future guarantees an Iraqi unwillingness to sever ties completely. This enables the USSR to cultivate the other power, Iran, which is intrinsically more important as a neighbour with a long coastline on the Gulf. Iran offers better opportunities also for domestic penetration and, in its anti-Westernism, it is more congenial. Its importance for an Afghanistan 'settlement' is an additional asset. As the War continues to sputter it is conceivable that there will arrive a moment of truth for the combatants, necessitating resupplies or a ceasefire. The Soviet Union's involvement on a small scale on both sides may enable it to retrieve some influence at that time.

## The US and Iran

The United States' initial involvement in Iran after the Second World War was military. By the 1960s the relationship had expanded to encompass other areas, but the military aspect remained a symbol of US 'responsiveness' toward a friendly state. By the 1970s arms transfers were expected to increase as an element in the Nixon Doctrine. With Iran they indicated a US commitment and served, it was assumed, as an alternative to a direct involvement. The arms transfer relationship took on some of the attributes of a treaty relationship.

American expectations about the benefits of arms transfers as such can be exaggerated. The relationship developed on the assumption of a continuing overlap of interests. It was recognized that, in the 1970s, the relationship would be more equal, based often on unstated *quid pro quos*. The responsiveness of the US was considered important by the Iranian government and Iran's influence in the region could in turn be helpful to the US. It was assumed that the arms supplier would retain a measure of influence over the actual use of the arms supplied, particularly in an intense conflict[1] occurring before the arms were assimilated or stocks had built up. Finally the arms supplied to Iran were seen primarily in their regional and above all in their Soviet context. Foreign not domestic contingencies were seen as the appropriate basis for evaluating decisions on transfers.

In practice the United States found itself unable to check the pace or determine the content of the arms sold to Iran. Furthermore the scale of the sales necessitated initially an increased physical presence and

---

1   See Staff Report on *Arms Sales to Iran*, US Senate, Congress Washington DC (1976).

involvement. As a policy tool, arms transfers were not easily manipulable. Withholding would be seen as a change in policy with domestic political implications far broader than a purely technical decision would normally entail. At the same time the arms transfers constituted an implied commitment. Artful attempts at semantic camouflage could not make politically real distinctions between defence involvement and defence commitment.[1] The revolution in Iran demonstrated that several criticisms of the earlier arms sales programme had been largely erroneous. There was no automaticity of involvement in conflict due to a presence. The 'hostage' theory of US military advisers was an extrapolation of the Vietnam experience and little else. The dependency of the recipient in war for functioning on a day-to-day basis was seen in 1980–81 to be a matter of degree. For full utilization of its resources this may have been true but, with cannibalization and improvization and for sub-optimal use, Iranian resources were adequate.

Over the longer term, US influence will be dependent on the level of fighting which will condition the amount and type of arms needed and the emergence of a government which sees its interests as not threatened by renewed supplies. For the United States a commitment to Iran had been antecedent to the supply of arms and the arms supplied have been the consequence not the cause of that commitment. A willingness to continue to supply arms even in a period of revolutionary upheaval represented a belief in the persistence of this interest and in the efficacy of arms sales as an instrument in achieving them. The sustained efforts by the USSR to prevent such a *rapprochement* suggests that Moscow too believes that the arms relationship, while reflecting the political temperature, also has a life of its own.

## The US and Saudi Arabia

The dependence of Saudi Arabia on the US for security is great. As the salience of external security threats grows, so will that of the US connection. It has been argued that the relevance of the outside power connection is limited insofar as it relates to other sources of instability, particularly domestic. But its importance, though limited, is nonetheless real:

1   As a deterrent against militant regional states (the PDRY).
2   As reassurance for the Saudi regime in Arab politics, which provides a tacit demonstration of the US stake in Saudi Arabia.

---

1   How else to explain the shattering of US credibility with the fall of the Shah? Note for example the illusory attempts of Richard Pranger and Dale Tahtinen, *American Policy Options in Iran and the Persian Gulf*, American Enterprise Institute, Washington DC, 1979, p.22.

3   As a favoured partner in the region (for technology, etc.).

The US connection through arms, security assurances, and skilful diplomacy, is capable of assisting in reducing the pressures and defusing the conflicts unsettling Saudi security. As a supplier of technology and knowledge, the US remains an important ally.

The contribution of the outside power to the local power's needs can thus be considerable but not total. The relevance of the outside power to the priorities of the local state will be critical. This will depend on a congruence of interest and a recognition of their respective roles, as well as on the policies pursued, and the outcome of politics within each state. For example, the US and Saudi Arabia share an interest in containing radicalism in the Persian Gulf. The US role may extend to deterring military adventures by radical states whereas Saudi Arabia's may be in shoring up moderate elements within those states, tempting their leadership with financial inducements, or isolating them in Arab councils. Policies in other areas affect both the stability of the relationship and the security of the two states. A Saudi action in OPEC that did not consider the impact on the world economy would result in basic Western reappraisals. Similarly a close alignment by Washington with Israel would raise similar incentives for readjustment by the Saudi leadership. The pattern of overlapping interest and reciprocal influence underscores that the issues rarely relate to raw leverage, but to adaptability and adjustment to divergences. Hence the *quality* of the relationship is as important as the relative power of either party on a specific issue. The degree of US 'influence' is not fully comprehended by reference to the provision of specific services. For the Saudi leadership, the US remains the only acceptable choice as a security partner. While this psychological dependence breeds excessive expectations which are doomed to occasional disappointment, the choices are stark and uninviting. Nonalignment or reinsurance with militants at this stage would severely limit her freedom for independent policies.[1]

Though not a 'balanced' partnership, the Saudi leadership has few alternatives. Other postures may remove some threats but not others (and may indeed create new threats). The relationship thus needs to be flexible to allow for divergences. For the US some of the policy instruments available may aggravate local problems. For example Saudi military modernization and conscription could undermine traditional sources of support for the Saudi dynasty. Industrialization may contribute to social problems of alienation and focus hostility on the

---

1   On the other hand, it is the inhospitable regional political environment that generates pressures for the US connection. The emergence of a security alternative for coping with regional threats (e.g. Egypt/Turkey) may generate greater freedom of action *vis-à-vis* the US.

US for disrupting age-old patterns of interaction.[1] US identification with the regime may as easily undermine as buttress it.[2] Sensitivity to Saudi concerns may dictate a more activist or acquiescent US regional policy than would otherwise be the case.

For the Saudis too, the relationship with the US requires flexibility. The Kingdom cannot be identified with US initiatives which are unpopular in the Arab world, such as Camp David. Under these circumstances Saudi silence or token opposition is inevitable. The Saudis cannot afford to look like a 'regional *gendarme*' or US 'agent' and so the Saudis must often be seen to take independent decisions divergent from that of the US. Military pacts or the provision of military bases are therefore refused. An obtrusive US military presence on Saudi soil is similarly avoided.[3] The Saudis must stress also their cultural identity and strength, and their distinctiveness. As Guardians of the Holy Places, the Saudi leadership places great emphasis on the future status of Jerusalem.

In short the US–Saudi relationship has had to accommodate divergent interests and priorities while maintaining essential links. The benefits have sometimes appeared uneven. The Saudis keep oil prices down or increase production while the US fails to meet their security concerns.[4] Yet the manner in which differences are reconciled testifies to the resilience of the relationship. Issue-by-issue bargaining or linkage is eschewed; and specific questions are not elevated into make-or-break tests of the relationship (as was sometimes true under the Shah). The style of the relationship is different. Saudi leaders prefer the use of the carrot to that of the stick (as was seen in 1976 and in 1979). Displeasure is indicated subtly: a trip is cancelled, or a rumour not denied.

The durability of a relationship in which the partners 'agree to differ' depends nevertheless on the persistence of a solid core of mutual

---

1 The relevance of economic development and large-scale industrialization to the needs of the populace will have to be clearly demonstrated in the light of Iran's reaction to a 'cardboard economy'.

2 Related to this is the narrowing of US policy choices by entanglement with regimes which may, or may not, be overthrown.

3 Saudi MAAG size was reduced from 133 to 80 between February 1974 and 1978. This understates the number of US military present which was as of March 1981, some 400. Semi-official assistance through the Vinnell Corporation, the Army Corps of Engineers and British Aerospace is still large at 2,000.

4 'You're asking too much. You're asking us to produce more oil, to keep the price down and to accept your inflation. Yet you didn't help us with our political problem in the region. It's not a balanced relationship' the Saudi Finance Minister Muhammad Aba al-Khayi has said. See *The Wall Street Journal*, 11 June 1979.

interest. This can change as a result of shifts in political values over time or with the preferences of a new ruling elite. The most durable relationship is a broad-based one in which the fruits of the partnership are seen to be reciprocally beneficial. In the Gulf states this must encompass the populations of the region and not just their leadership if it is to survive regime changes. Commercial relations in which economic 'white elephants' are visible or military sales which result in no observable improvement in defence capability,[1] will only undermine the relationship over time. The choices between short- and medium-term interests will need to be carefully weighed by the outside power. Short-term oil needs may dictate pressure on the regional partner to increase production, but this may expose it to domestic and regional criticism. Similarly the inclination to tighten leverage on the regional state may dictate encouragement of projects which increase its dependency while the longer-run optimum goal for both states might be a diversification of relations with outside powers, even at the cost of dilution of the leverage of the superpower partner.

Reference was made at the outset to the question of elite orientation in the regional states. None of the leaderships are truly monolithic or hold identical values. While there may be agreement on the need for regime stability, there is seldom unanimity on how this can be best achieved. This is clearly evident in the turmoil in Iran, but equally present in the Ba'ath leadership in Iraq and in divisions within the Royal Family in Saudi Arabia. Outside powers' policies can exacerbate factionalism and strengthen the hands of those arguing in Saudi Arabia, for example, for a more 'pro-Arab' rather than 'US' policy; for a more 'rejectionist' or more pro-Soviet stand in Iraq; or for greater balance in relations with superpowers in Iran.

These actions need not be deliberate; indeed often they are inadvertent. An insensitive public statement (such as the US search for 'bases' in Saudi Arabia) or public leaks about divisions within the Royal Family in Saudi Arabia (July 1979) can weaken the leadership in these states. Intrusive demands for statistics from ARAMCO by the US Treasury Department for anti-trust purposes (December 1979) lends ammunition to those in Saudi Arabia accusing the regime of being 'puppets' of the US. Particularly given the political atmosphere in the region in the aftermath of the Iranian revolution, much greater sensitivity is required by US policy makers. Improved co-ordination of policy machinery is essential if a smooth and consistent policy is to be sustained over time. Just as the Saudi leadership is vulnerable to

---

1 In which 'dependency' itself may come to be seen to be a 'cure' worse than the illness it seeks to combat, i.e. weakness.

political blackmail and intimidation through the threat of terrorism by its neighbours, so is it politically exposed to the charge of collusion with the West whether of acquiescence in Zionist policies, of weakening OPEC, or of indulging in anti-Arab, anti-Muslim or anti-National policies. It cannot afford to support firm US action *vis-à-vis* Iran although it may desire it and it must make ritual pronouncements against foreign military presence.

Improved co-ordination and greater sensitivity may be necessary but they will not be sufficient elements in US policy. A greater readiness to make quiet suggestions and to point out the manifold implications and interrelationships between the various strands of the development programmes under way is essential. Military modernization may require both foreign manpower and divert scarce skilled indigenous manpower away from the civilian sector. Some military weapons systems may be equally as effective as those being sought without such a major diversion. In such a case it may be necessary to make this clear to the Saudis. The cumulative impact of various programmes needs to be assessed for its effect on traditional social and power structures, on value systems and on the fabric of society. It is a delusion to believe that involvement in such an extensive development programme can be purely economic and that its political implications can be left to the host country. Oil has not yet brought with it the skilled human and organizational resources necessary for the producing state to make these studies and assess their implications. Unless they are made by the outside power they will not be made at all. The failure to anticipate the consequences and alternatives of current policies will then become extremely costly for both states. In short the outside power will have to steer carefully between the rocks of dictation and deference. It must eschew gratuitous and patronising advice but nonetheless must point out the full impact of decisions made in one sector on needs elsewhere, the interrelationship of decisions, the cumulative effect of small changes and the longer-run implications of decisions made today. To do this will require not only better knowledge about the region and more streamlined policy machinery, but also tact, consistency, commitment and a genuine involvement in the wellbeing of the regional partner. It may well be too much to ask.

# Index

173

Iraq (cont.)
post-1976 moderation of revolutionary regional policies, 88-9, 94, 152; proposes 'Arab defence organization' 1970, 151; rapprochement with Saudi Arabia 1979 and after, 89, 130, 153-4, 155, 156, 159, 160, 166; regional security agreements 1978-79, 89, 130, 153-4; rise and fall of Soviet influence, 77-8, 79, 94, 95-6, 103-6, 163; settles border clashes with Iran 1975, 87, 88, 152, 158; settles border disputes with Saudi Arabia 1975, 88; severs relations with USA 1967, 79; Soviet arms supplies, 74-9, 80-3 *passim*, 87; Soviet military advisers in, 81n, 83; Soviet pilots in, 81n; Soviet technicians in, 76; supports opposition in PDRY, 94; suppression of Communist Party, 84, 167; terminates Yemeni war, 93, 158; trade with Soviet Union, 76, 77, 104n; Treaty of Friendship with Soviet Union 1972, 7, 10, 80-1, 86, 91, 95, 112, 126, 128; unhappy about Iranian revolution, 92; *see also* Iran-Iraqi war 1980-81 and Kurds
Iraqi Communist Party, 89, 96, 105: Ba'ath's attitude to, 90-3; denounces Ba'ath regime, 91; exile of leadership 1979, 91; failure of national coalition containing 1972, 86, 91-2; purges of, 90, 91, 92; suppression of, 84, 167

Israel, 105, 128, 145: F-15 sales to 'balance' sales to Saudi Arabia, 48; question of arms for Saudi Arabia and, 49, 51, 54, 55; US aid for 1982, 55

Jackson, Senator, 51
Japan: dependence on Iranian oil, 17n, 19n
Jones, General, 50
Jordan: assistance to Gulf sheikhdoms, 140, 151, 152

Khaled, King, of Saudi Arabia, 49
Khomeini, Ayatollah, 16-19 *passim*, 32, 35: revolutionary philosophy, 18
Khruschev, Nikita, 84
Kissinger, Henry, 4, 10, 11: relationship with Shah of Iran, 12
Kosygin, Alexei: visits Iraq 1976, 82
Kurds, 105, 106, 114, 166: campaigns against, 79, 81, 84, 87, 88; Kurdish Democratic Party, 86
Kuwait, 125n, 126, 150-4 *passim*, 156: Iraqi claims on, 86n, 87, 88, 111

Libya, 97, 118: break with Saudi Arabia, 64n; Soviet arms supplies, 76, 78

Muskie, Edmund, 25

Nasir, Pres. Abdul, 38, 43, 85
Naval Arms Limitation Talks (NALT), 132
*New York Times*, 51
Nixon, Pres. Richard M., 4, 10, 11, 58, 114: relationship

United States of America (USA) (cont.)
during Iranian revolution, 14-16; pact with Iran undisturbed by oil price increases, 11; policy towards Persian Gulf security, 4-5, 112; poor co-ordination of government agencies, 69, 70; problem of freeing hostages in Iran, 18-26, 61; question of supplying F-15s to Saudi Arabia, 67; rapid deployment force for Persian Gulf, 122-6; reaction to Soviet invasion of Afghanistan, 61; relations with post-revolutionary Iran, 16-19; relations with Saudi Arabia, 6-7, 13, 14, 25, 36-42, 67-74, 161, 168-72; sanctions against post-revolutionary Iran, 20-1; security guarantor role in Saudi Arabia, 56-8, 63, 64, 145; support for Saudis in Yemeni conflict, 59-60;

United States of America (USA) (cont.)
tries rapprochement with Iraq, 100n; willingness to alienate allies, 75n

Vance, Cyrus, 50
Vinnell Corporation, 45, 170n

Yamani, Zaki, 54
Yazdi, Iranian Foreign Minister, 20
Yemen, North (YAR), 43, 53n, 60, 93, 122, 144, 158: Saudi aid, 158; Soviet aid, 126-7; US aid, 59
Yemen, South (PDRY), 10-11, 38, 39, 53n, 57, 79, 89, 90, 92, 93, 117, 118, 122, 125, 126, 163: gives sanctuary to Iraqi Communist Party, 94; invades North Yemen 1979, 59, 60, 144, 158; Saudi offers of aid, 158; Soviet aid, 75; Soviet power in, 126; Soviet restraint on, 125

180